Color My World

Ginger Marks

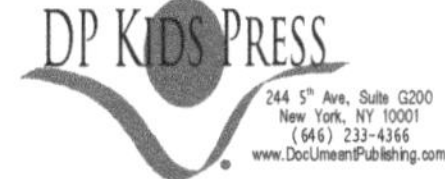

Published by
DP Kids Press
a division of DocUmeant Publishing
244 5th Avenue, Suite G-200
NY, NY 10001
646-233-4366
www.DocUmeantPublishing.com

Cover & Interior Illustrator: Ginger Marks
Editor: Philip S. Marks

Cover Design & Layout: Ginger Marks
DocUmeant Designs
www.DocUmeantDesigns.com

ISBN 9781957832258 (print) $19.95
ISBN 9781957832265 (digital)
Library of Congress Number: 2023948910

Introduction

For quite some time I have been sharing my drawings on social media. My preferred medium is black and white pencil. It seemed that with every posting the majority of comments suggested that I create a coloring book collection. This is the result of those requests.

This eclectic mix of original and hand drawn illustrations took me more than a year to create. In this volume you will discover mandalas, cartoons, tangles, dangles, steampunk, and much more. I have chosen not to order them in any particular sequence in the hope that you will not get bored with any one style.

Feel free to color them, in any order, within this book, or copy them on watercolor paper or other such medium for your personal use. I would love to see your finished results. Share them on my social media channels but please don't copy them to sell or share for commercial use.

Thank you,

Ginger Marks

Facebook: https://linkpro.cz/ukzQchd

Instagram: docupub

LinkedIn: gingermarks

Twitter: gmarksfl

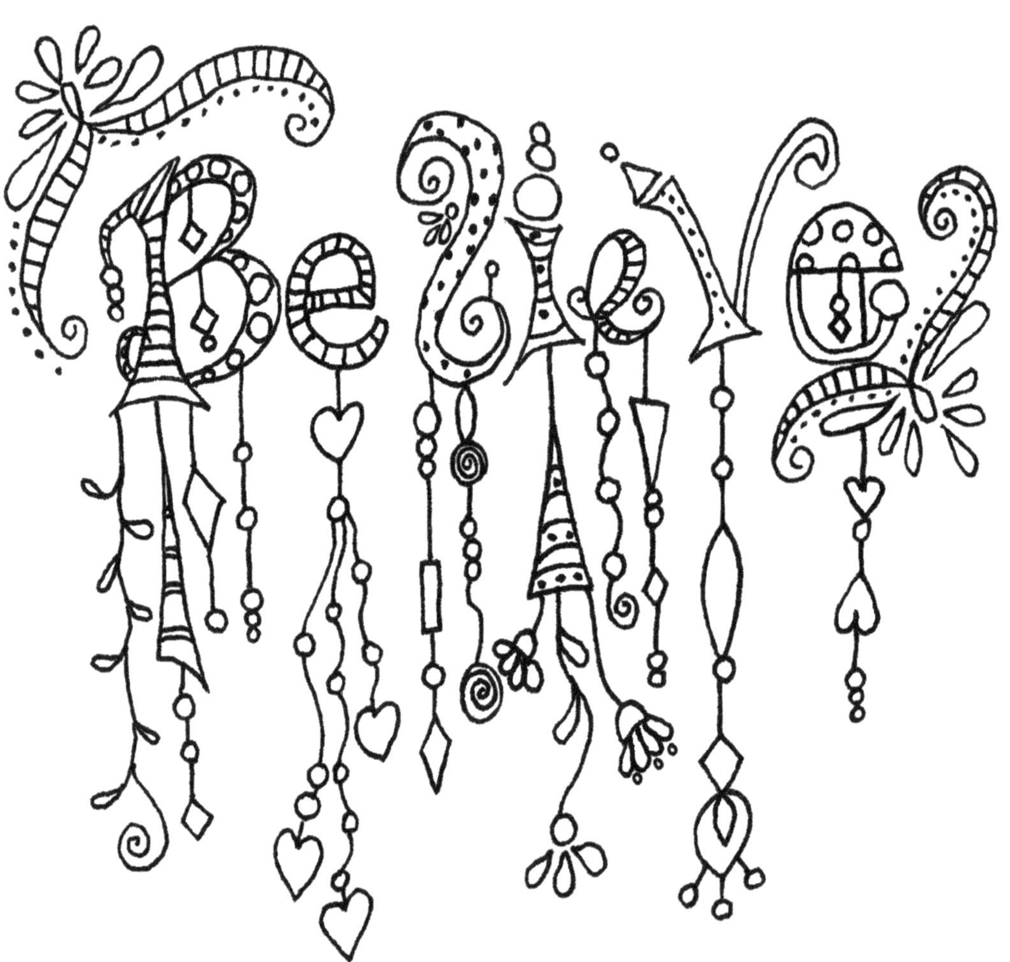
Believe

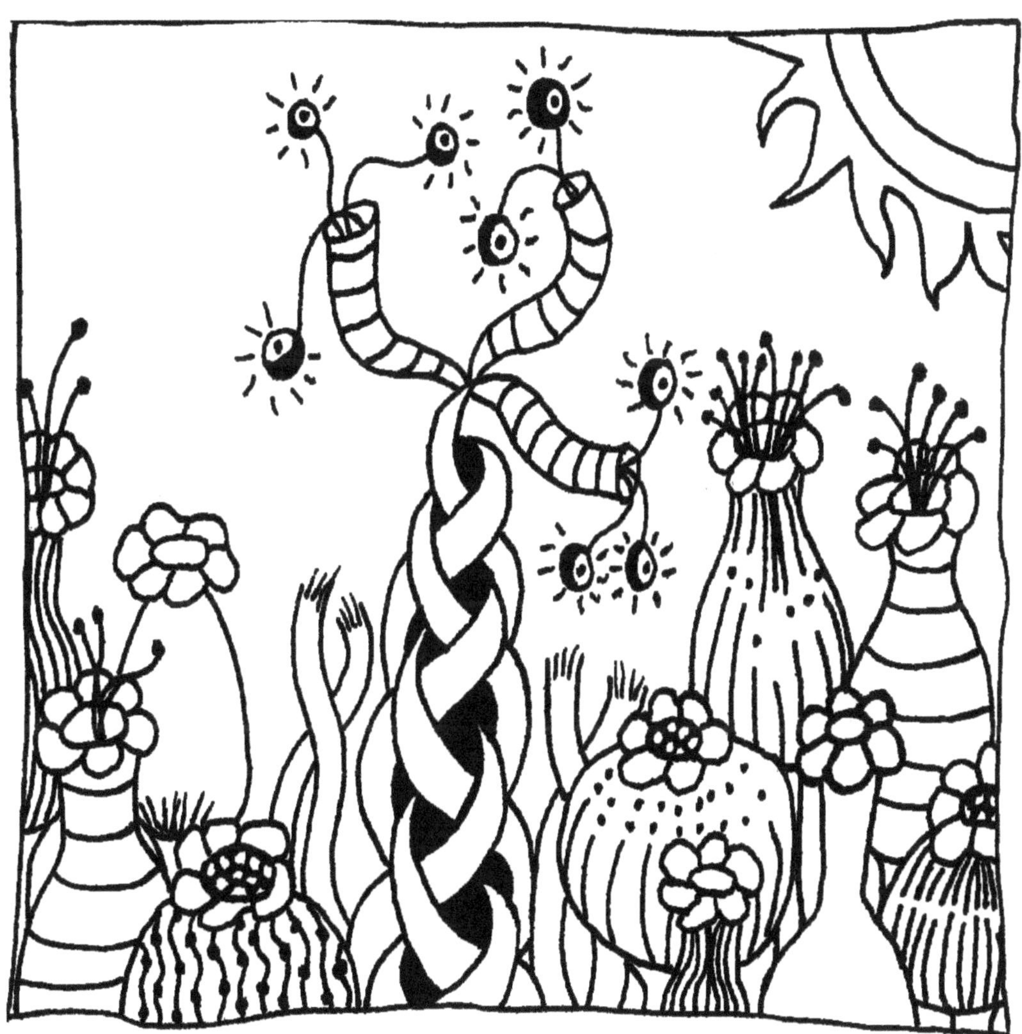

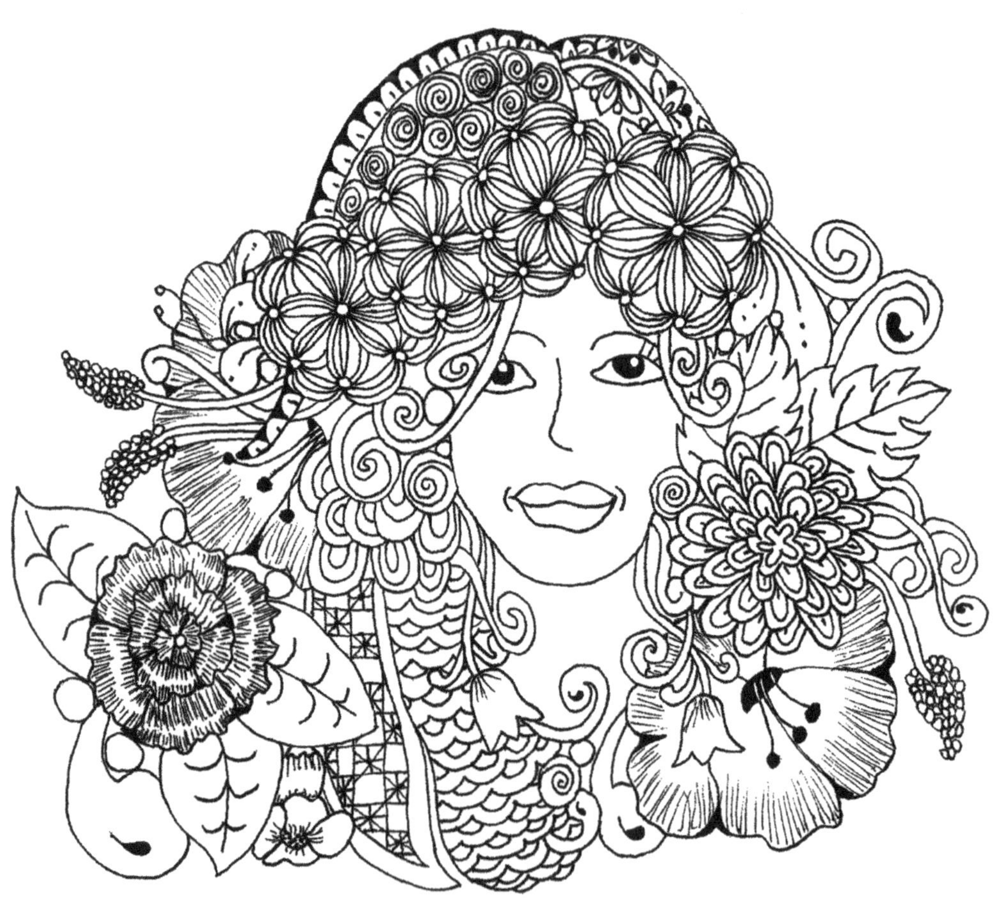

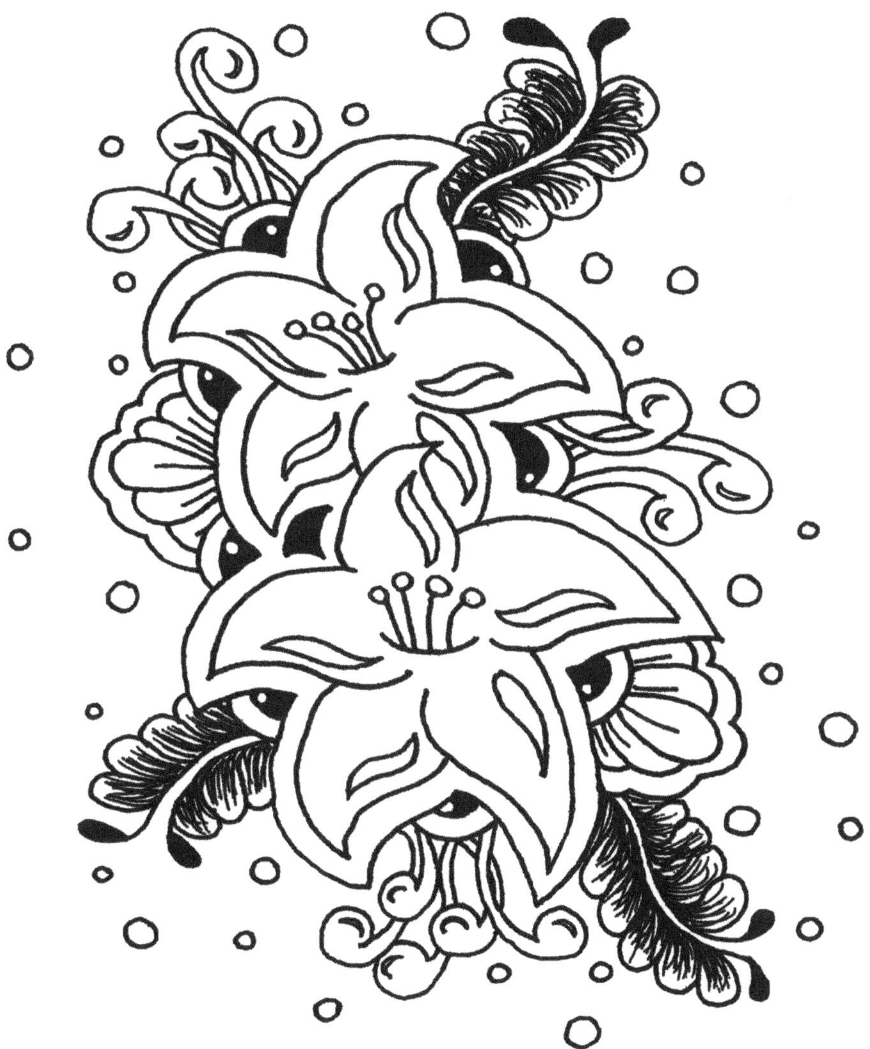

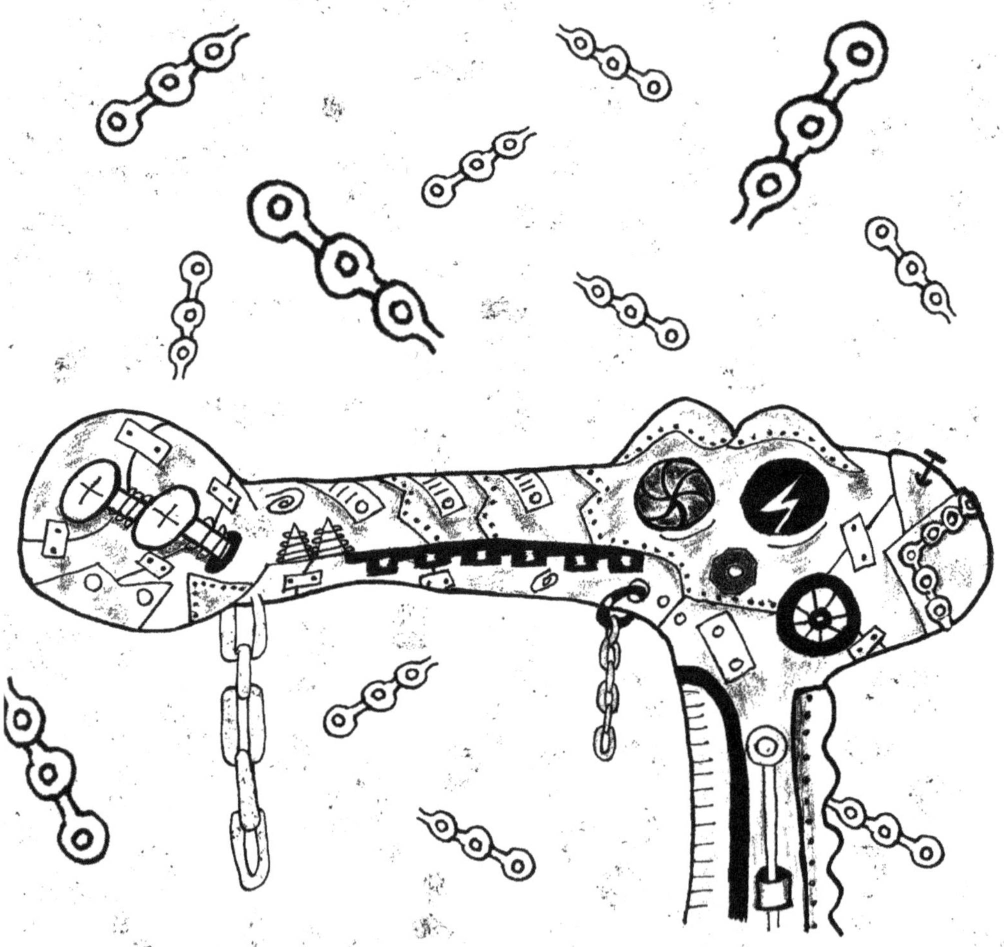

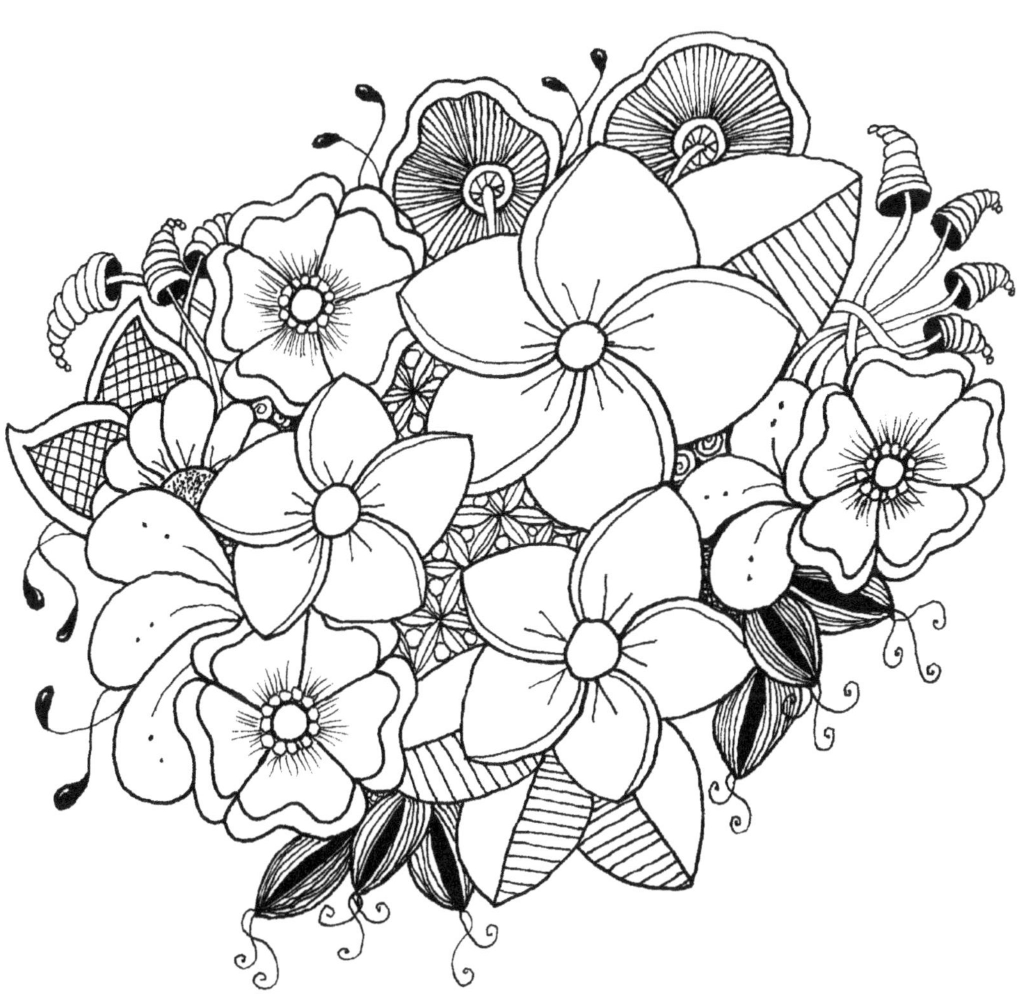

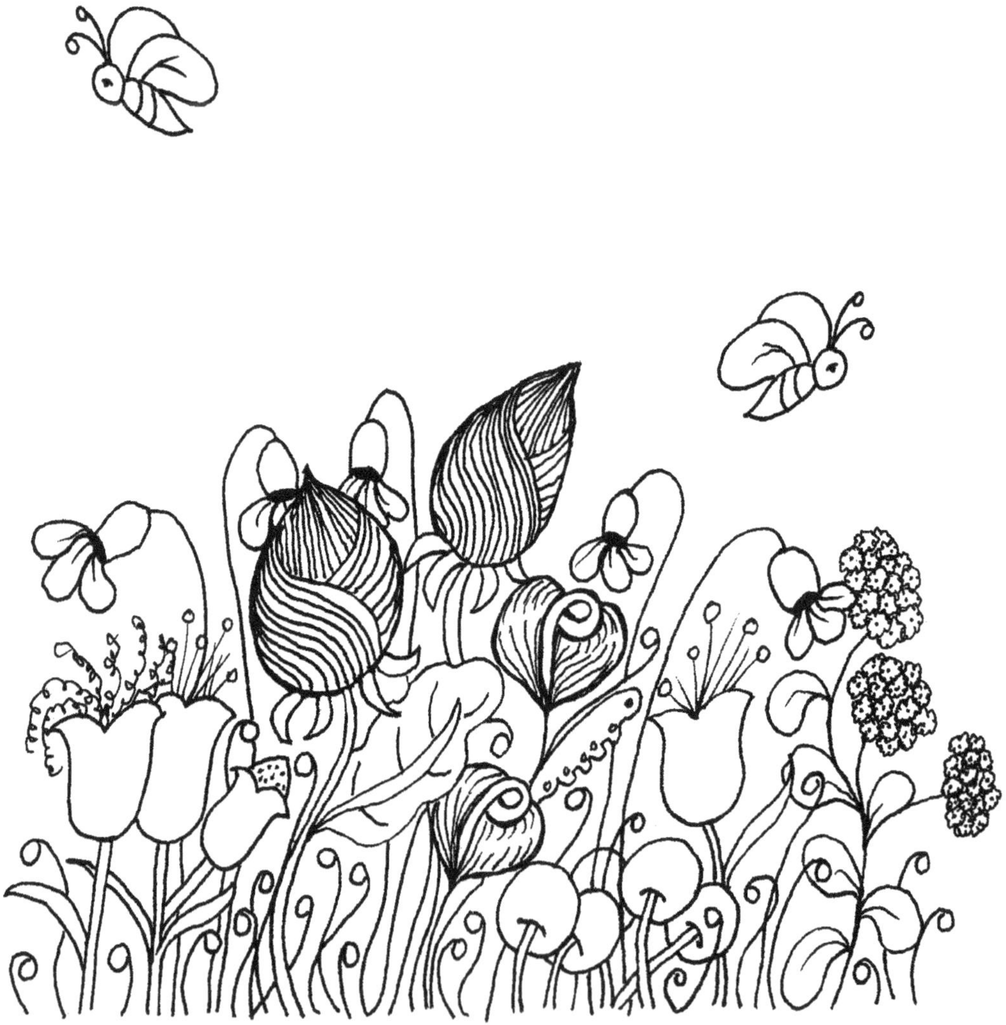

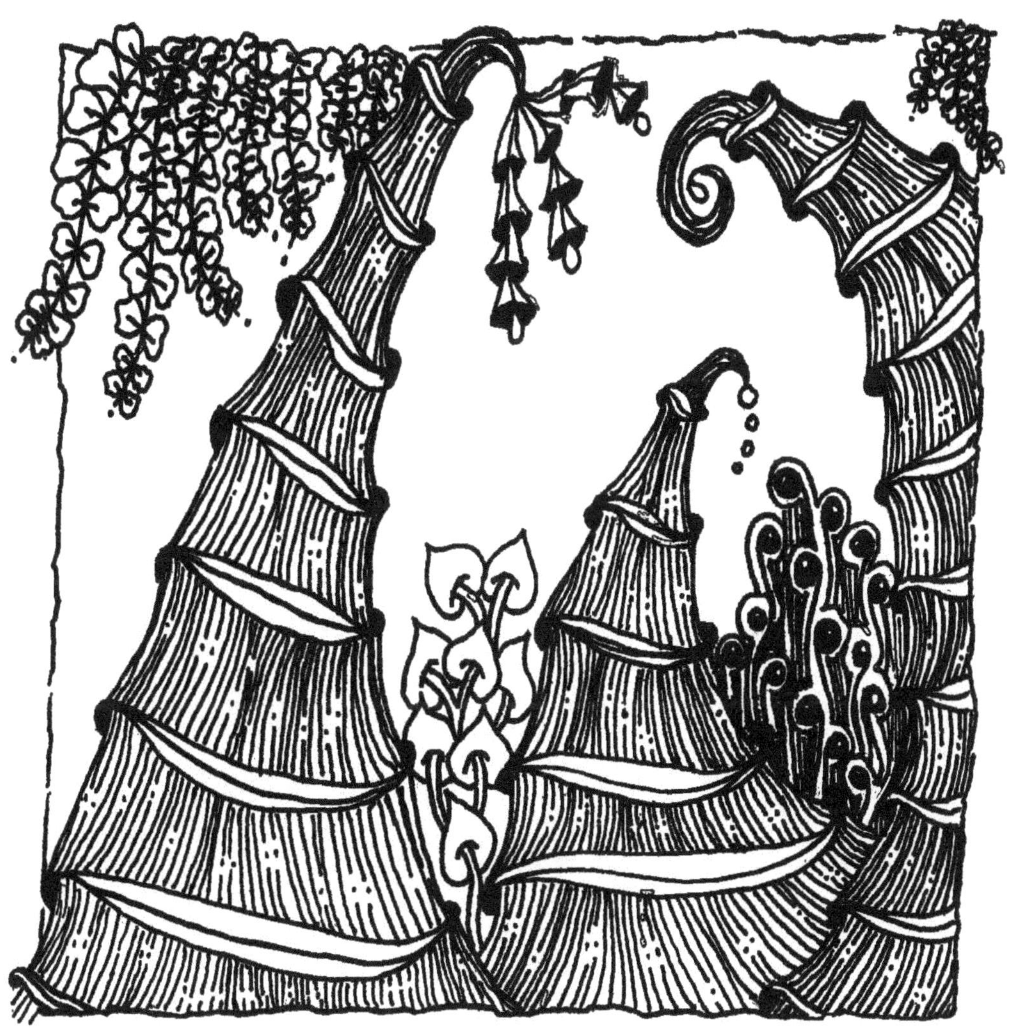

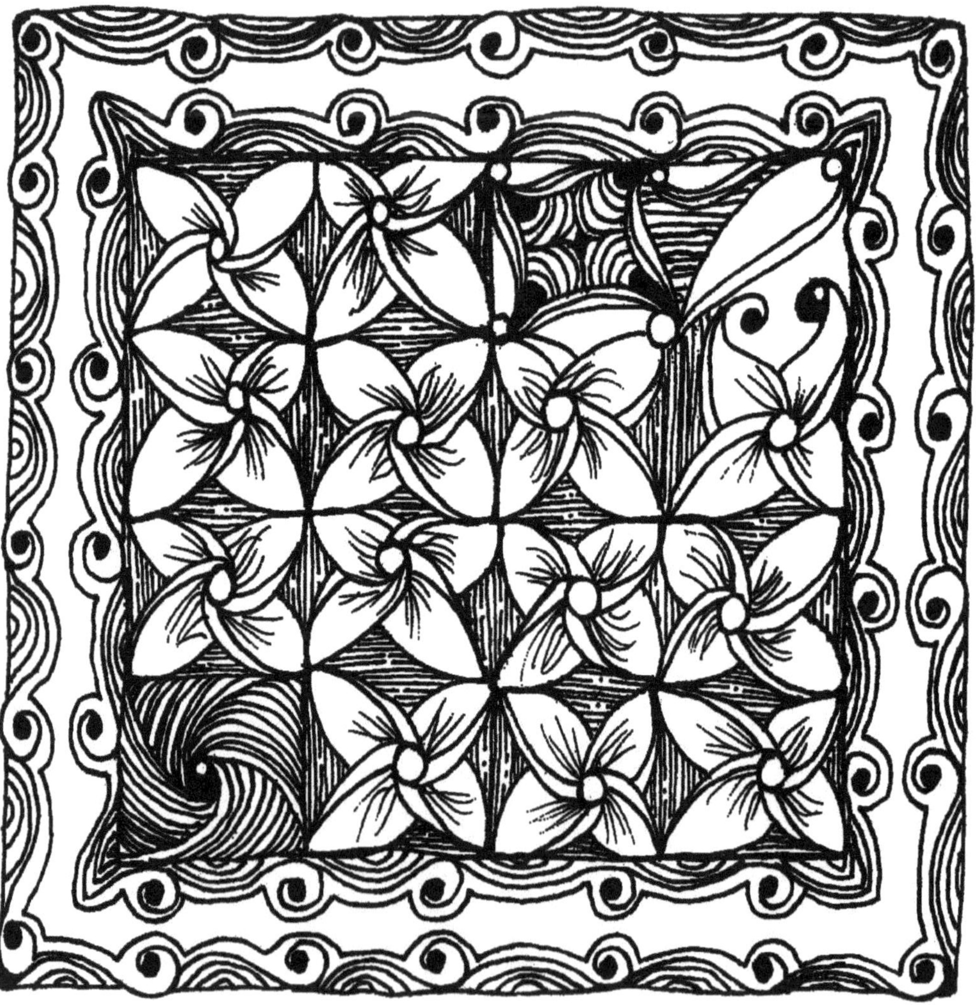

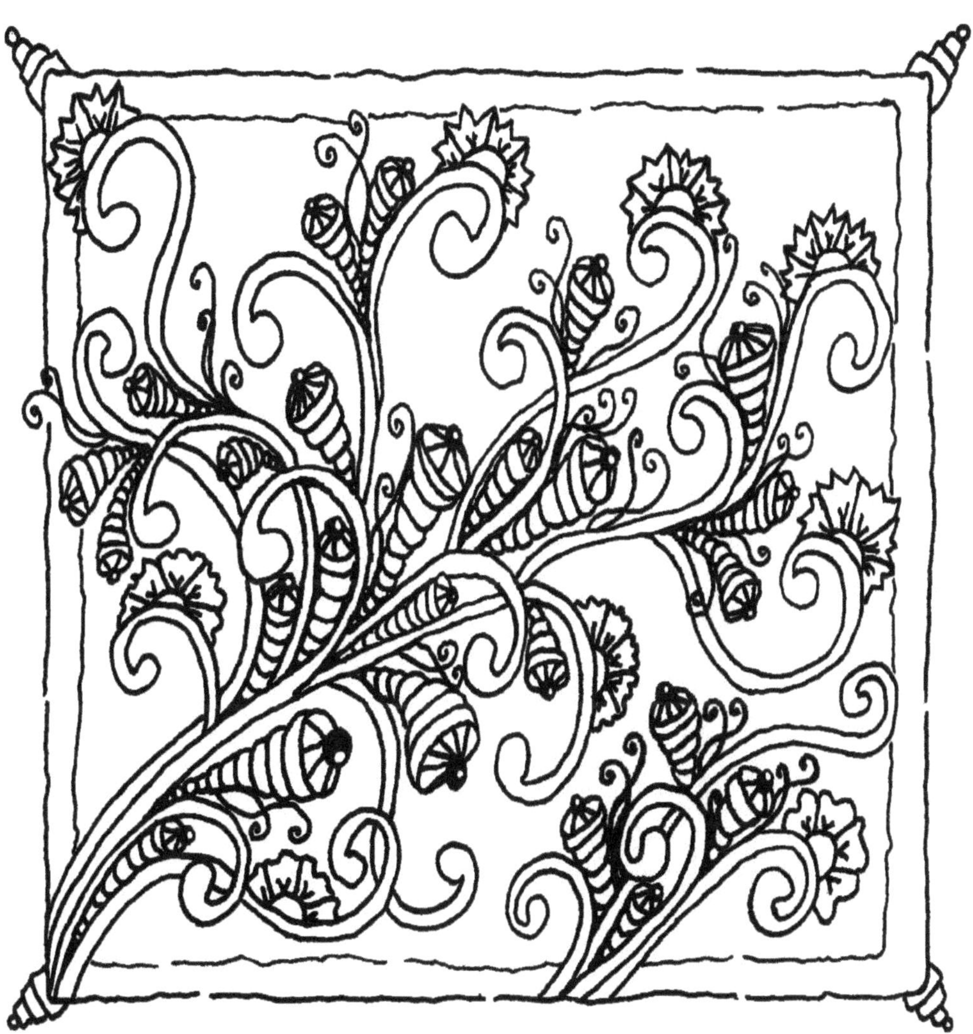

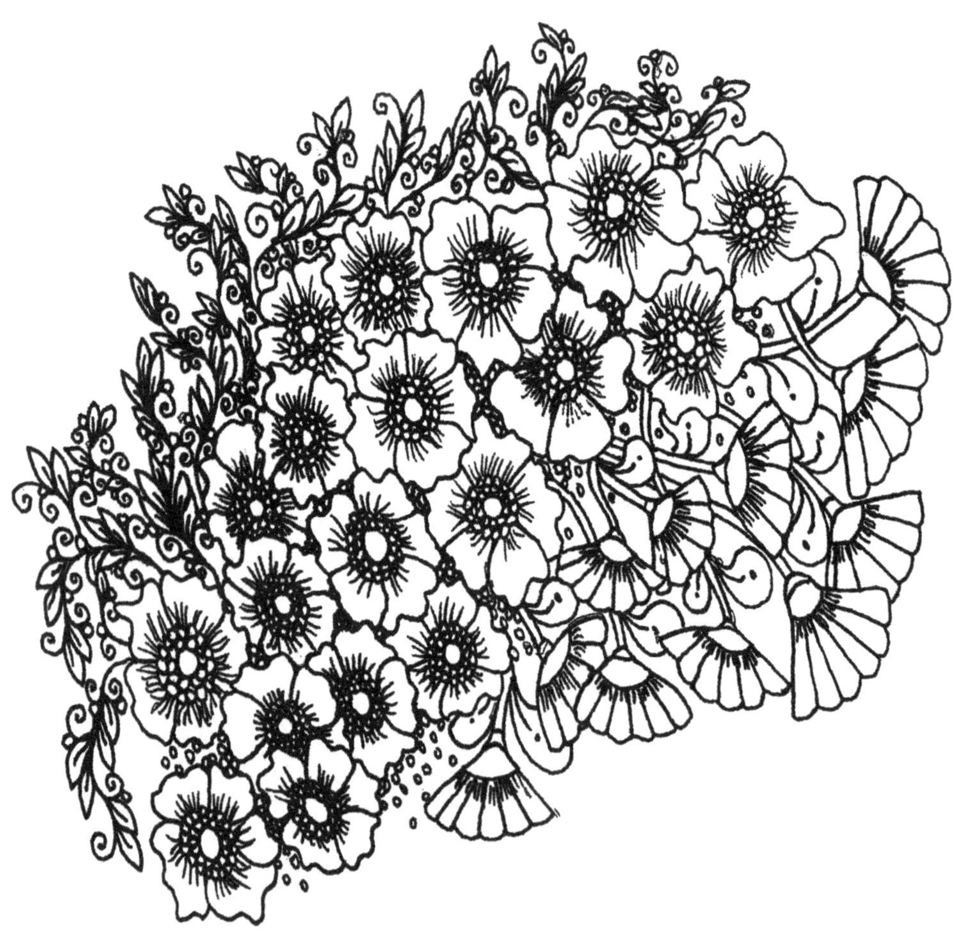

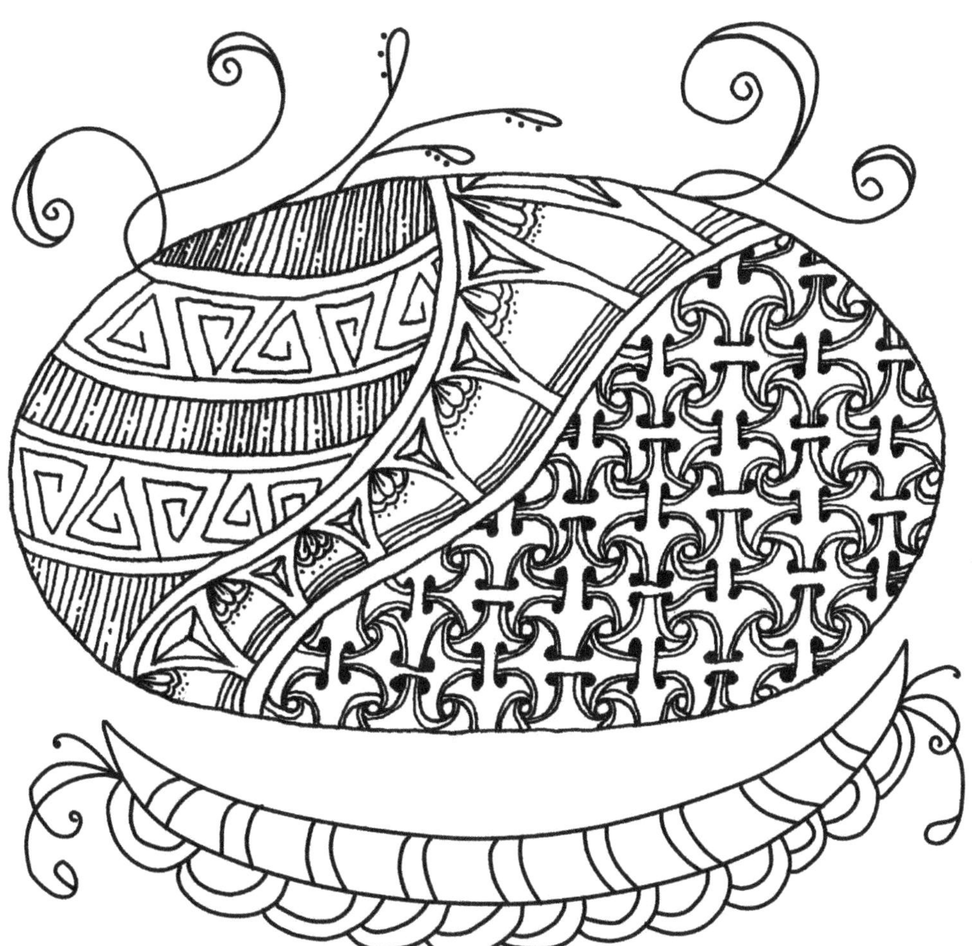

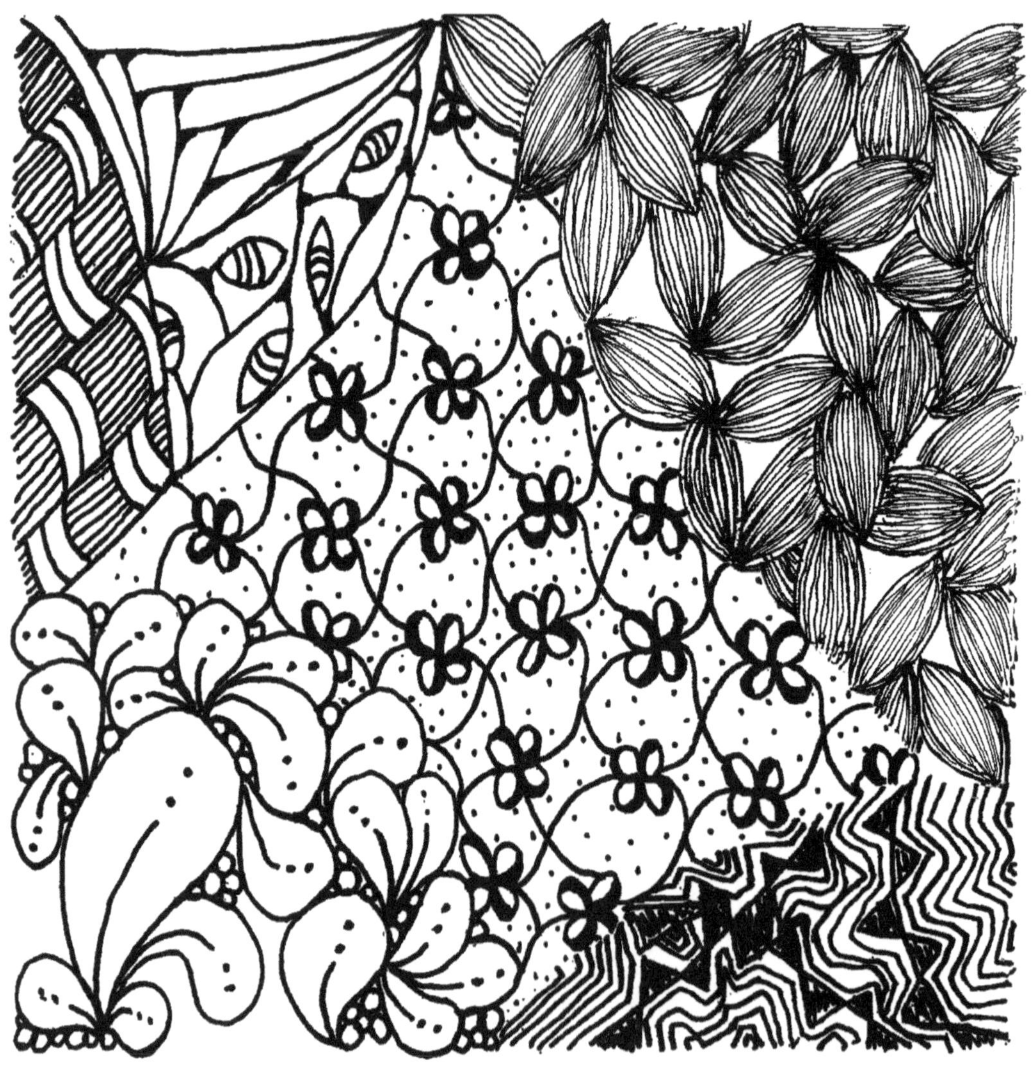

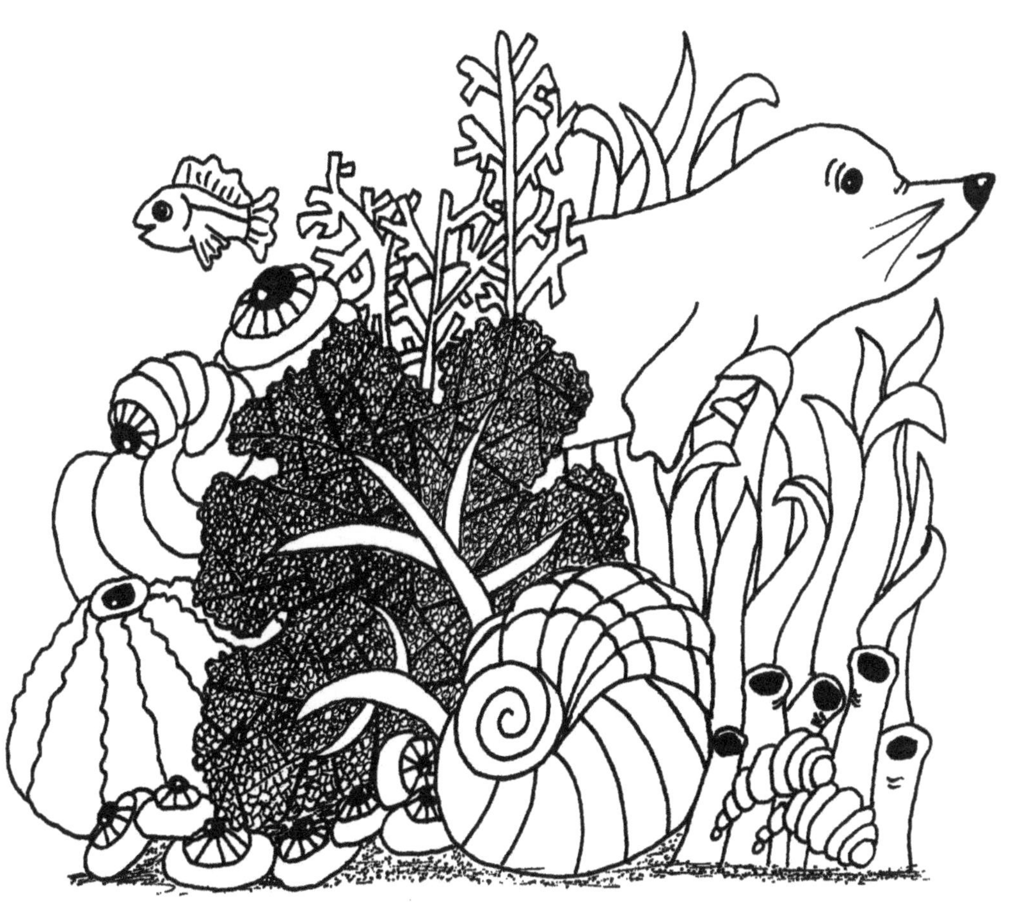

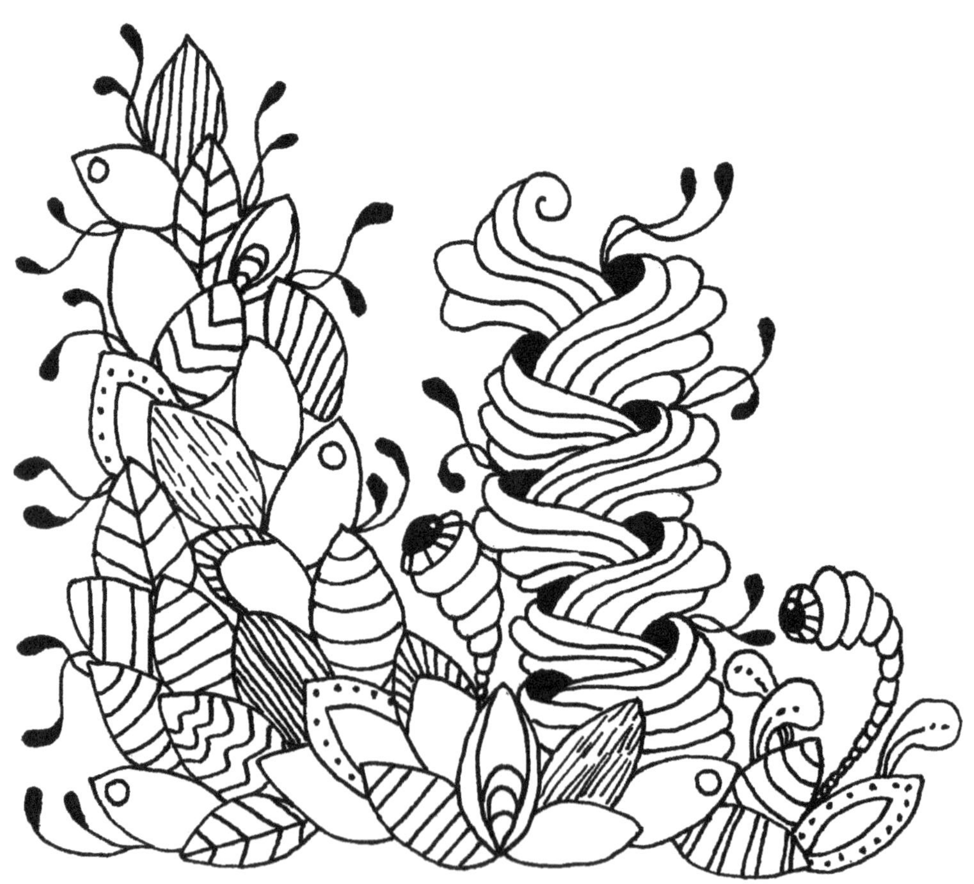

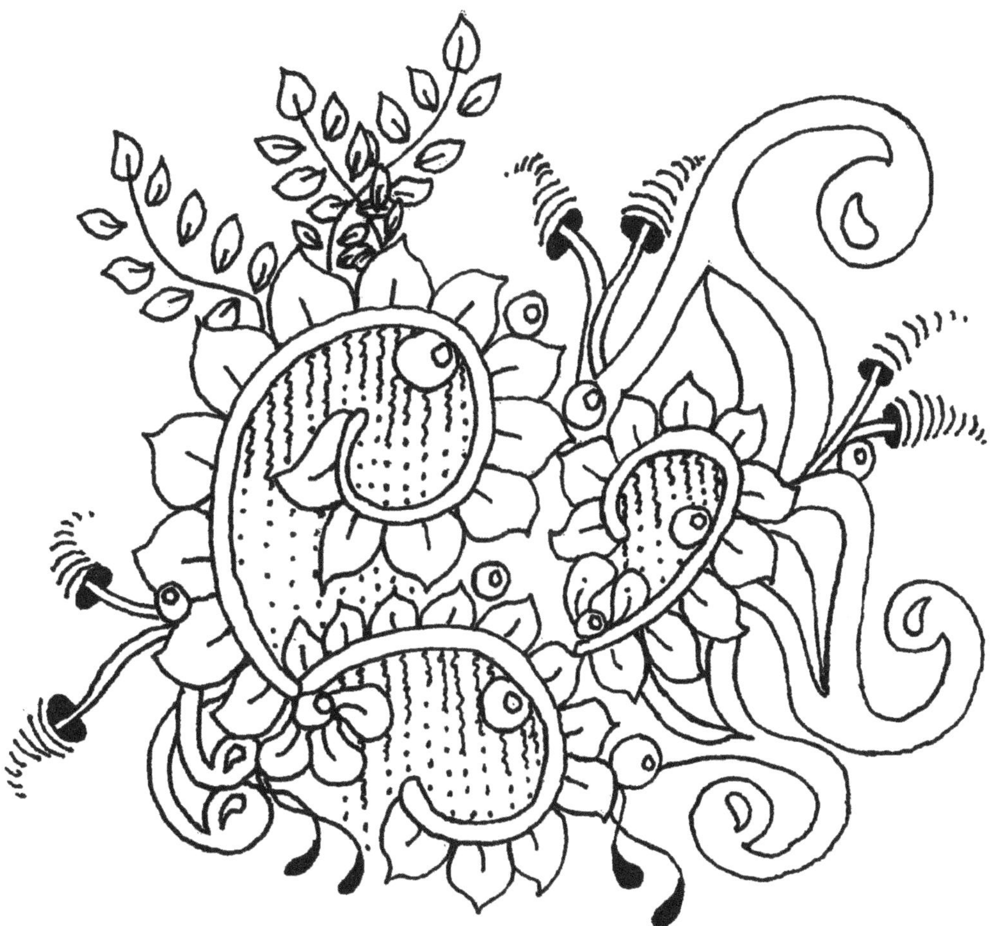

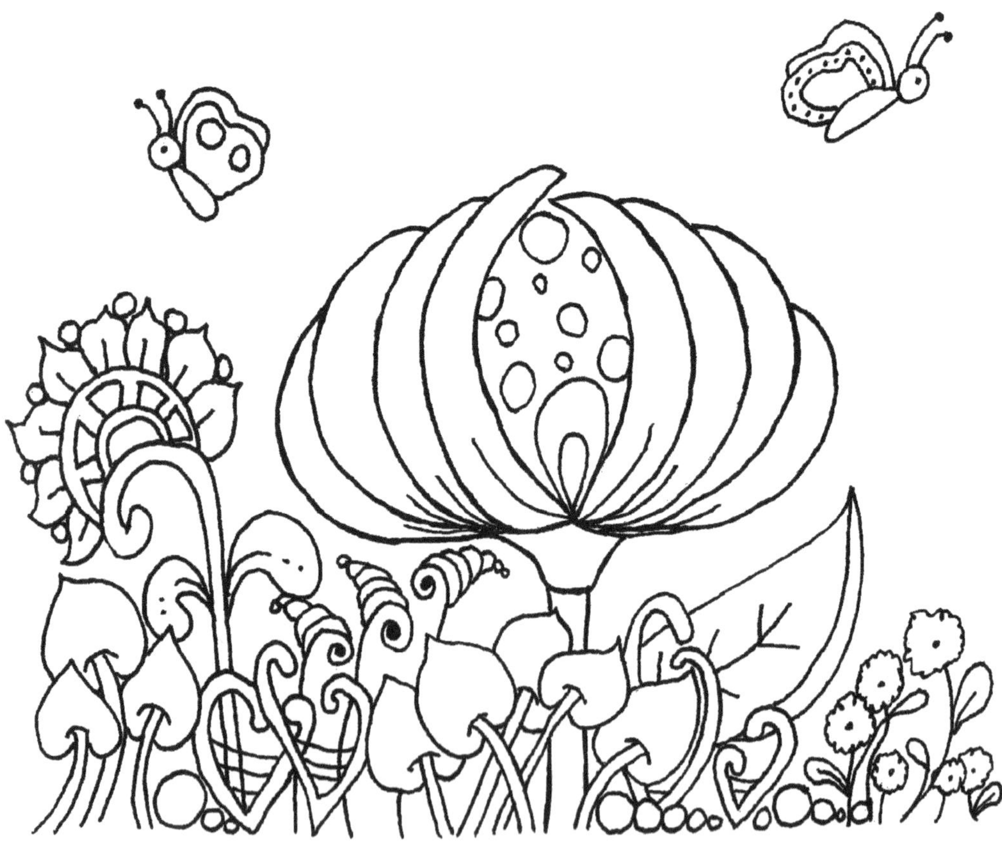

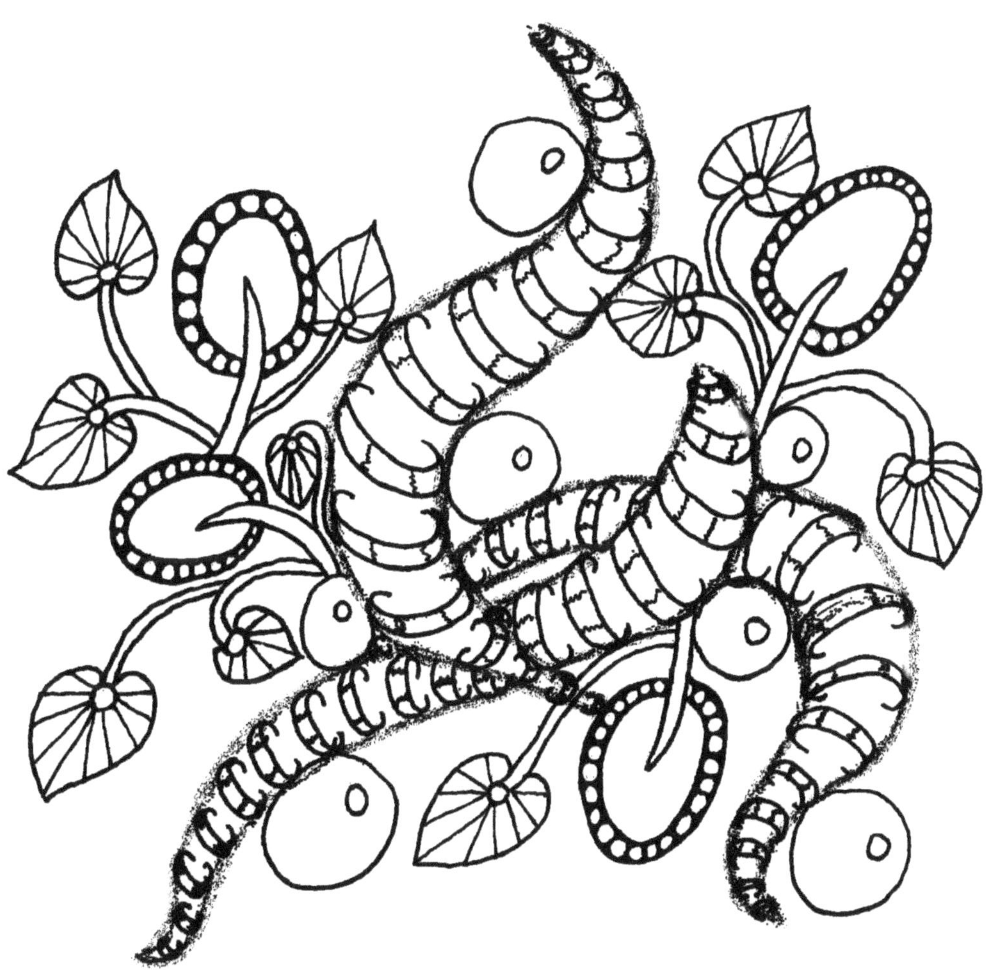

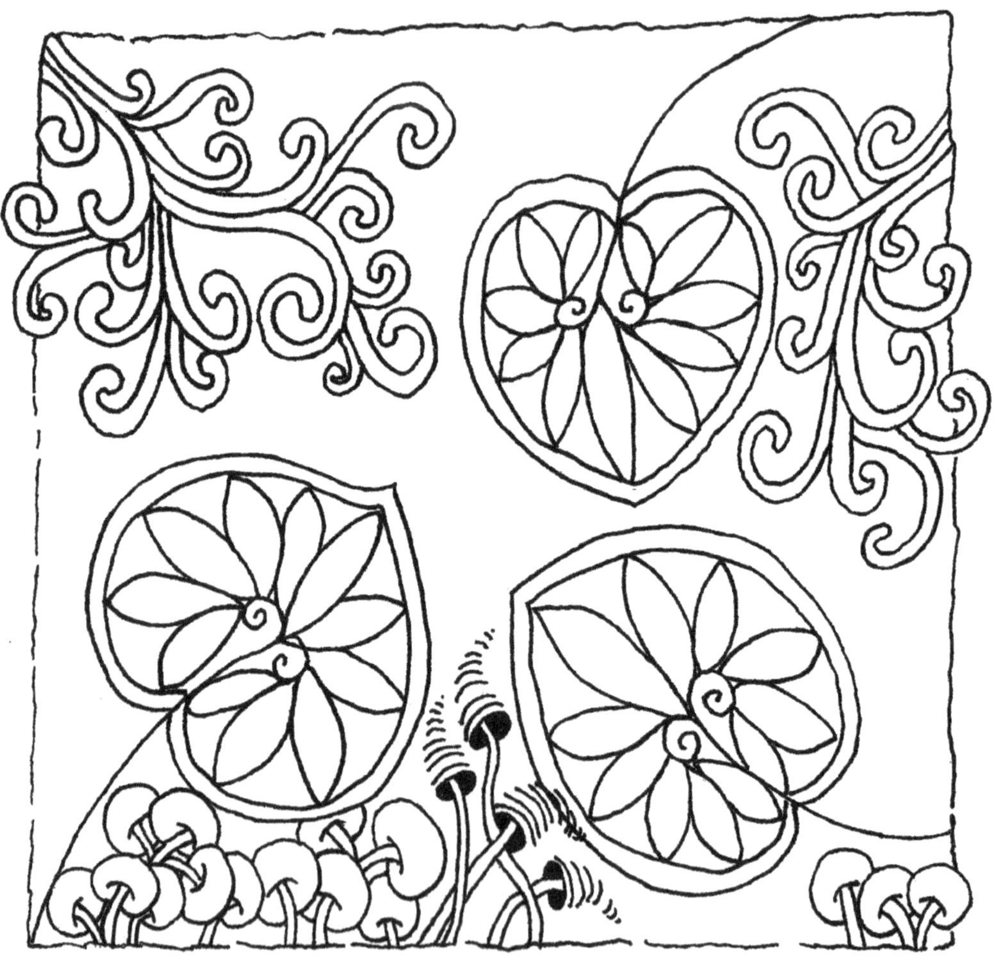

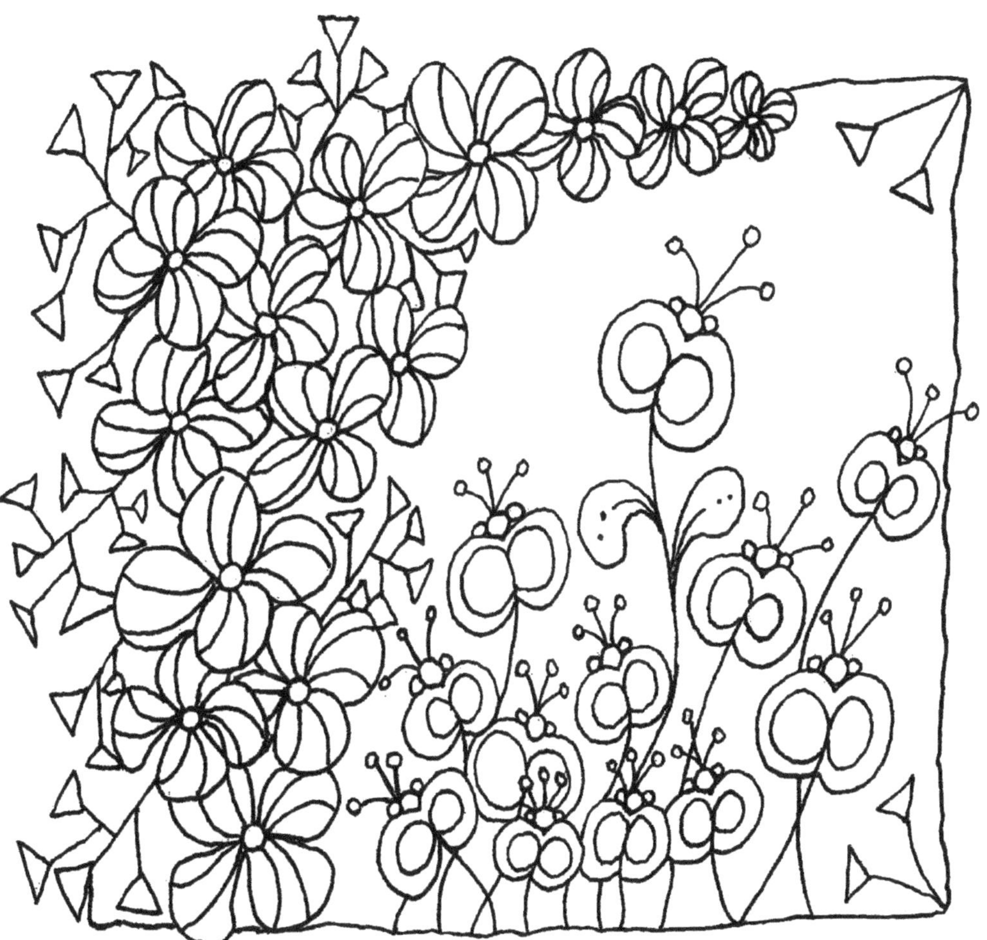

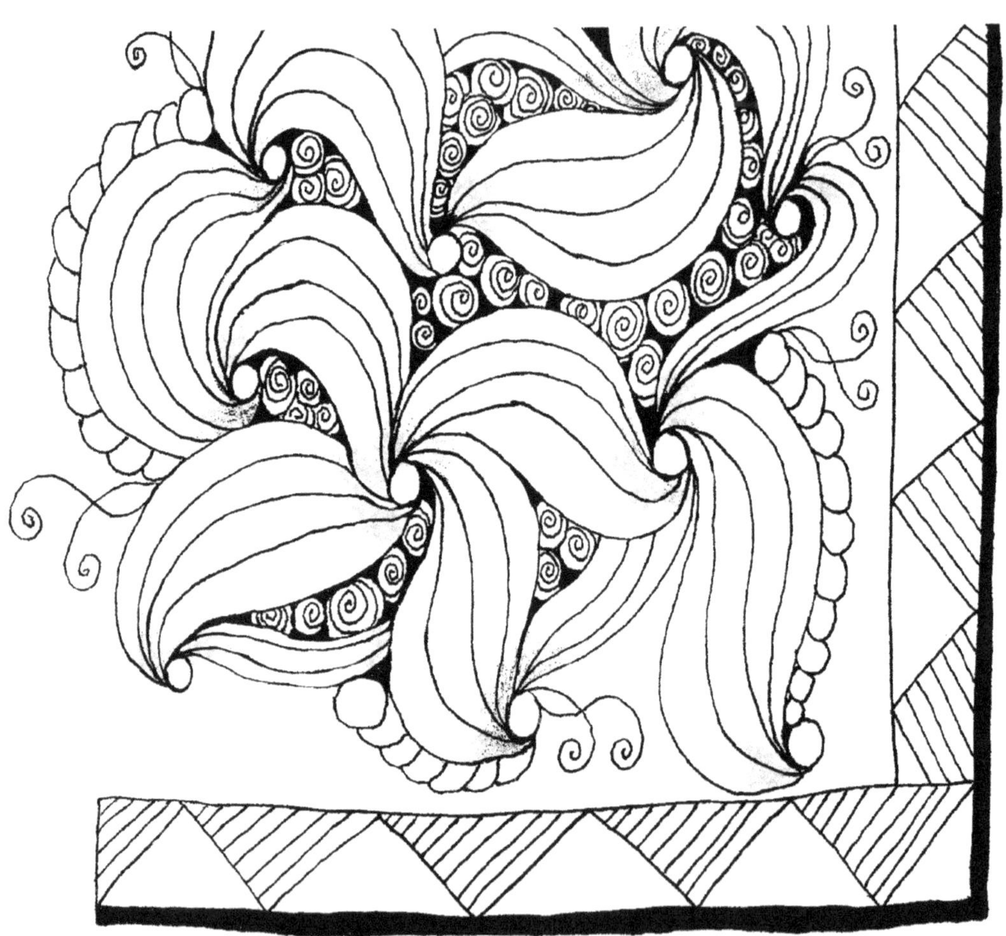

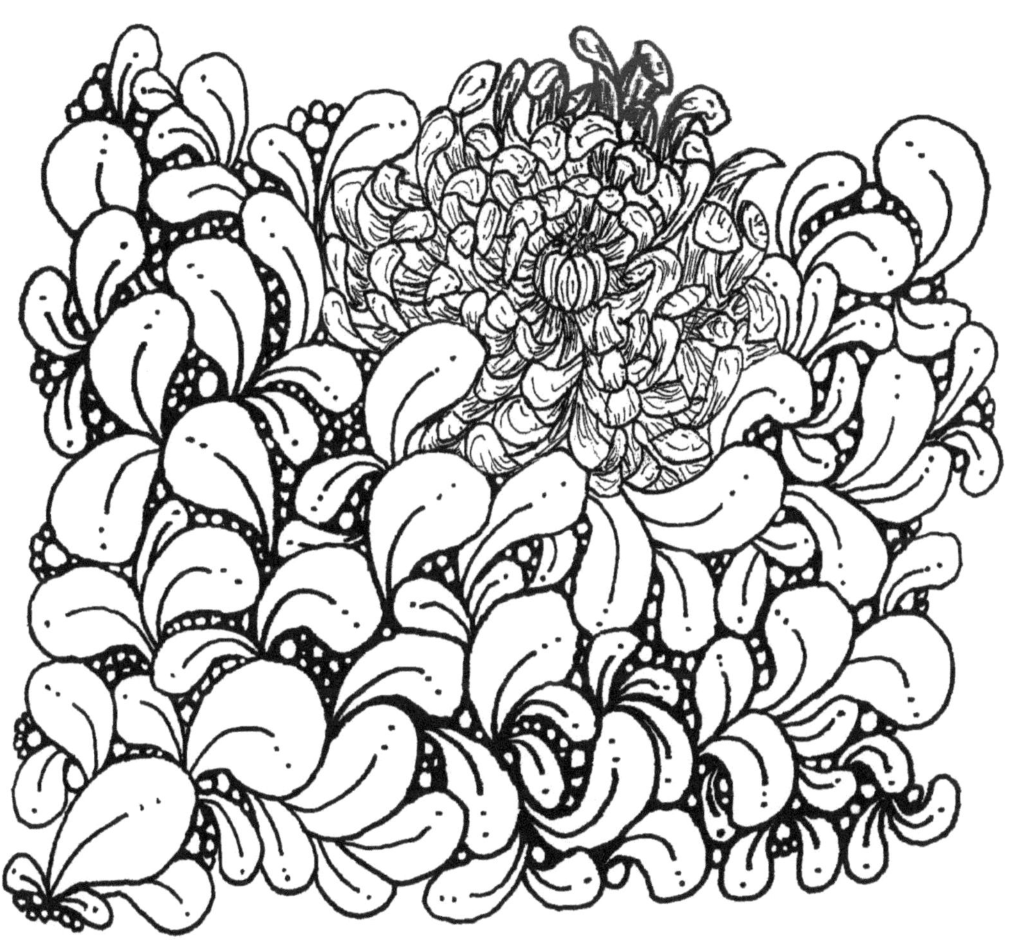

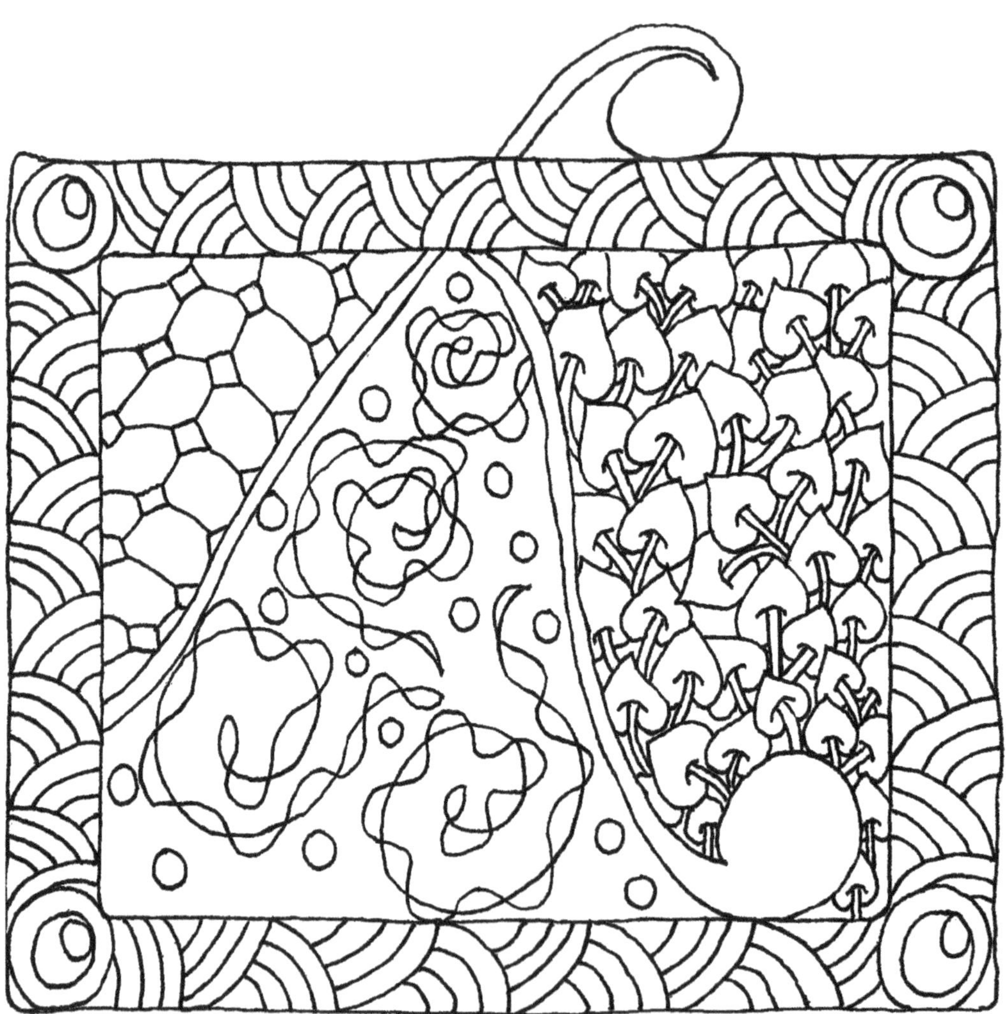

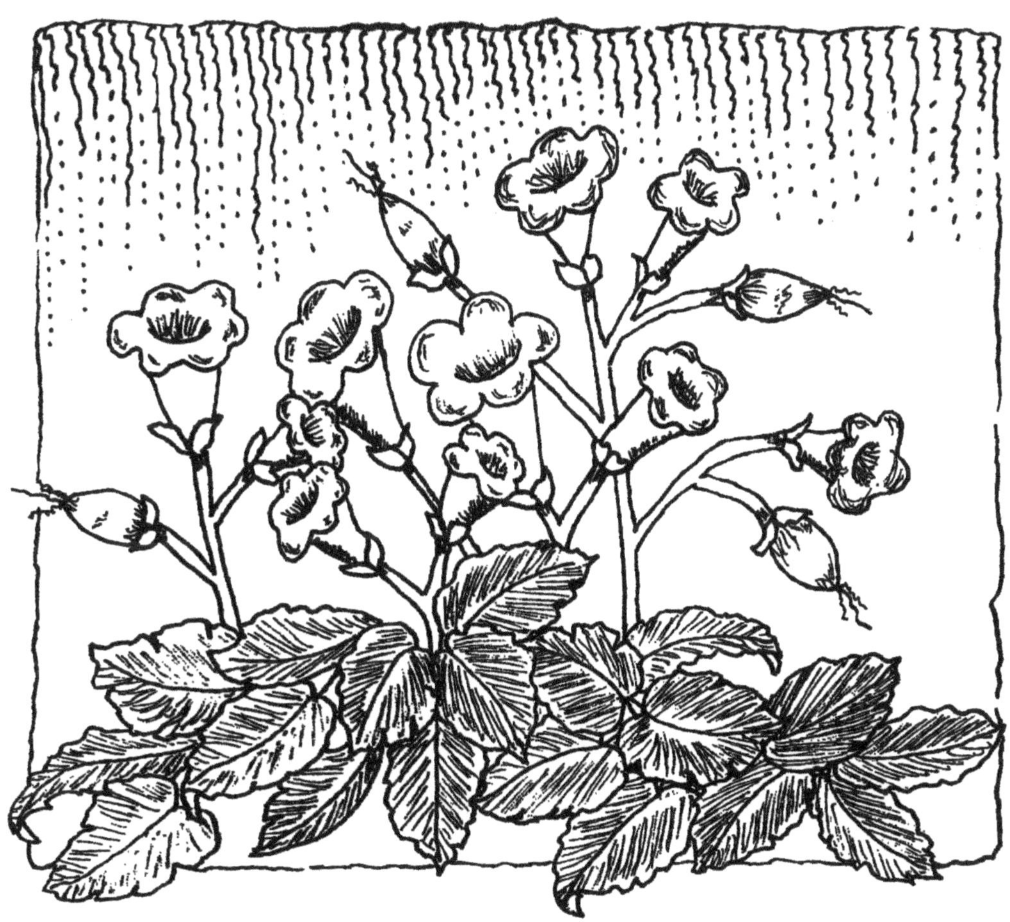

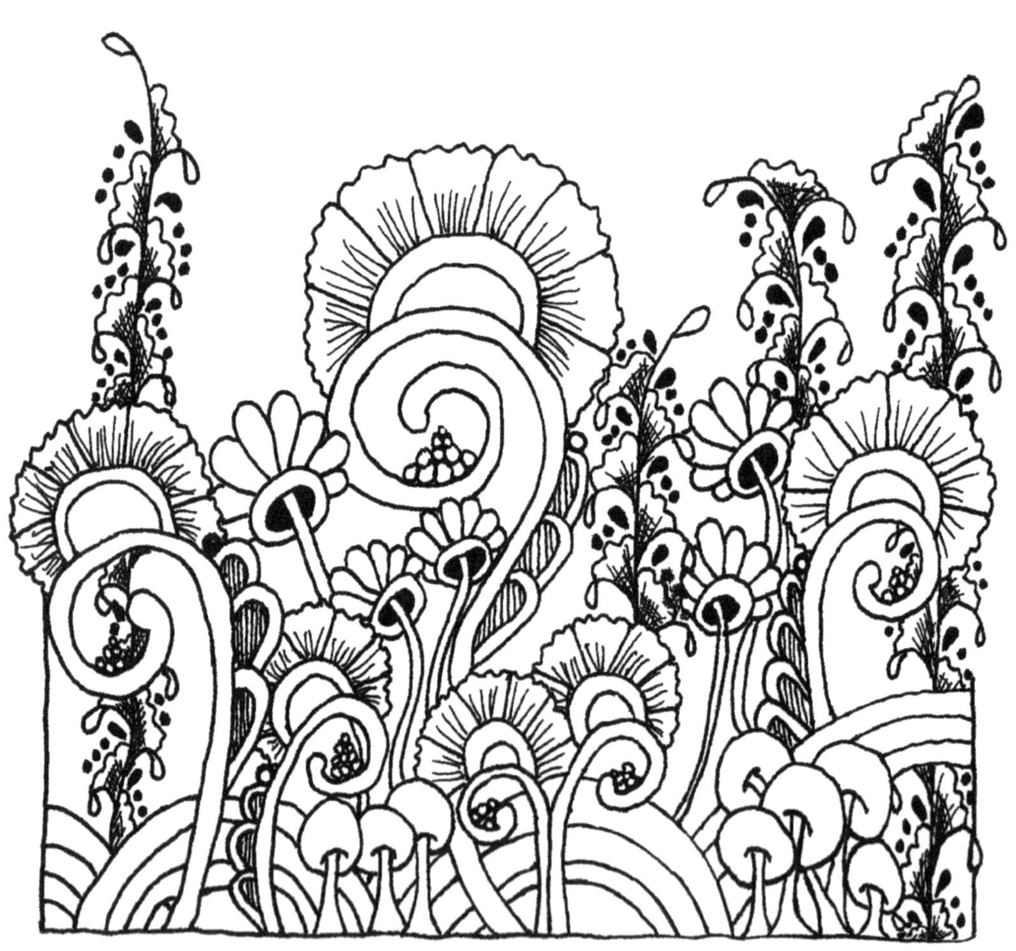

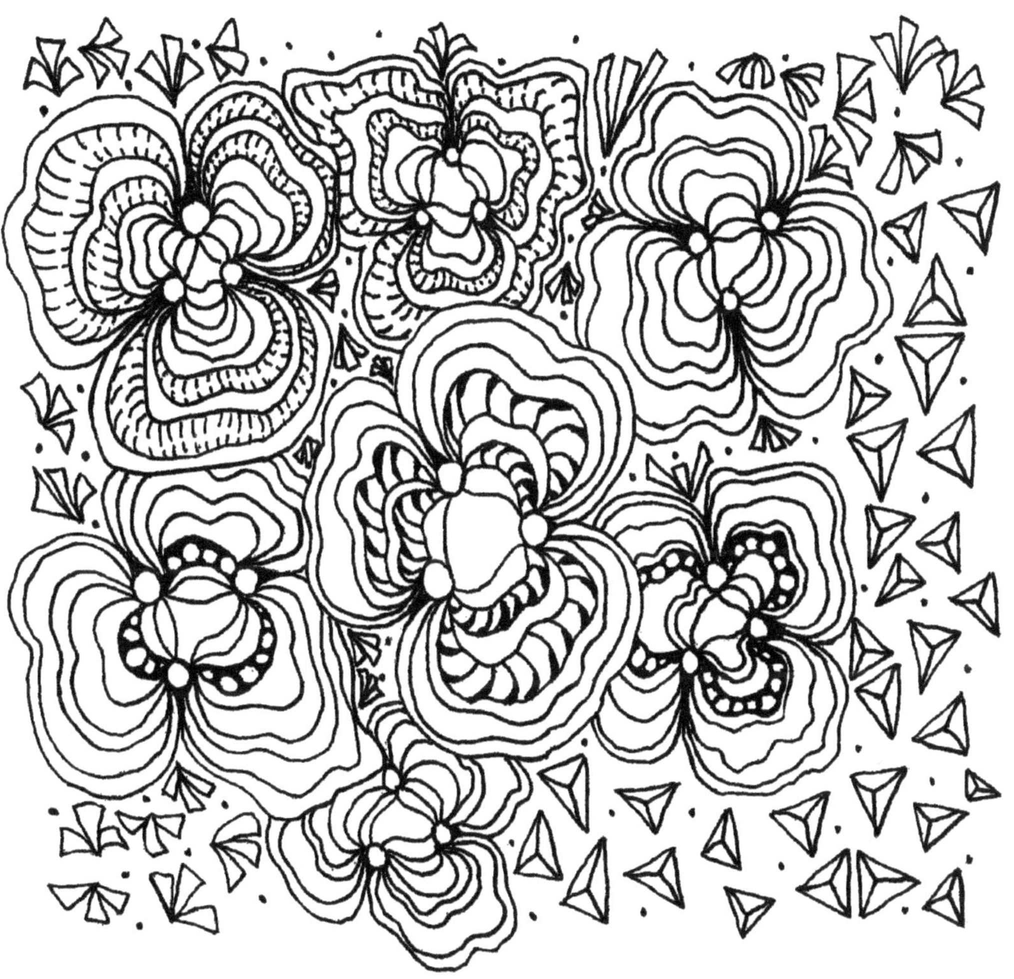

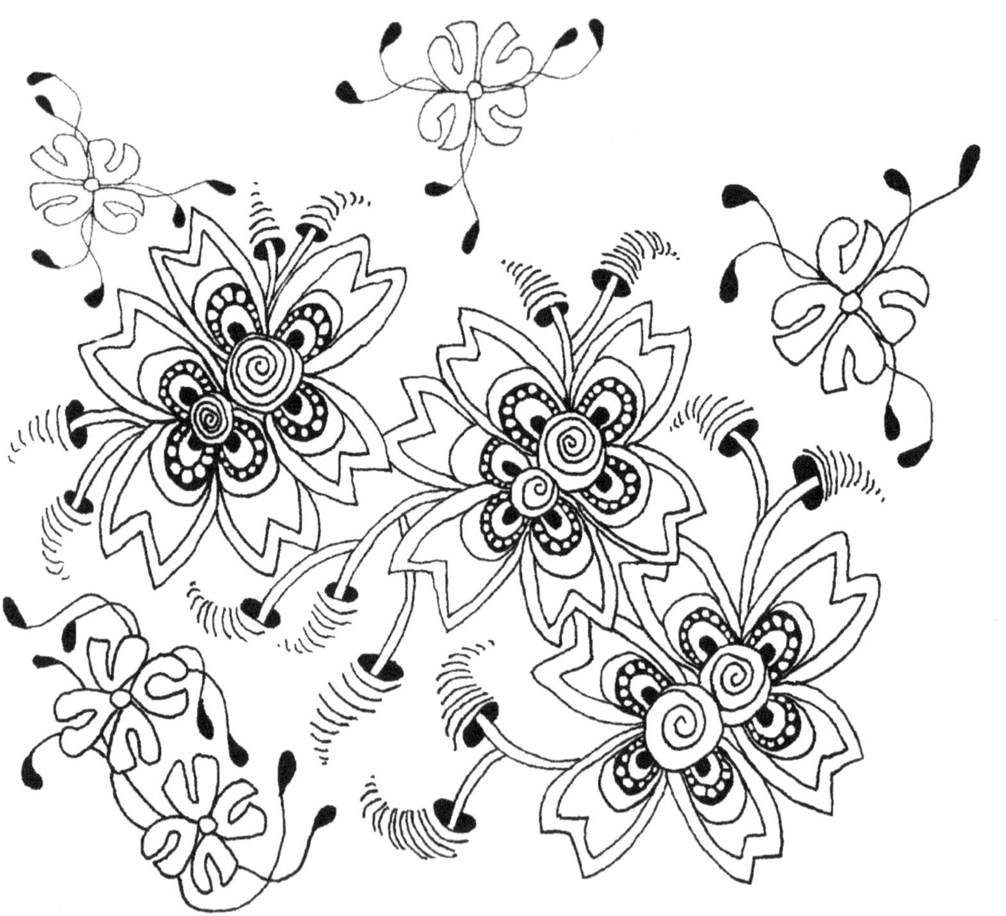

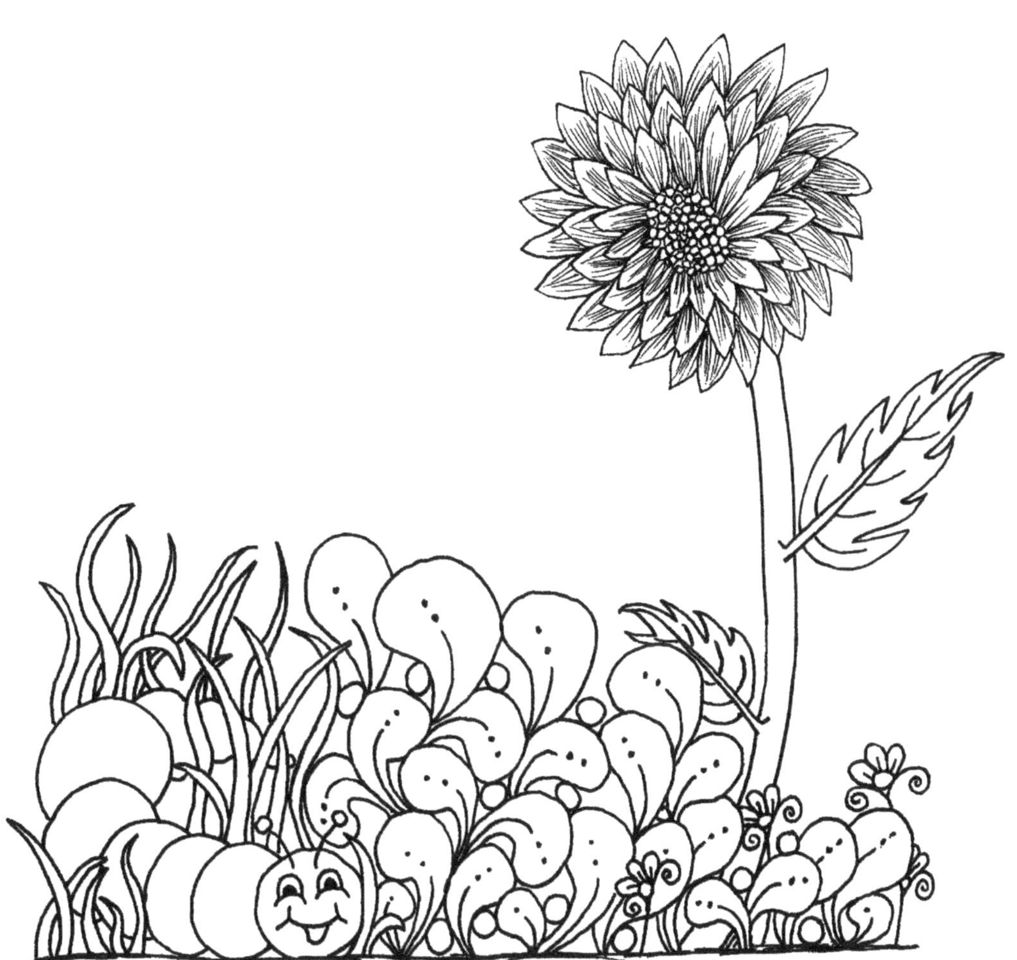

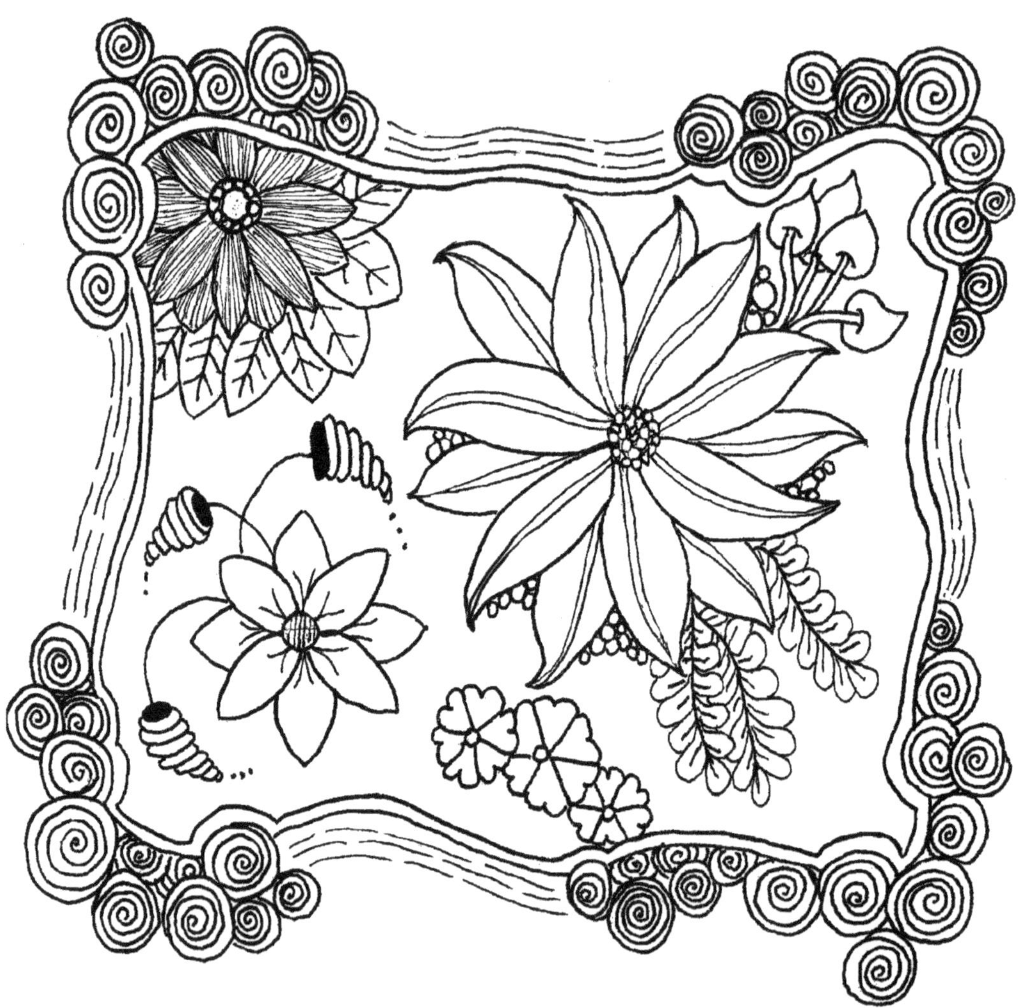

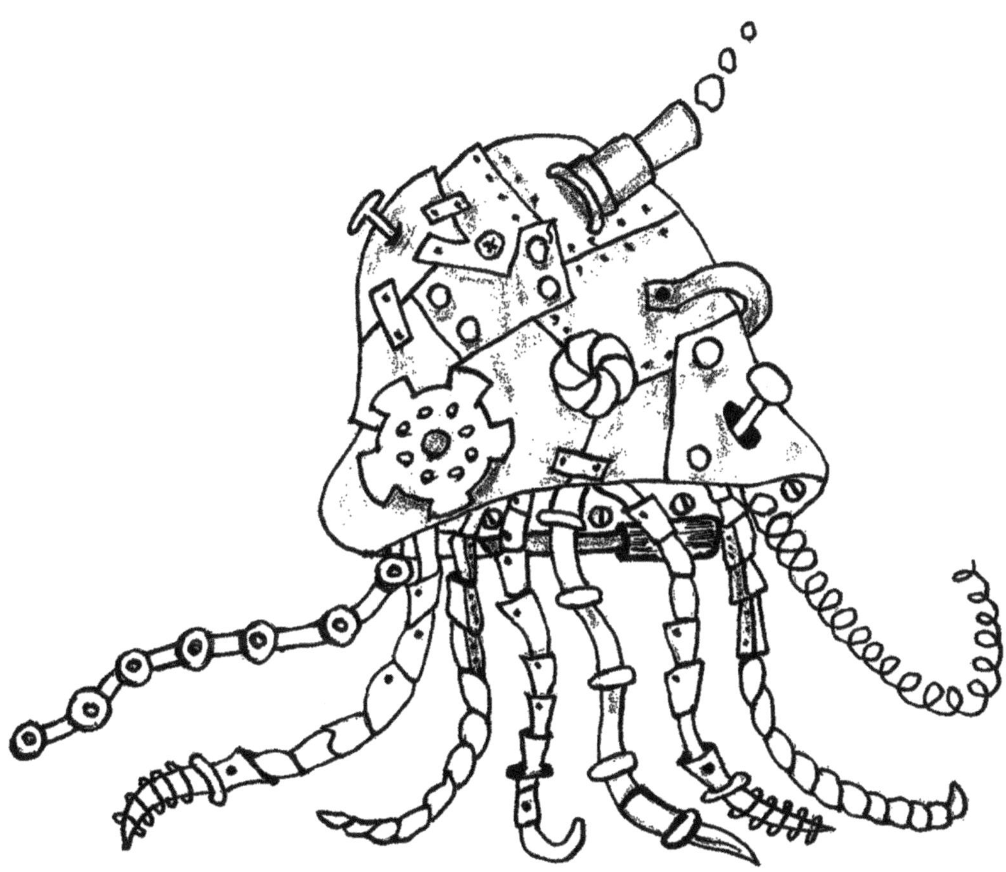

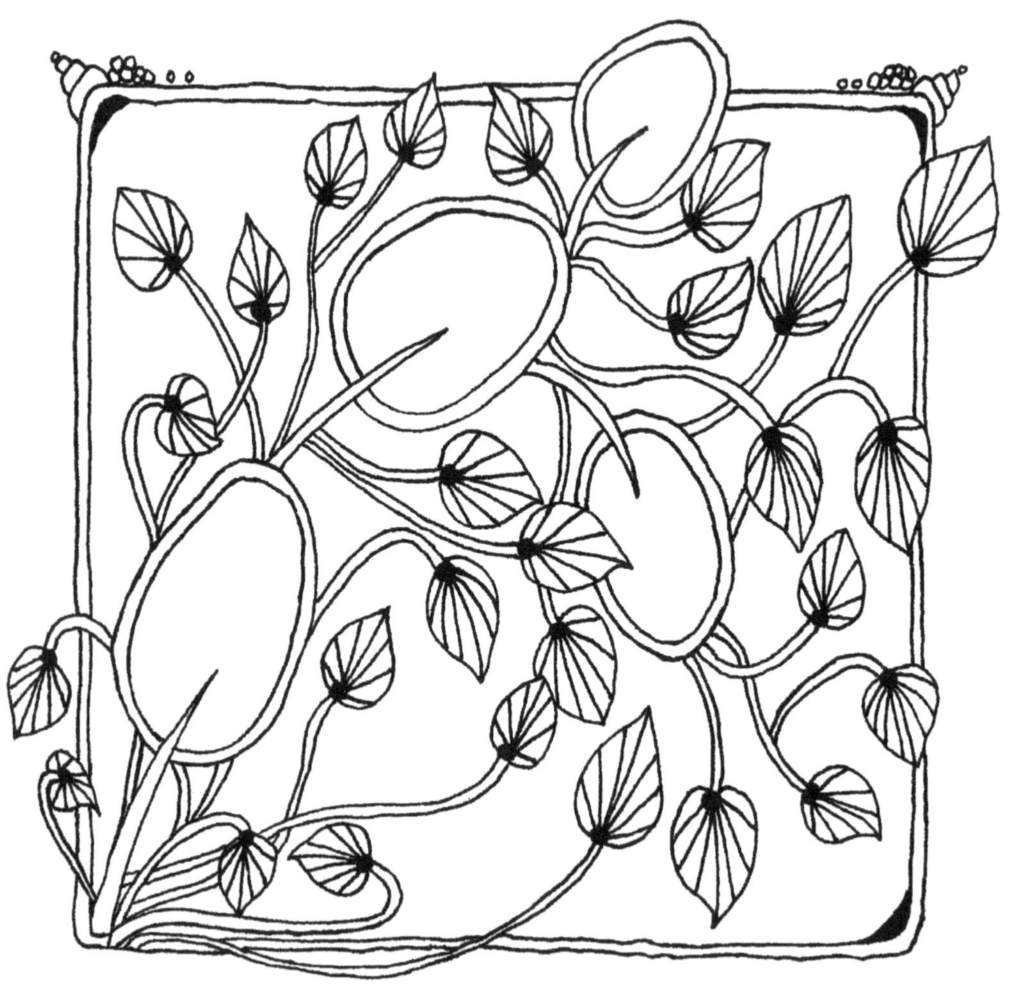

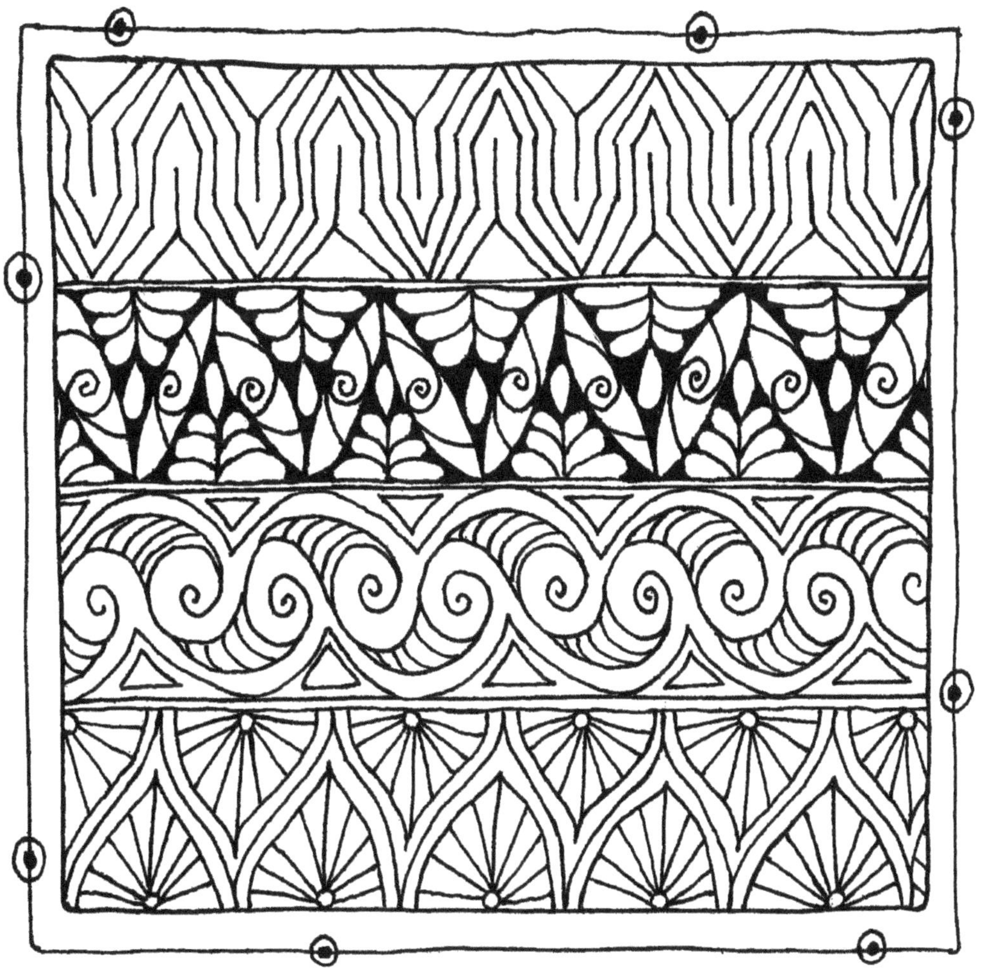

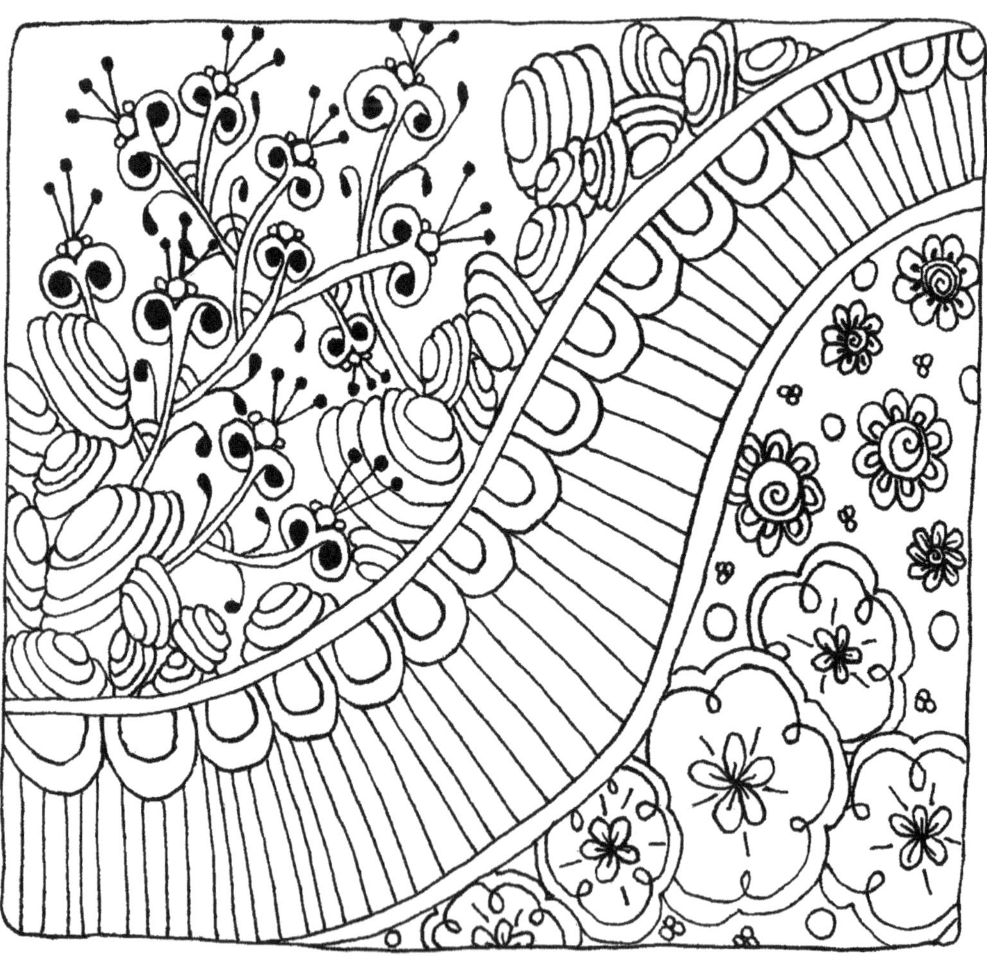

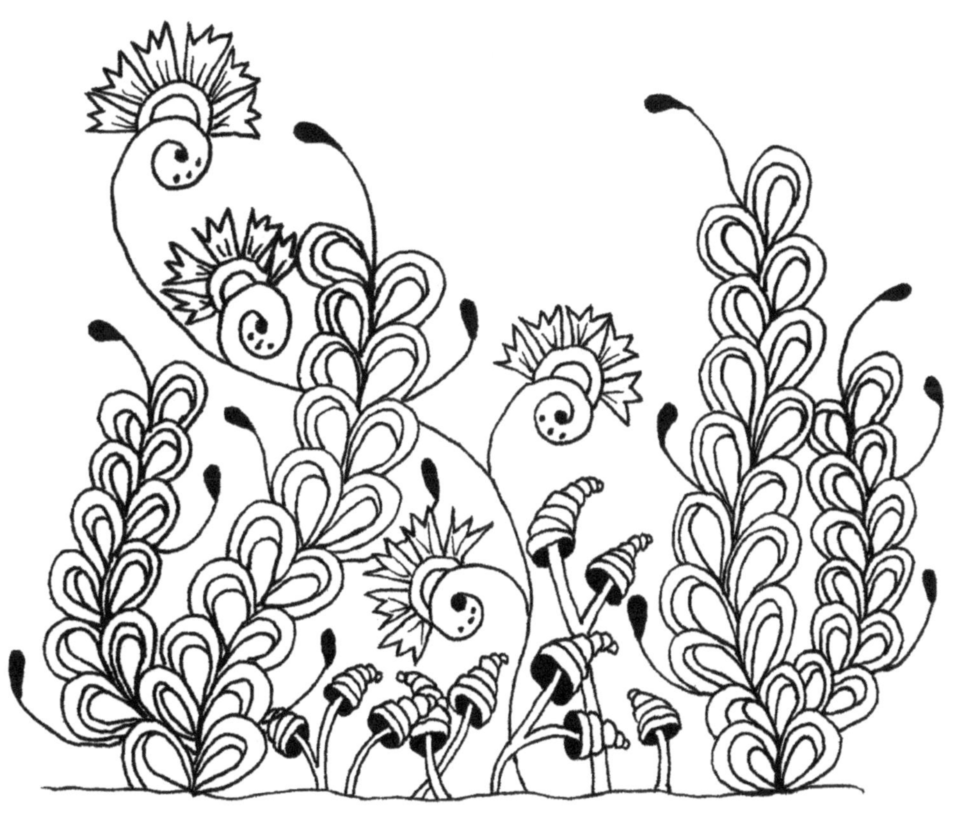

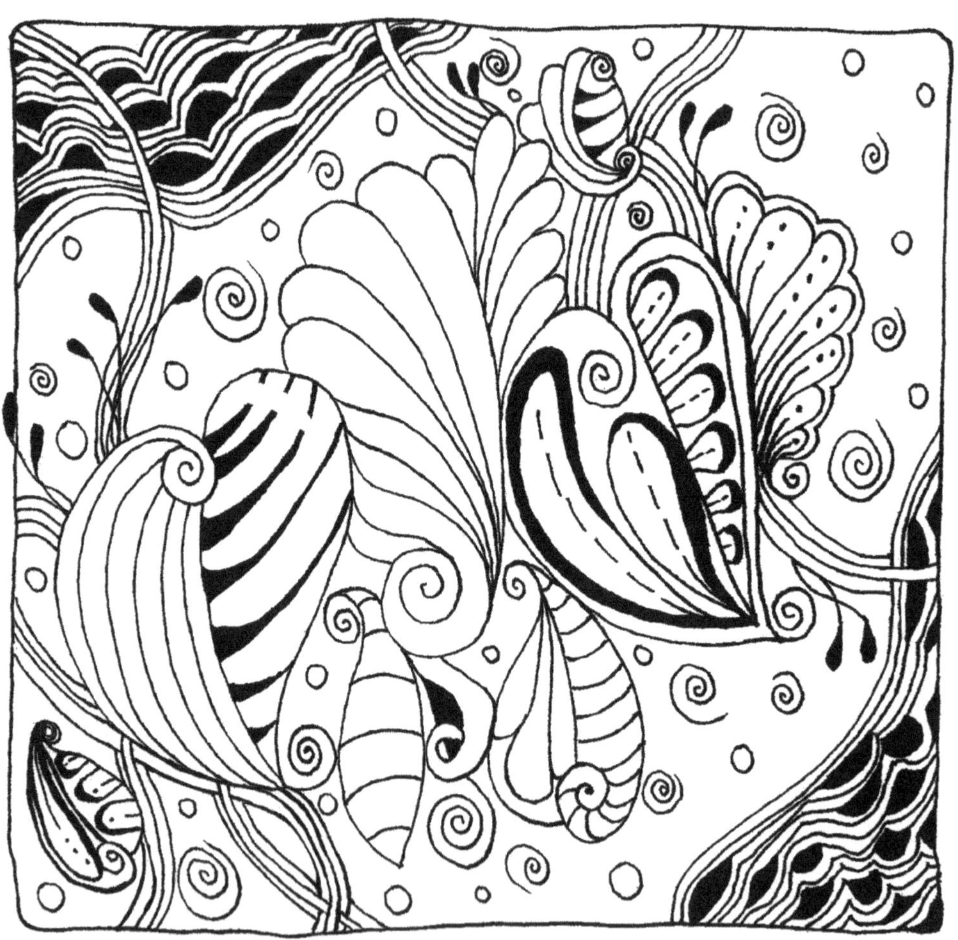

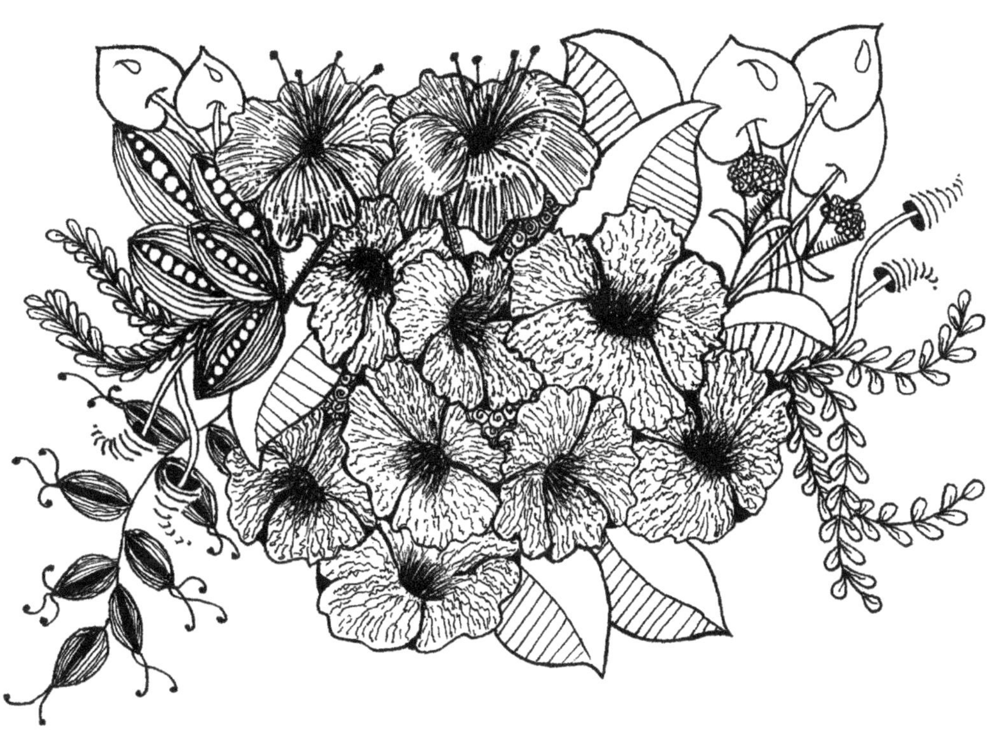

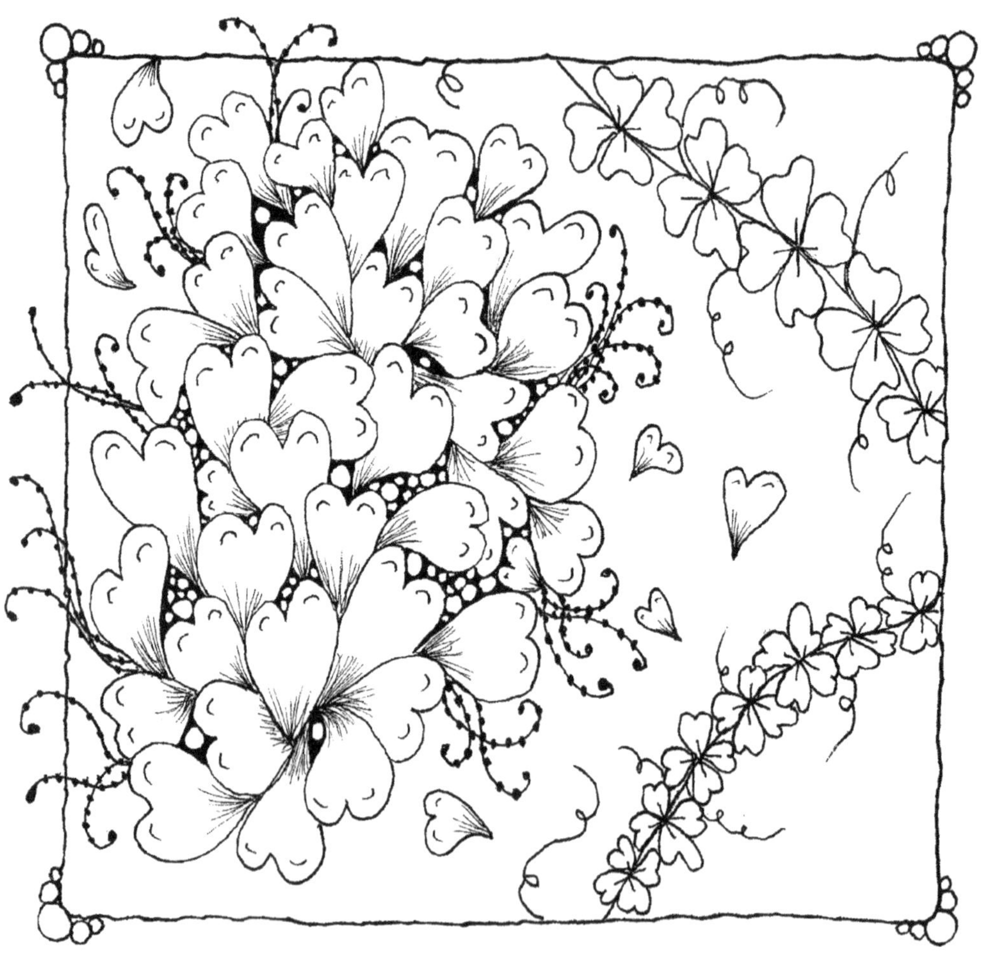

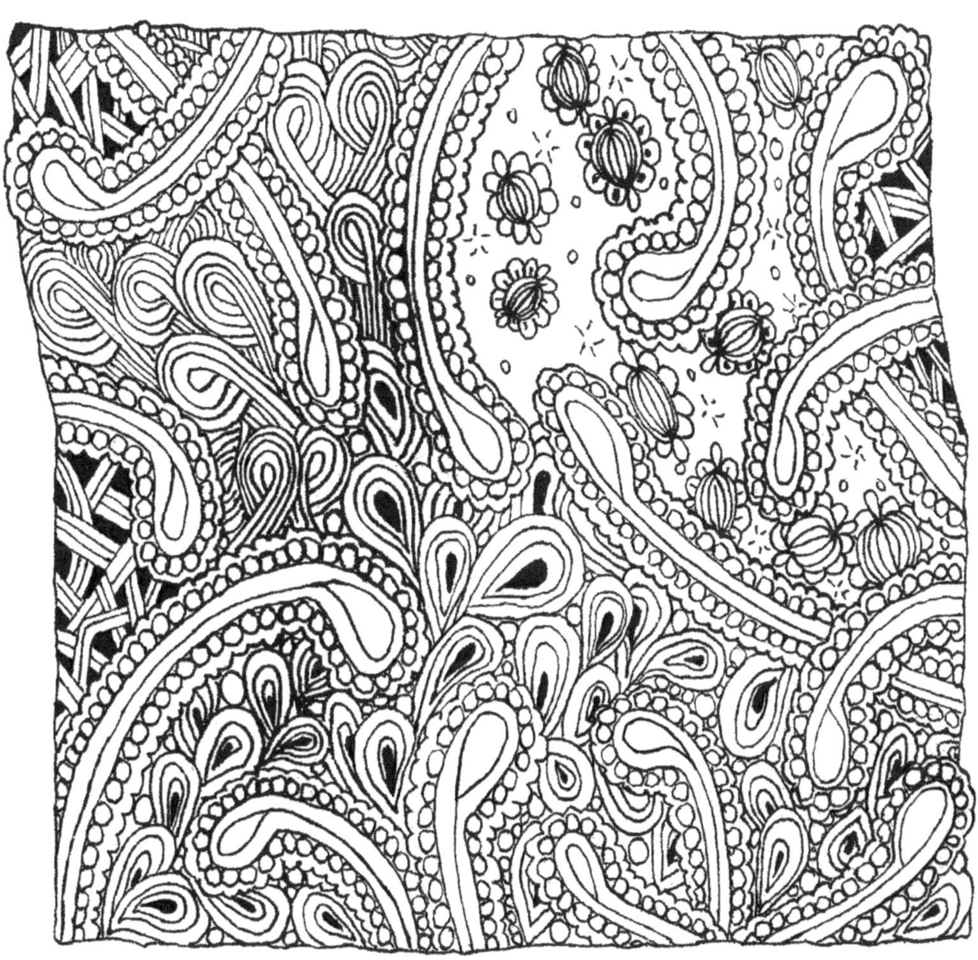

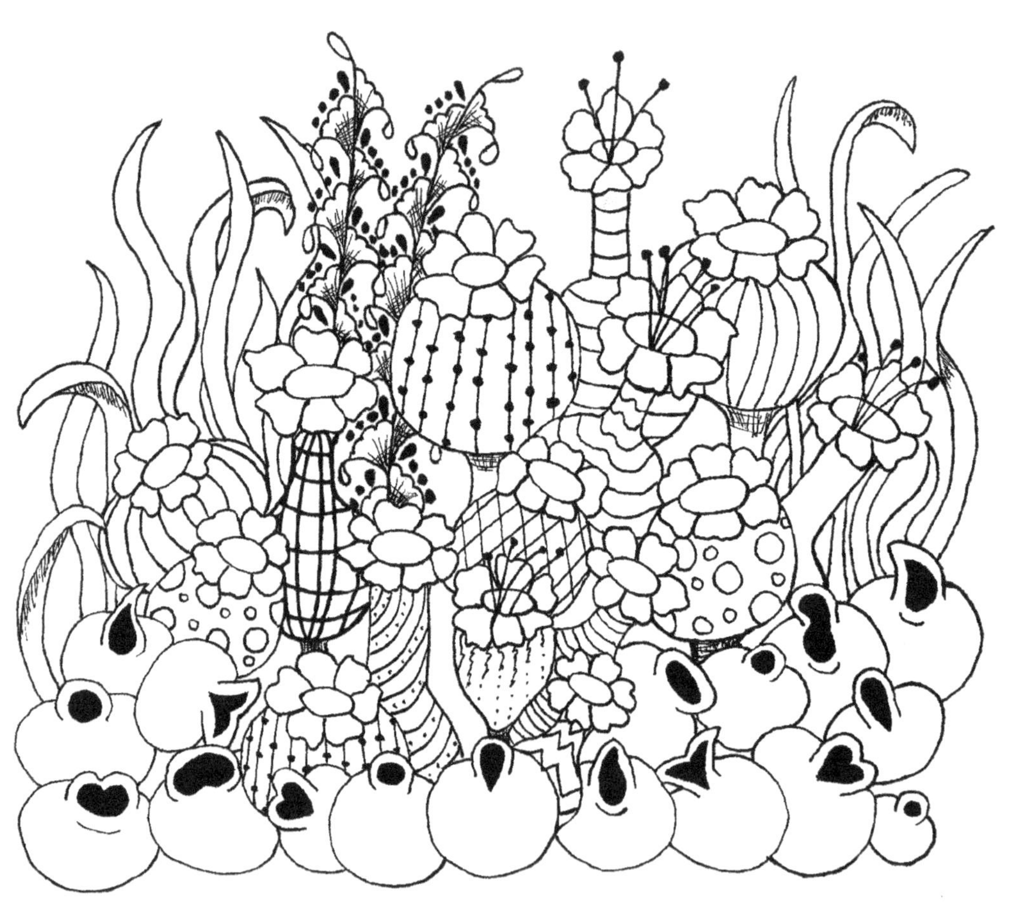

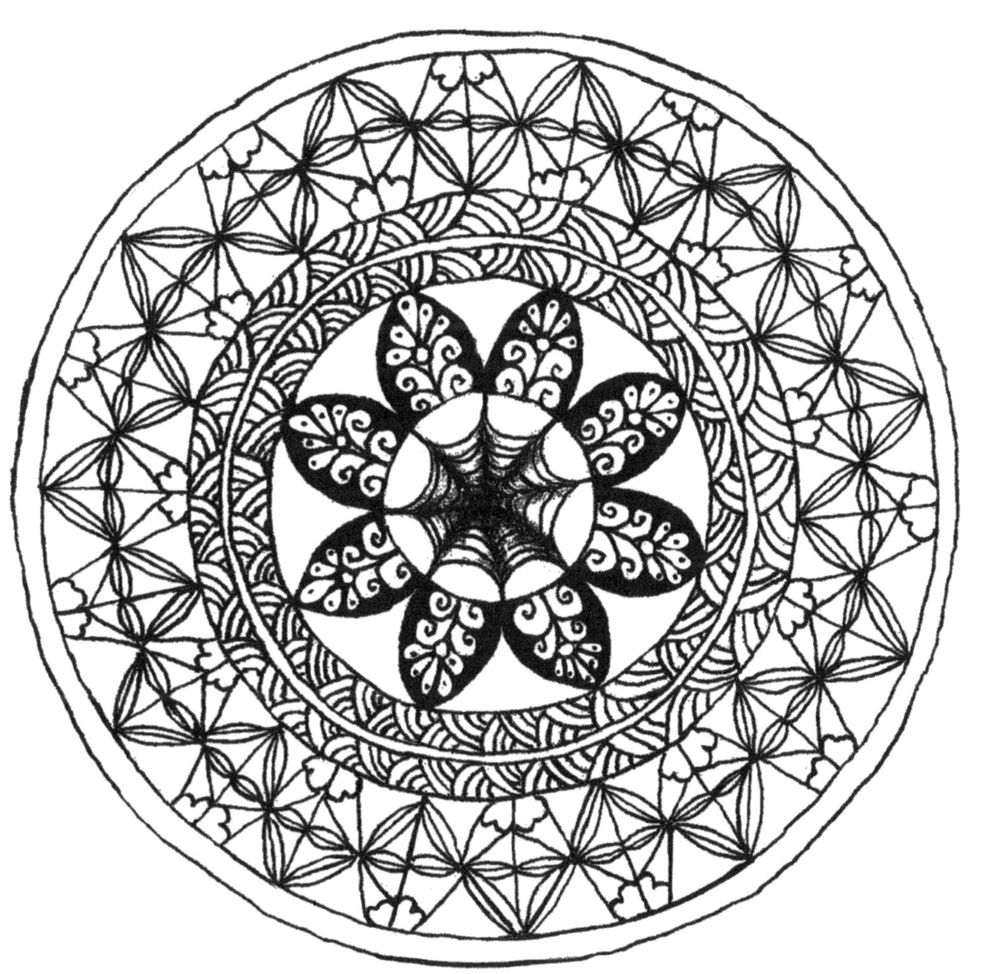

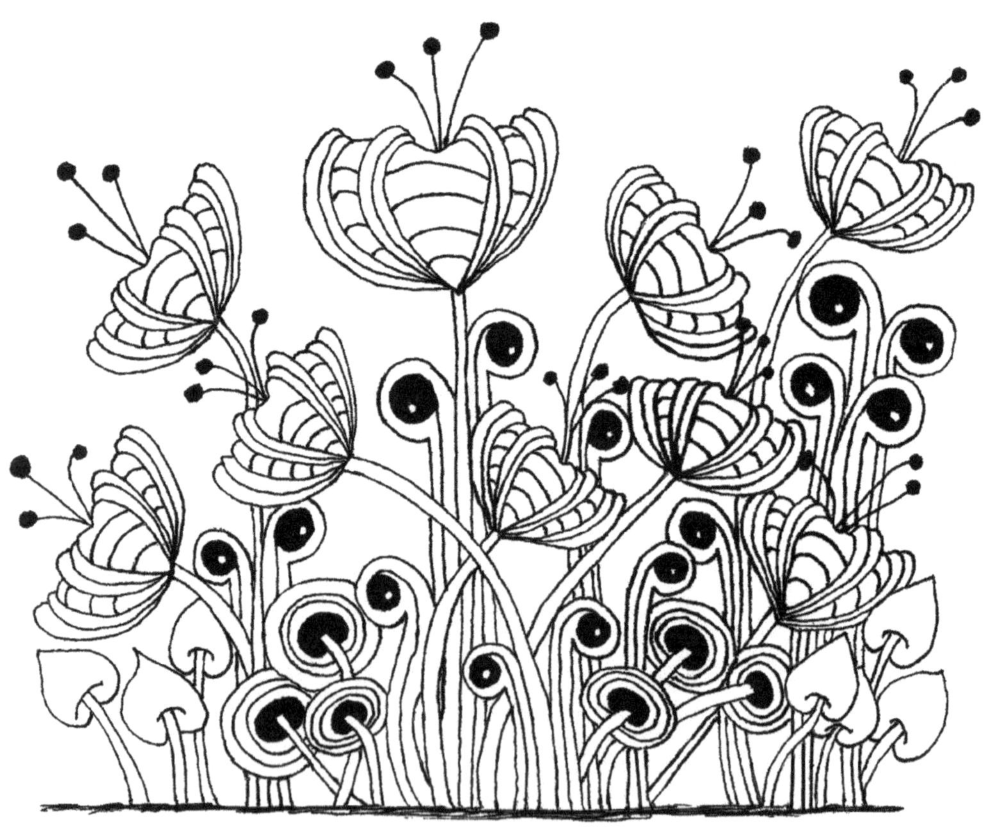

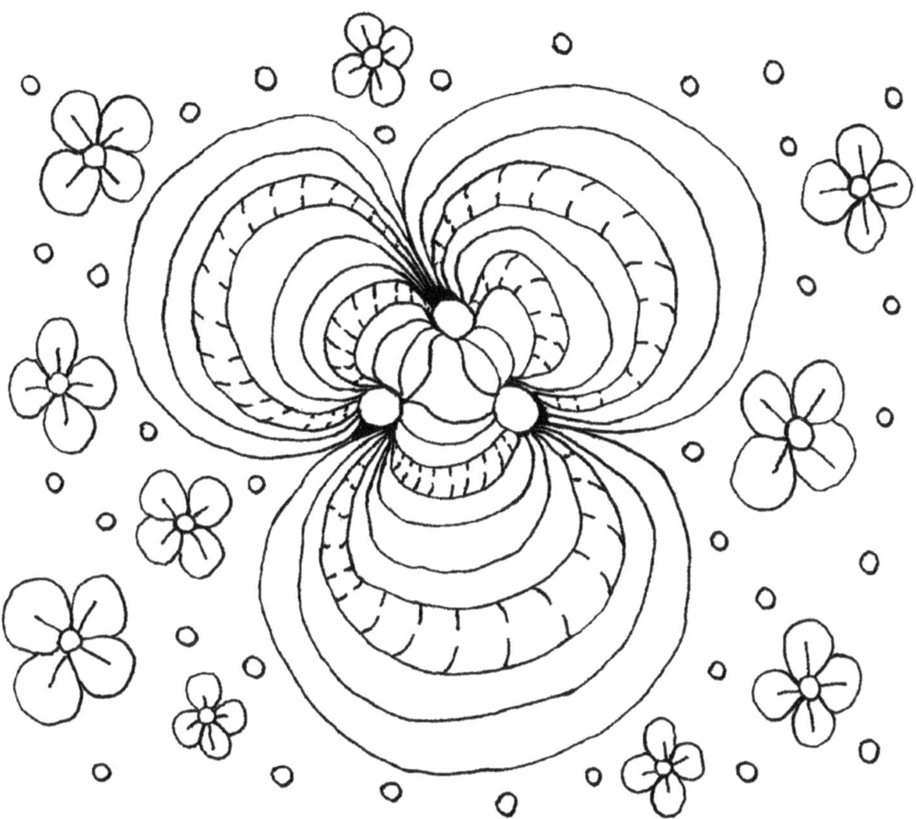

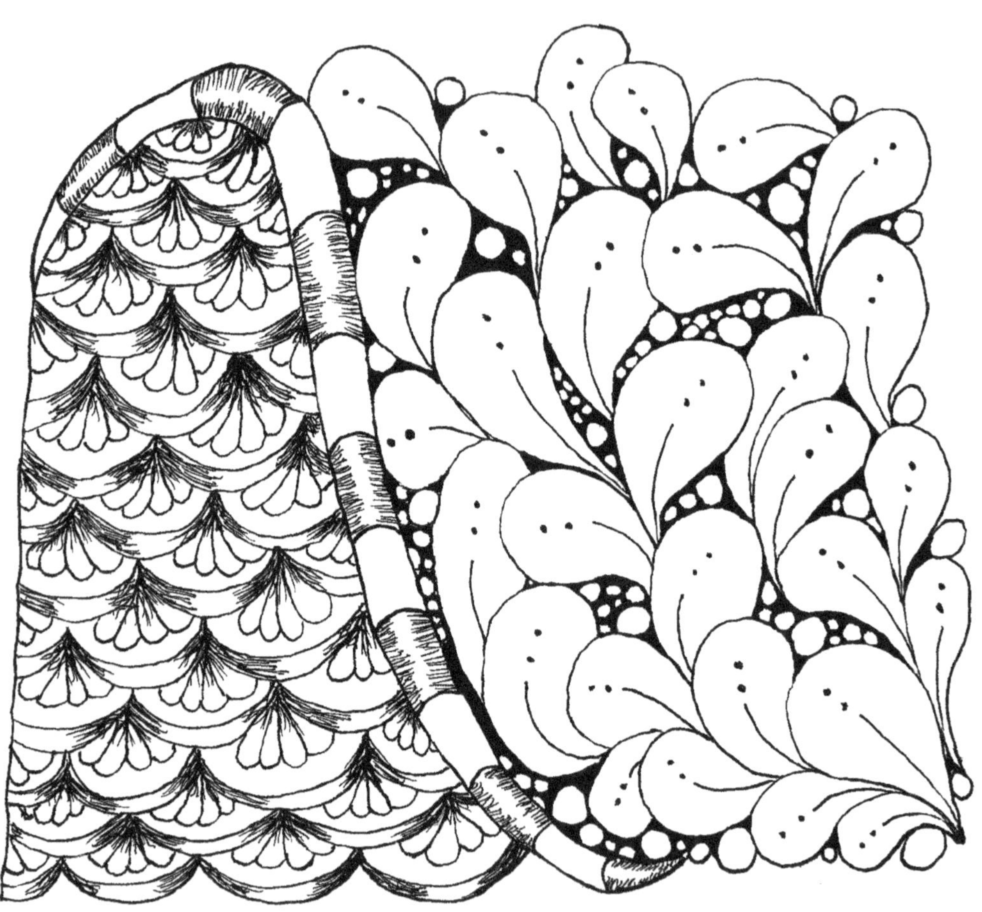

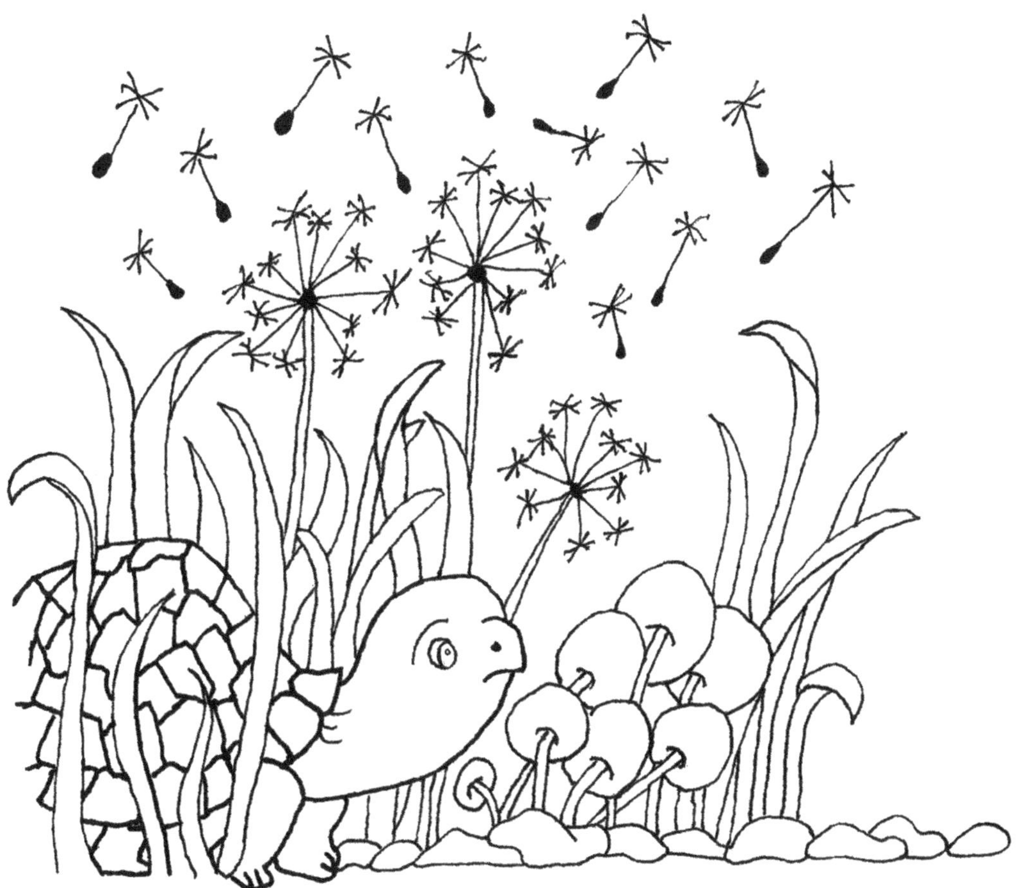

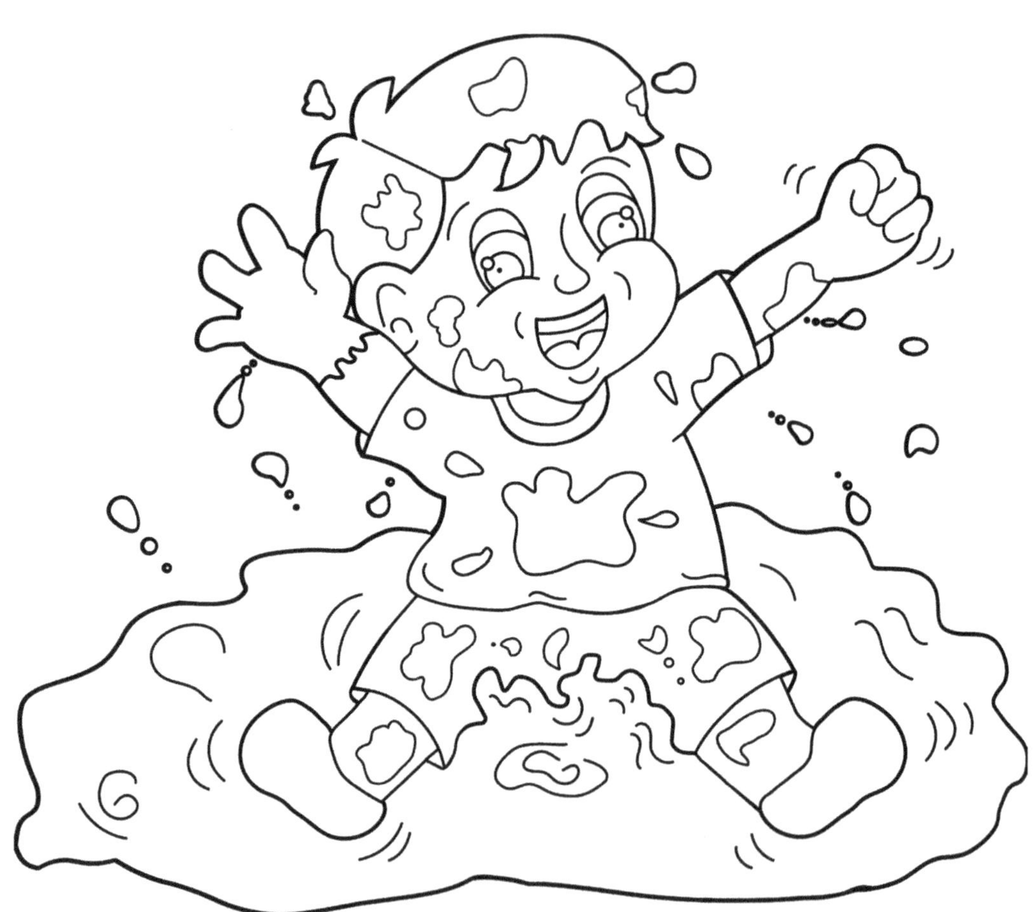

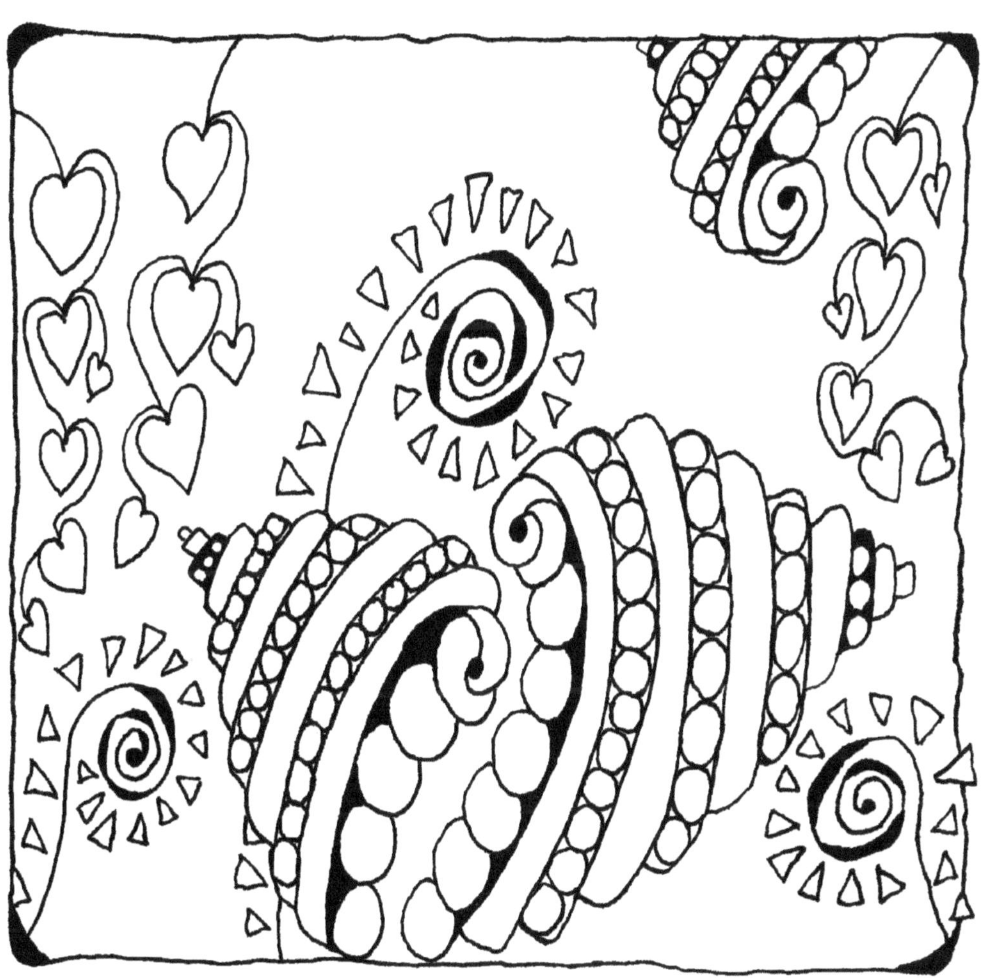

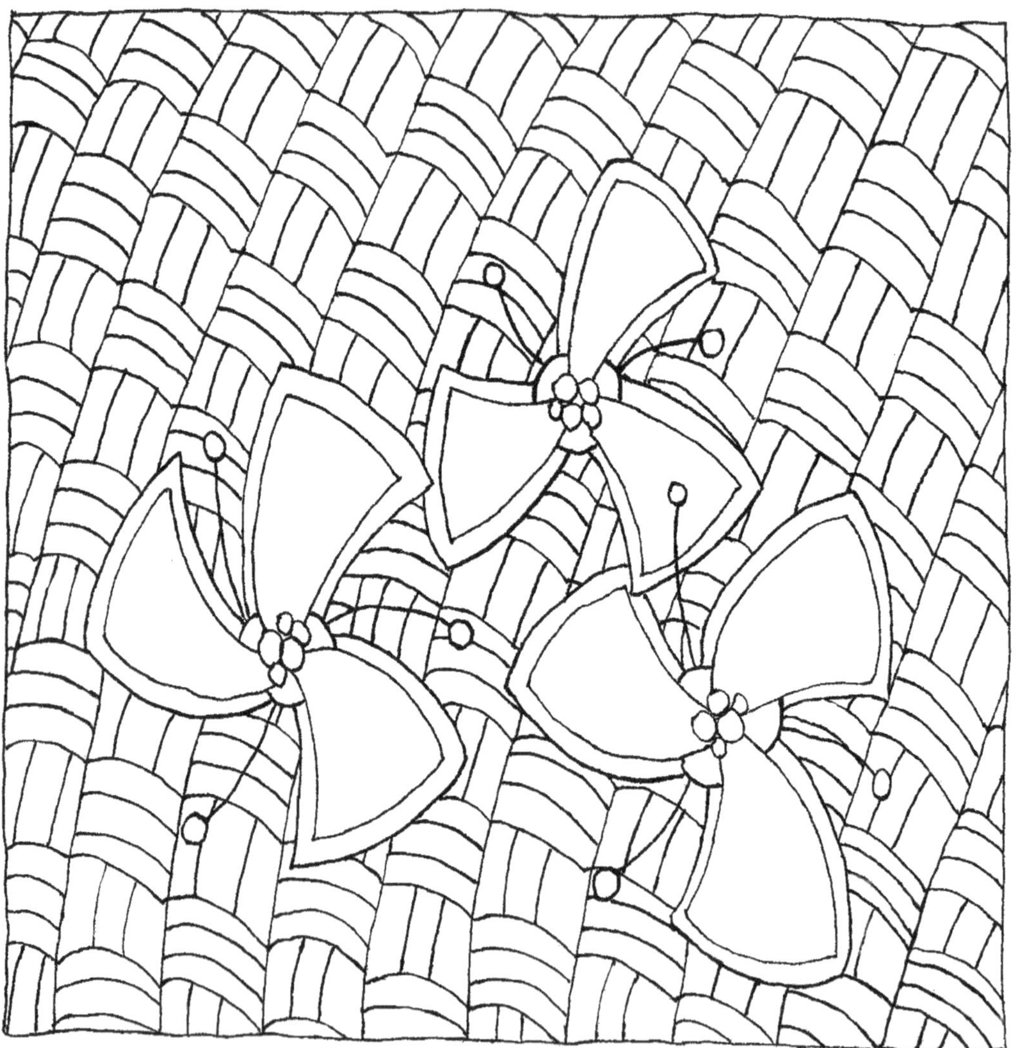

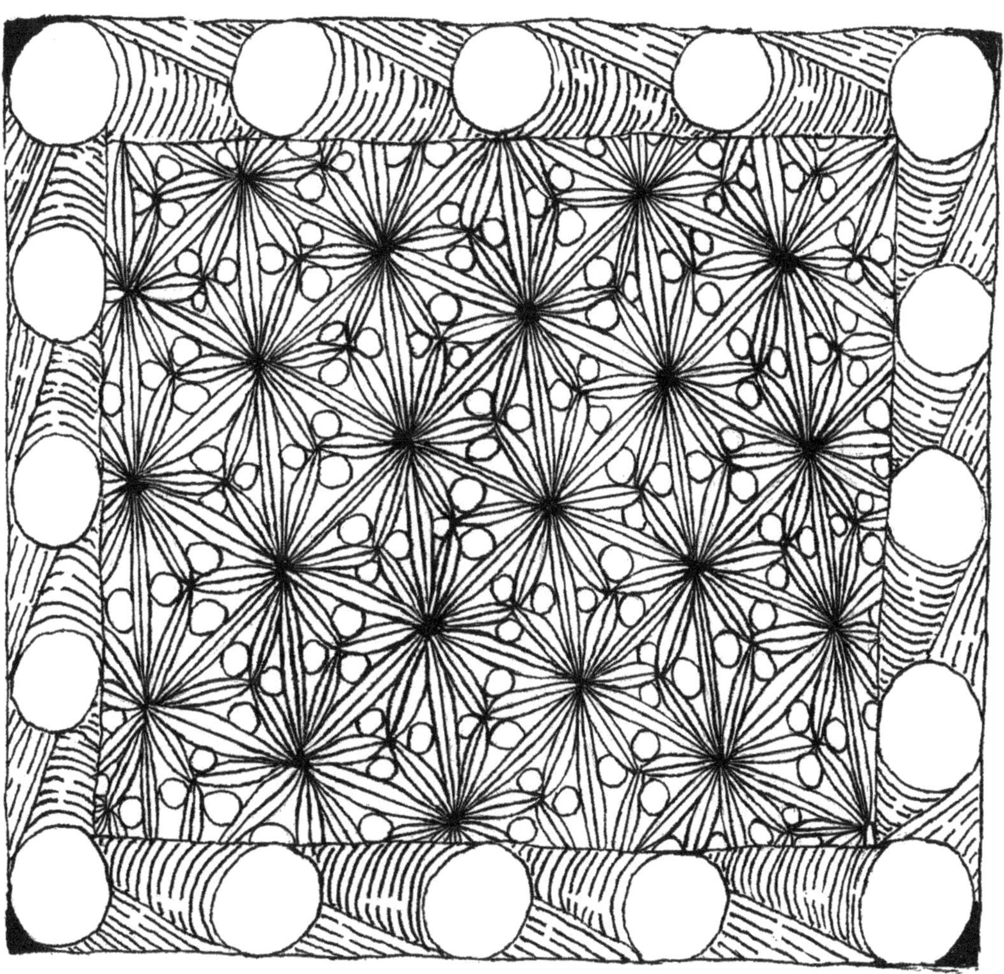

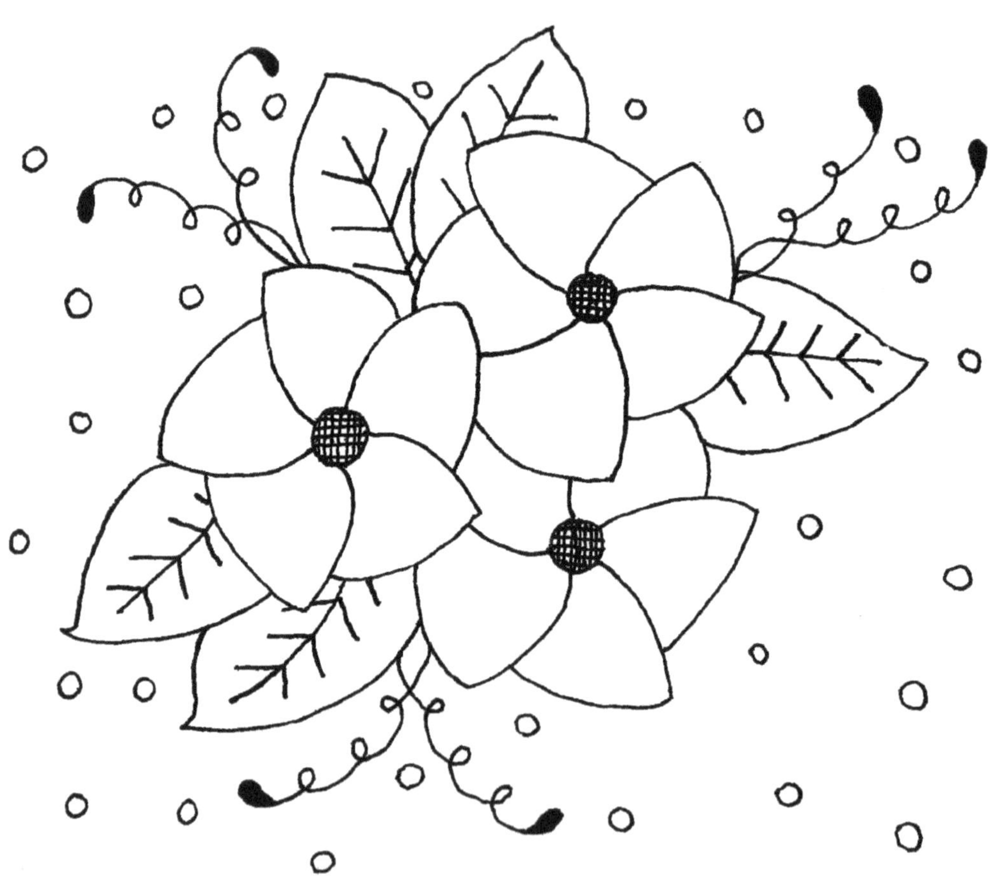

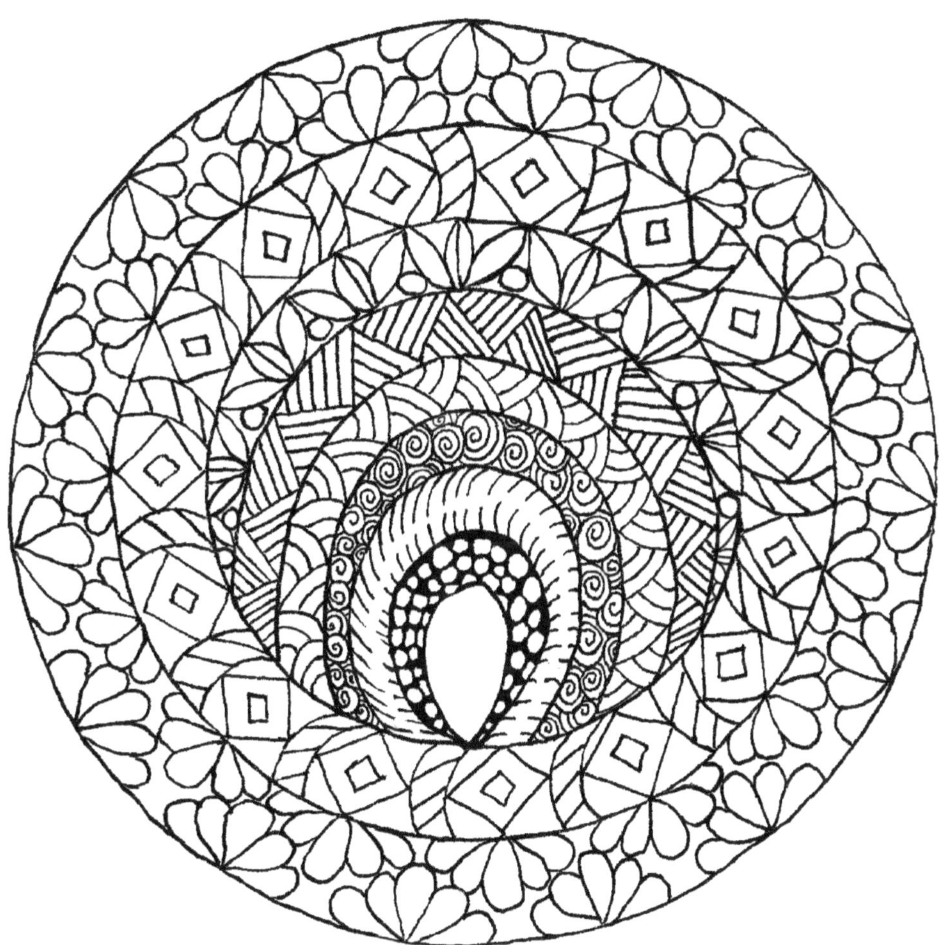

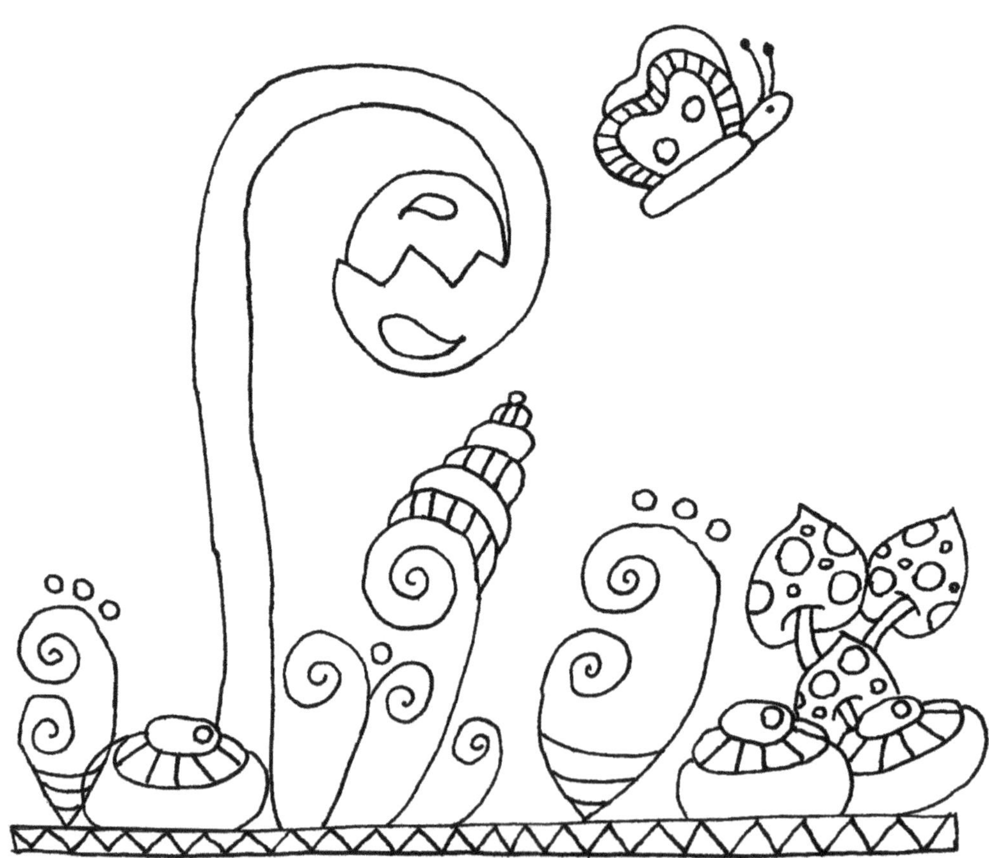

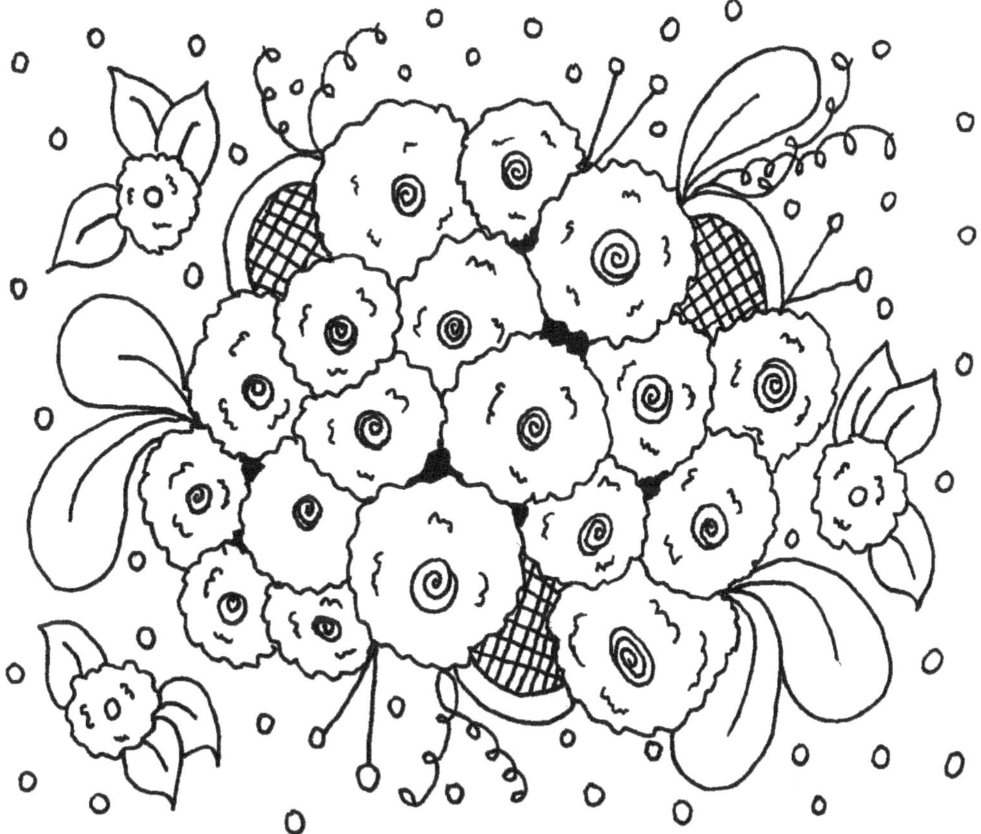

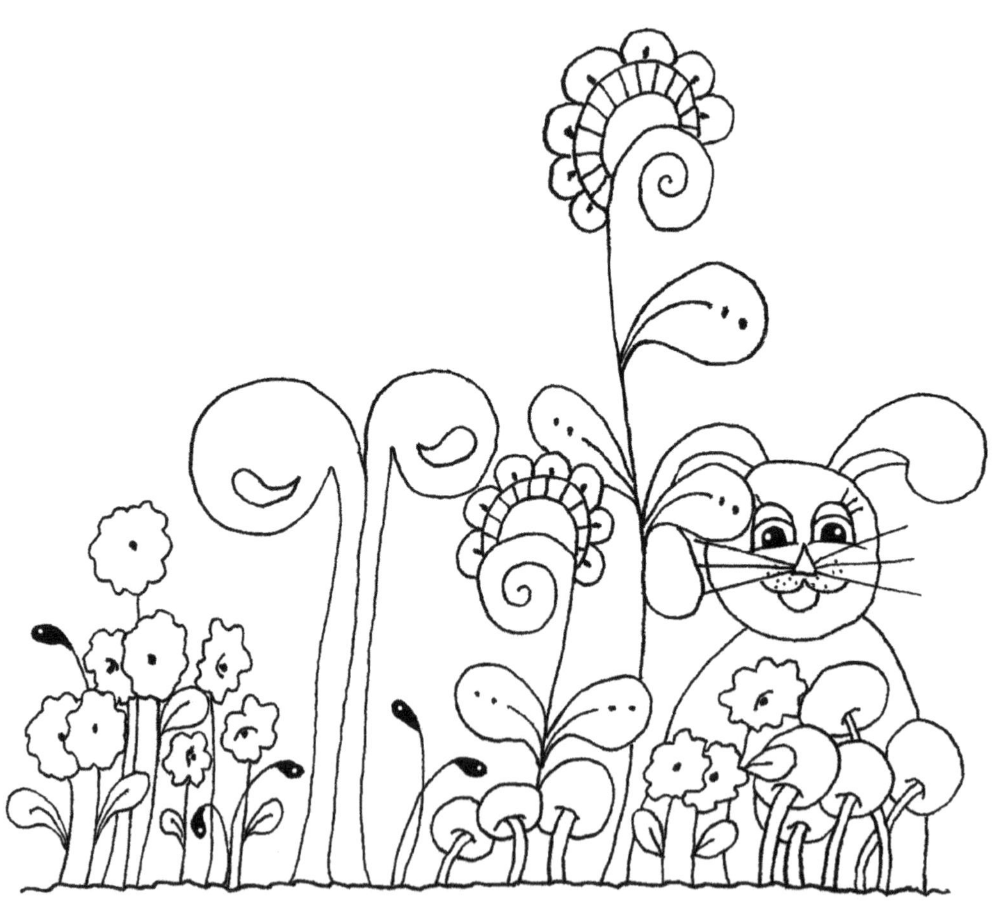

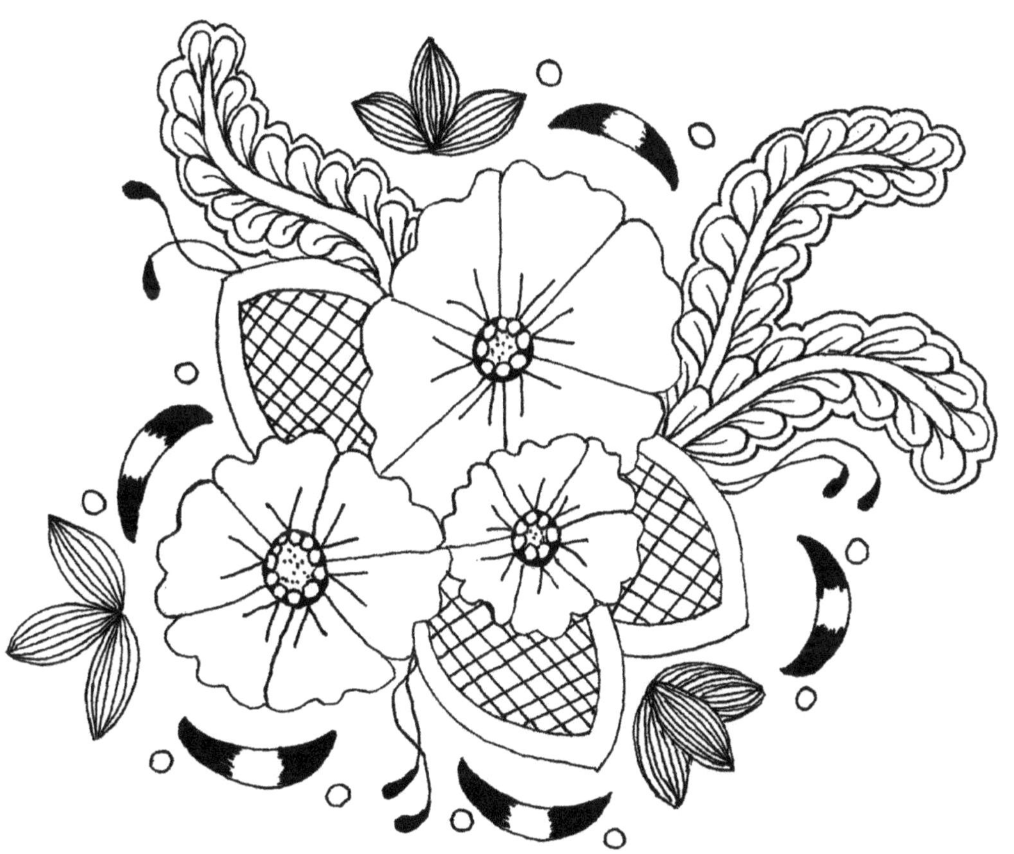

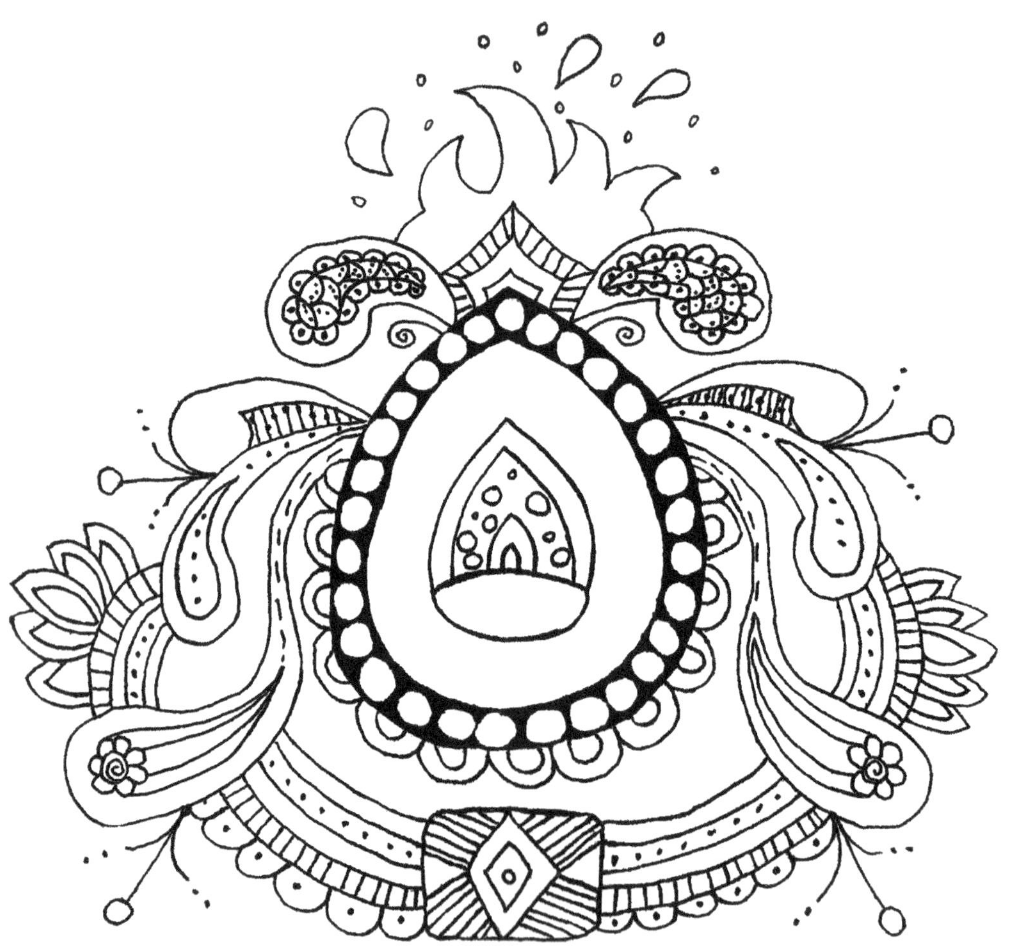

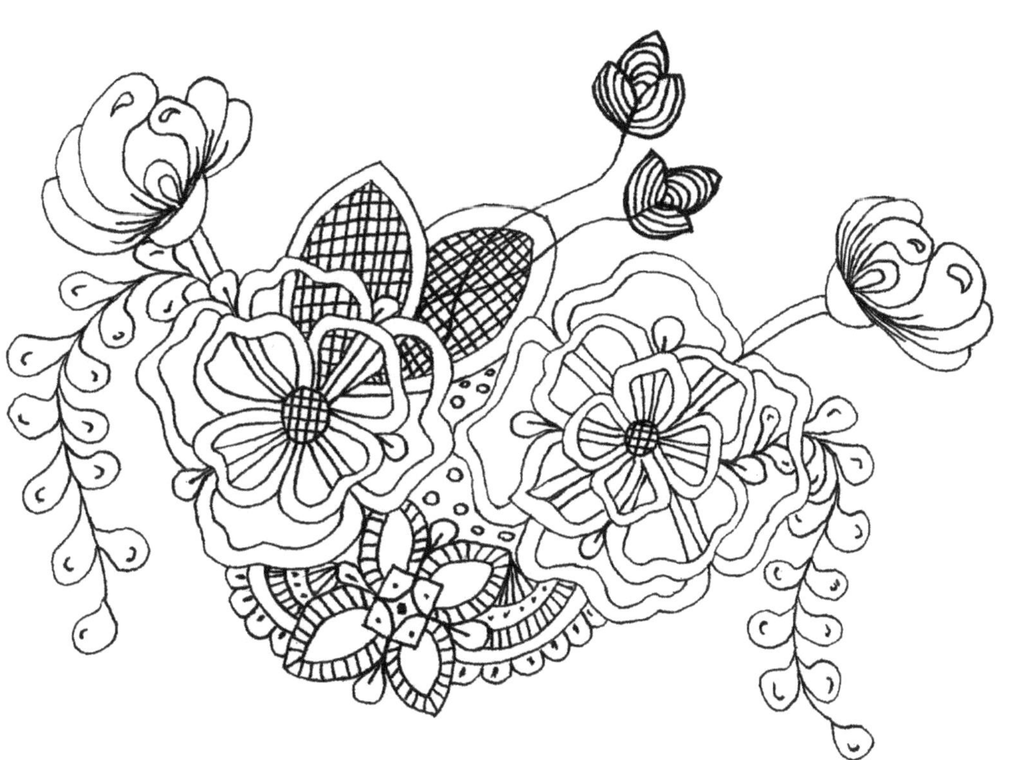

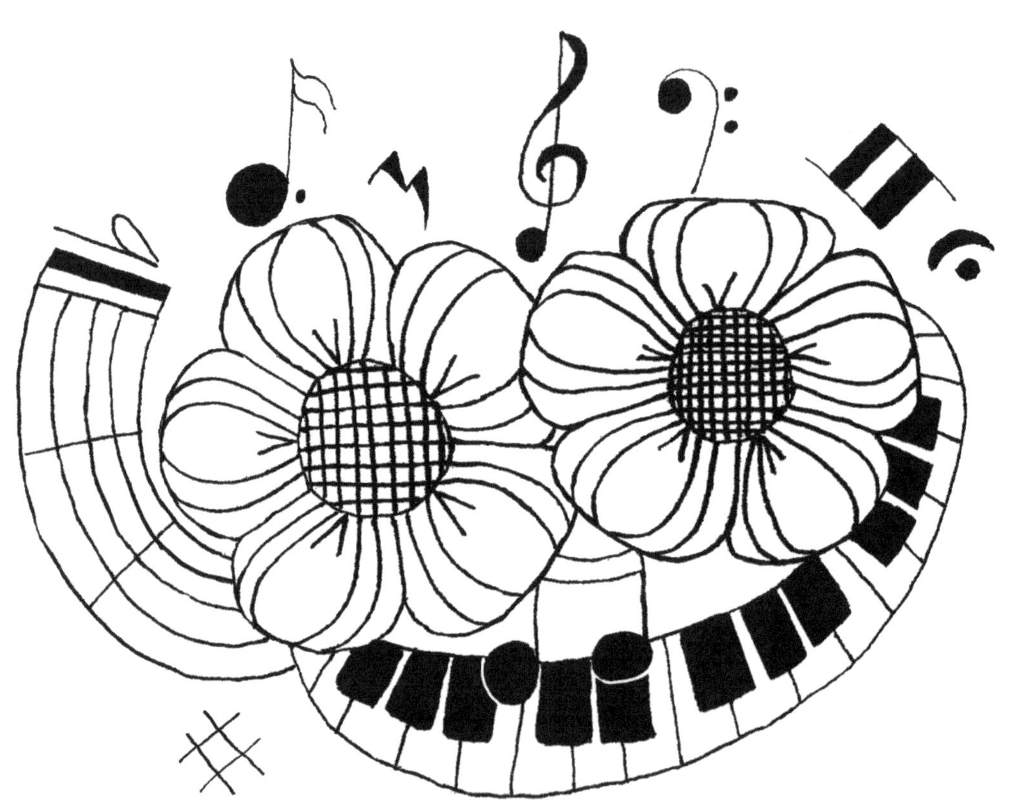

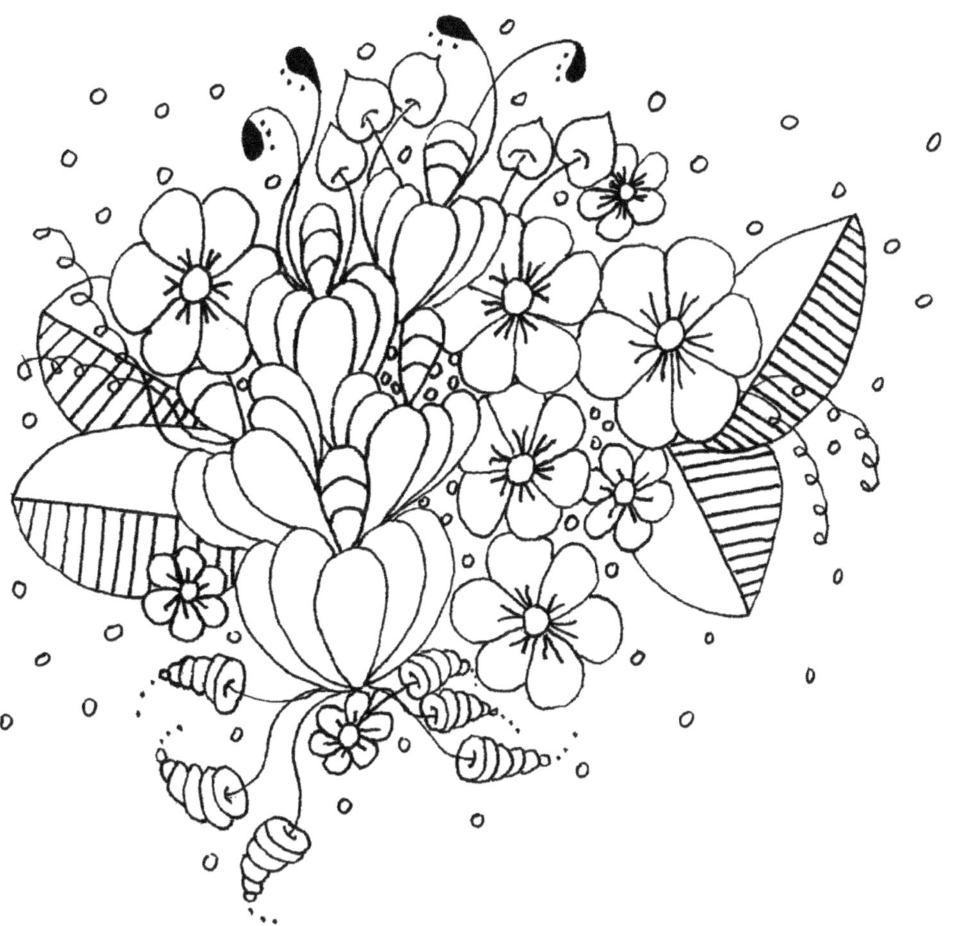

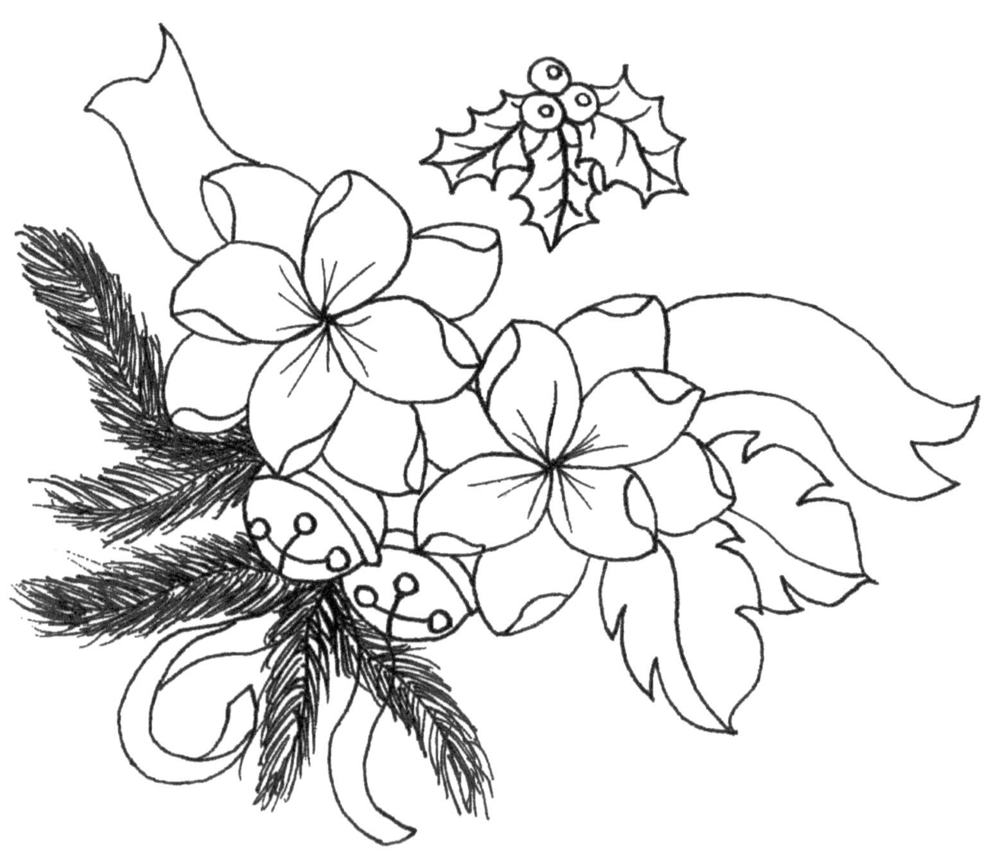

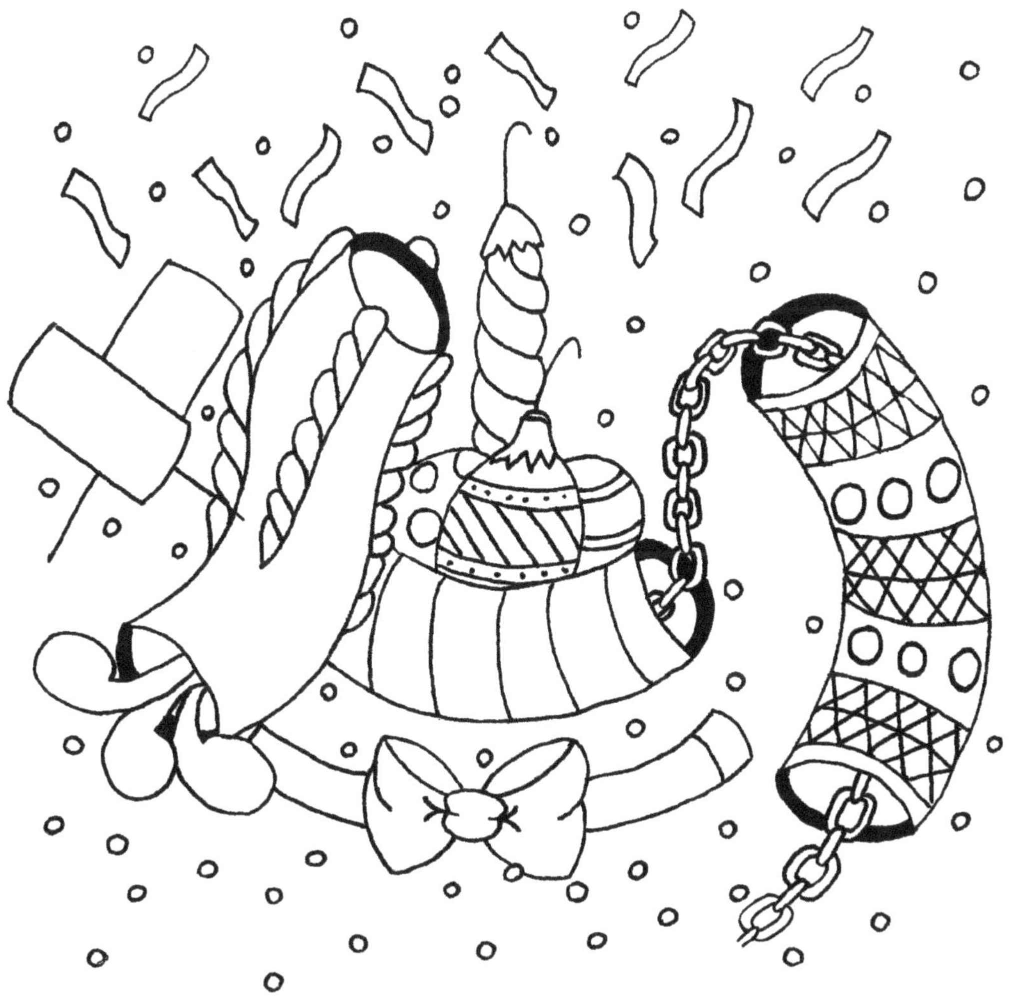

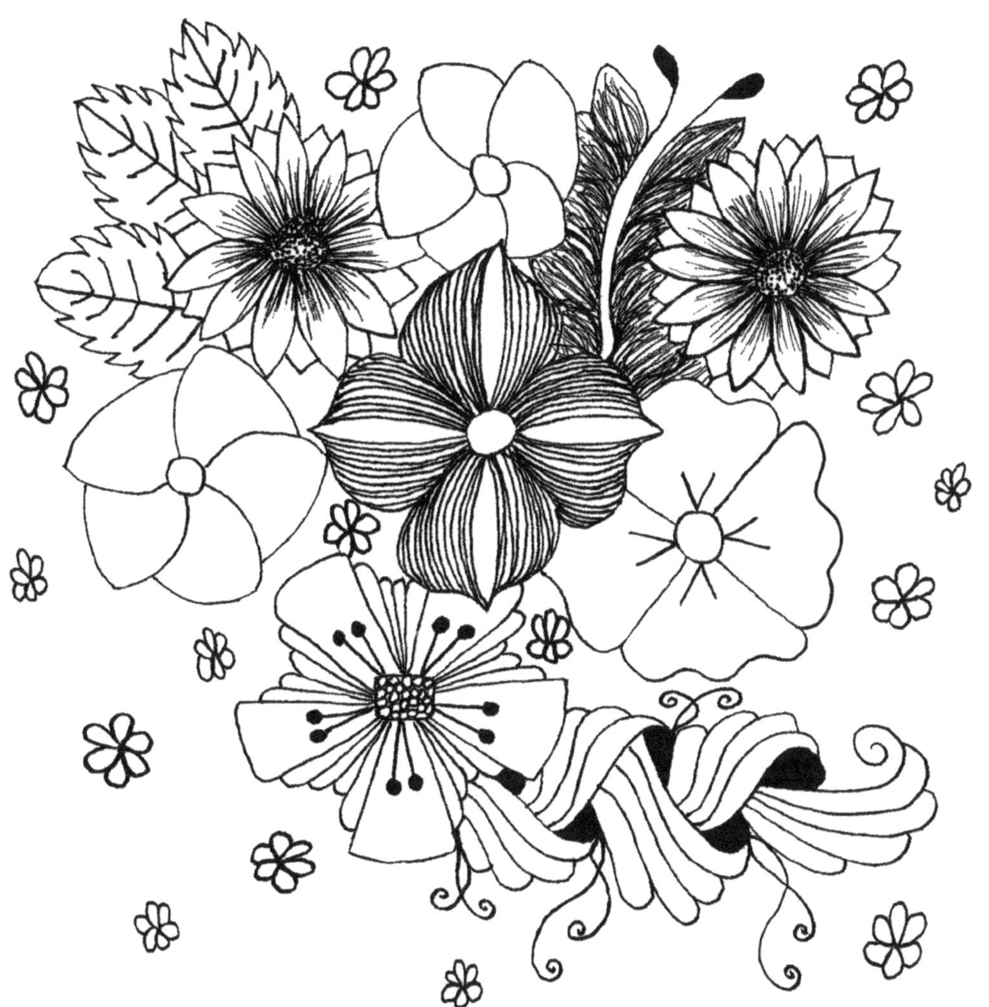

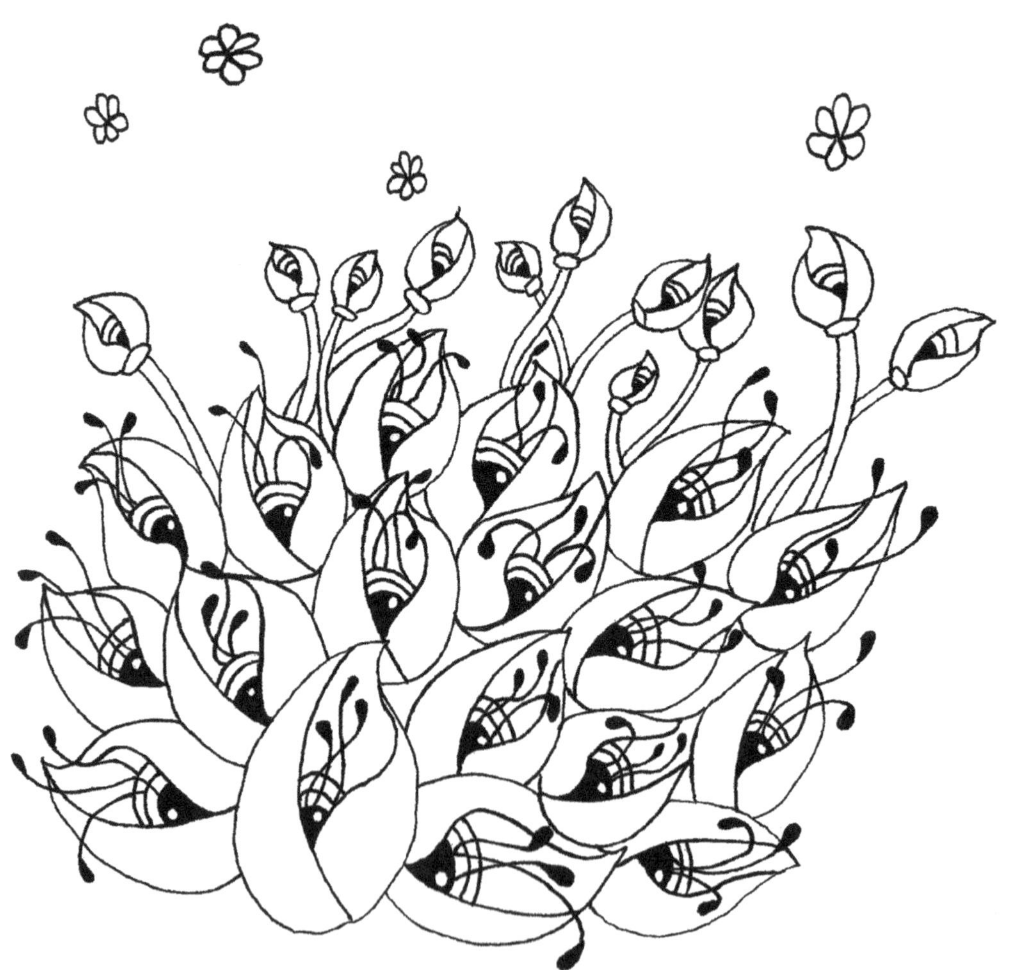

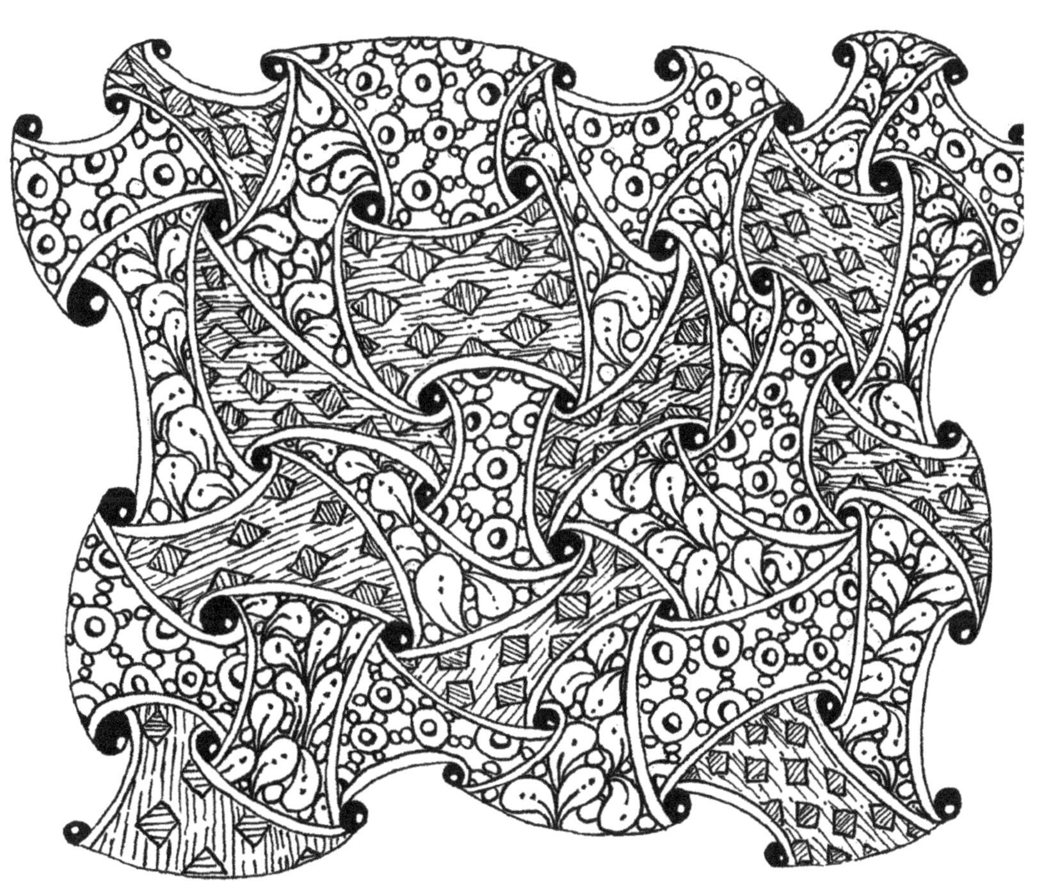

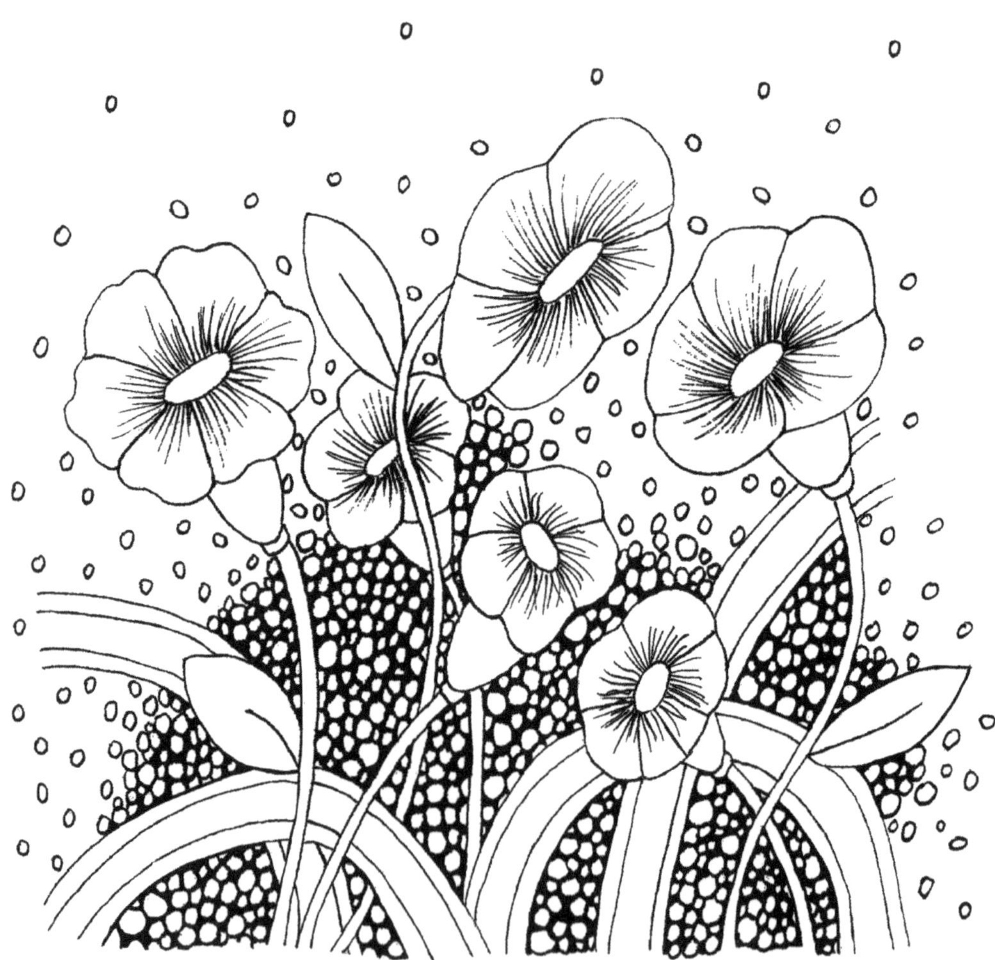

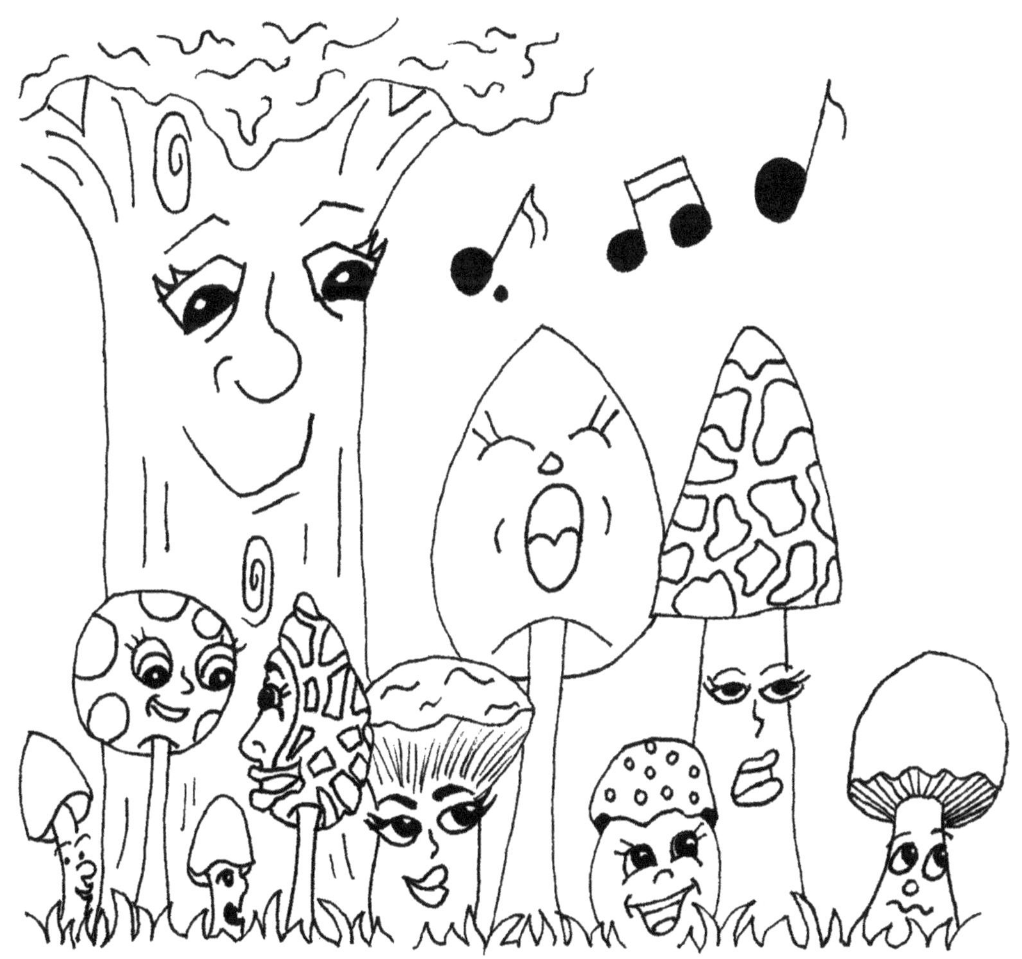

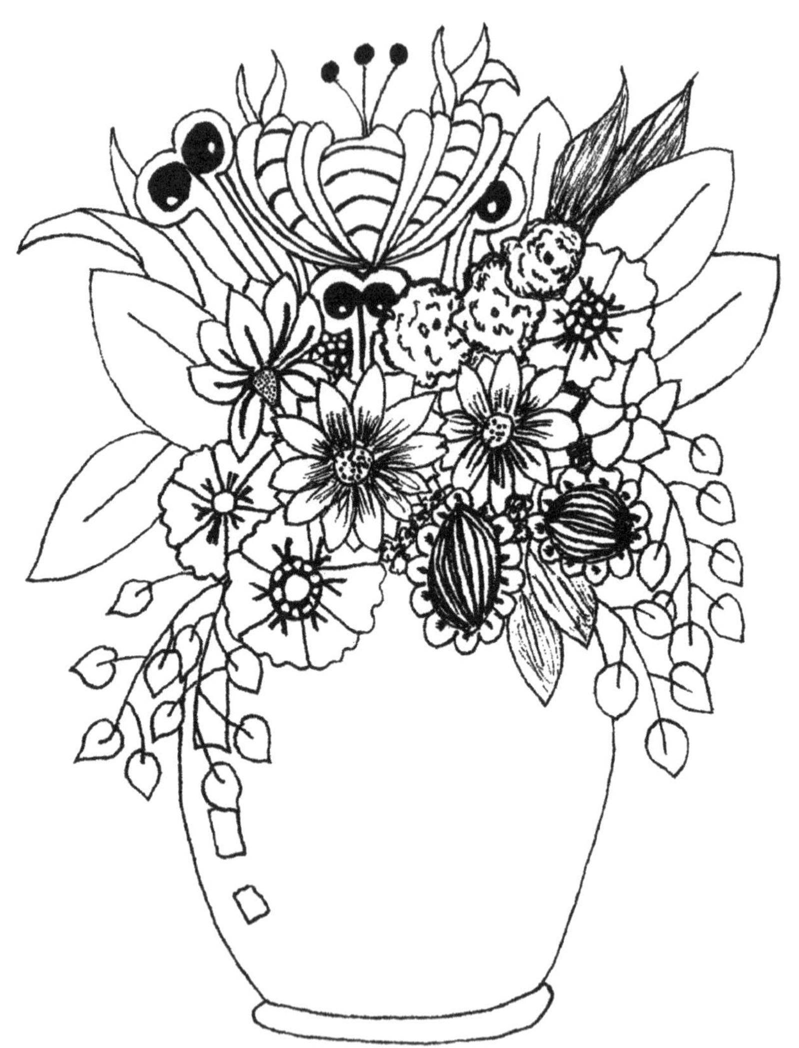

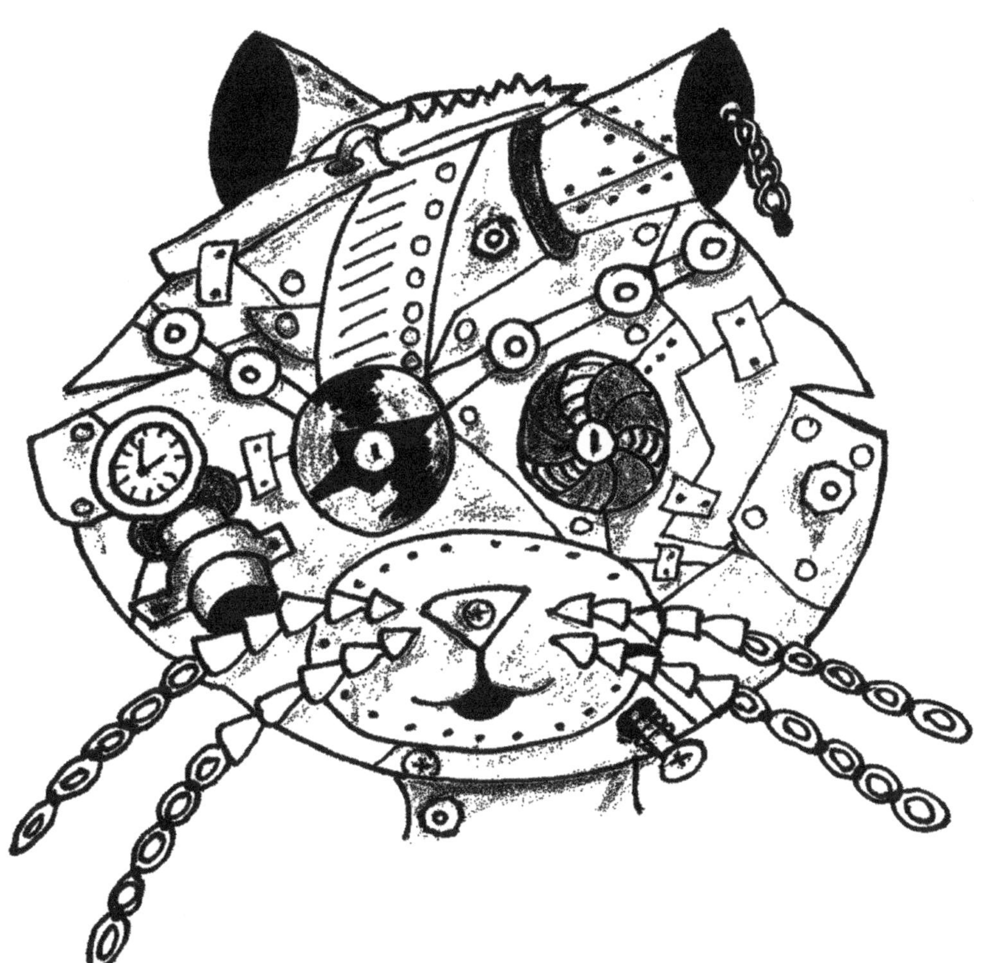

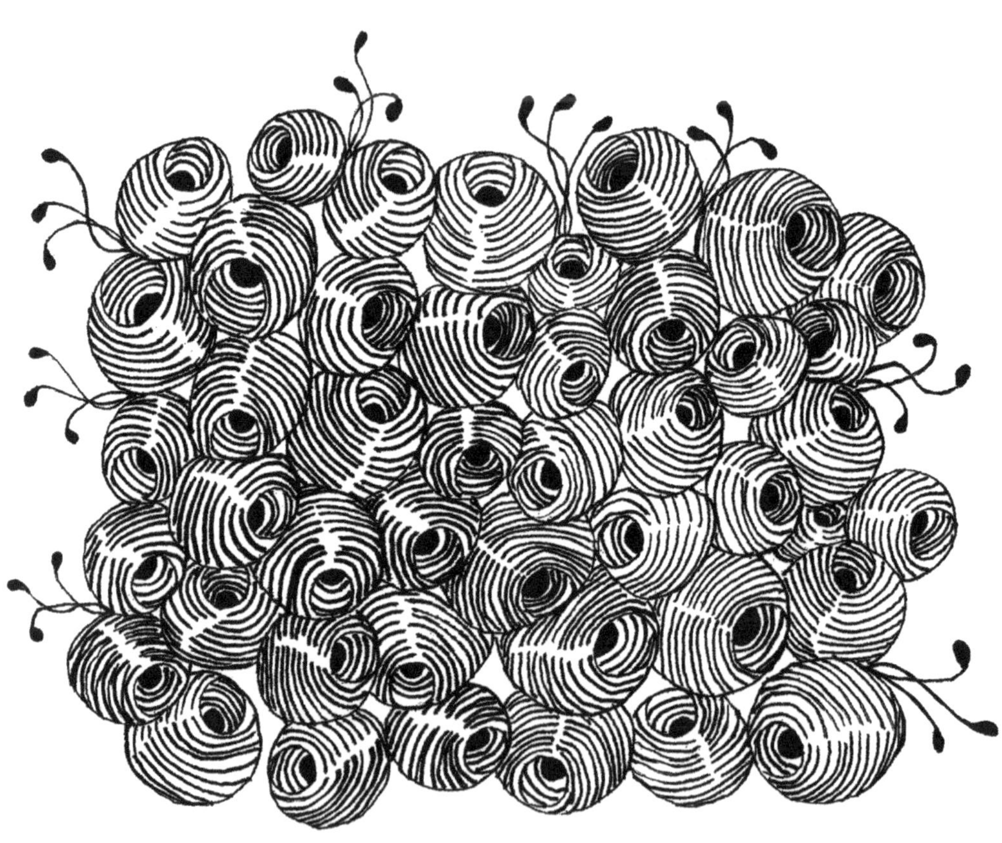

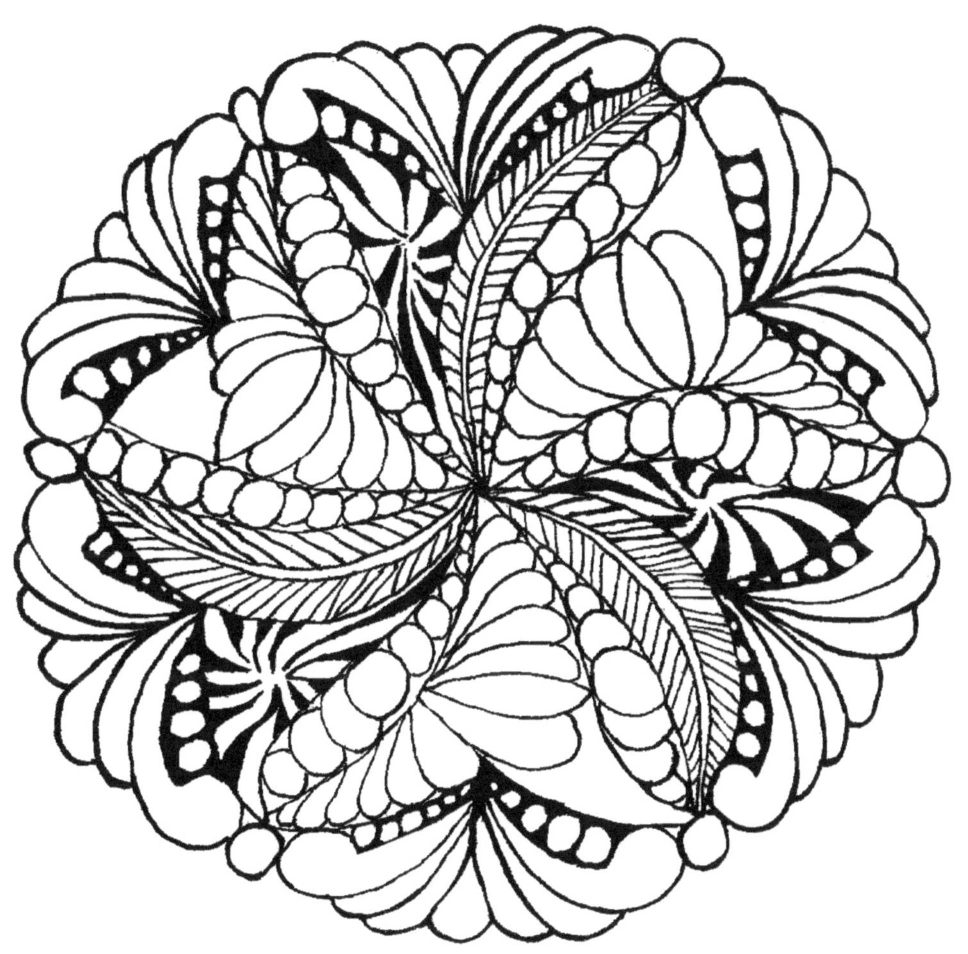

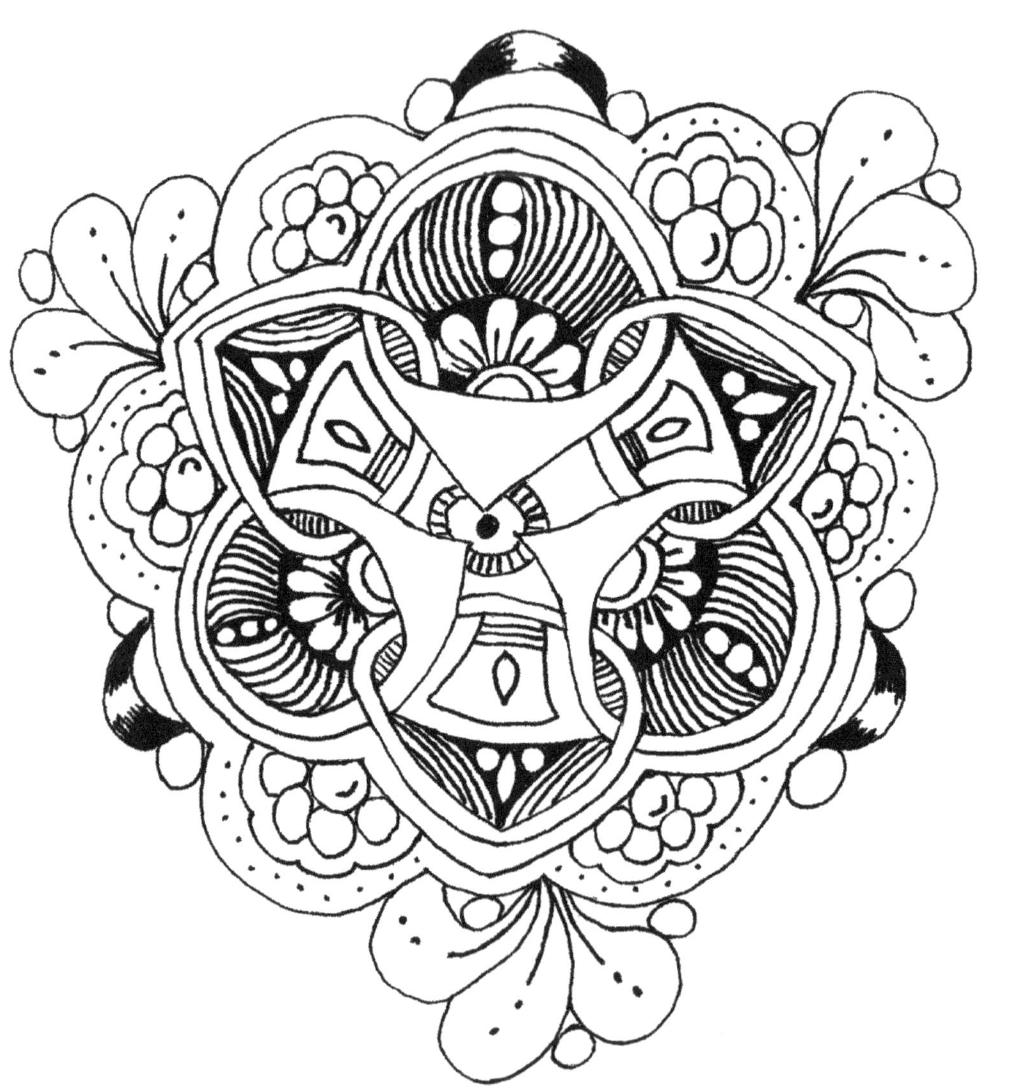

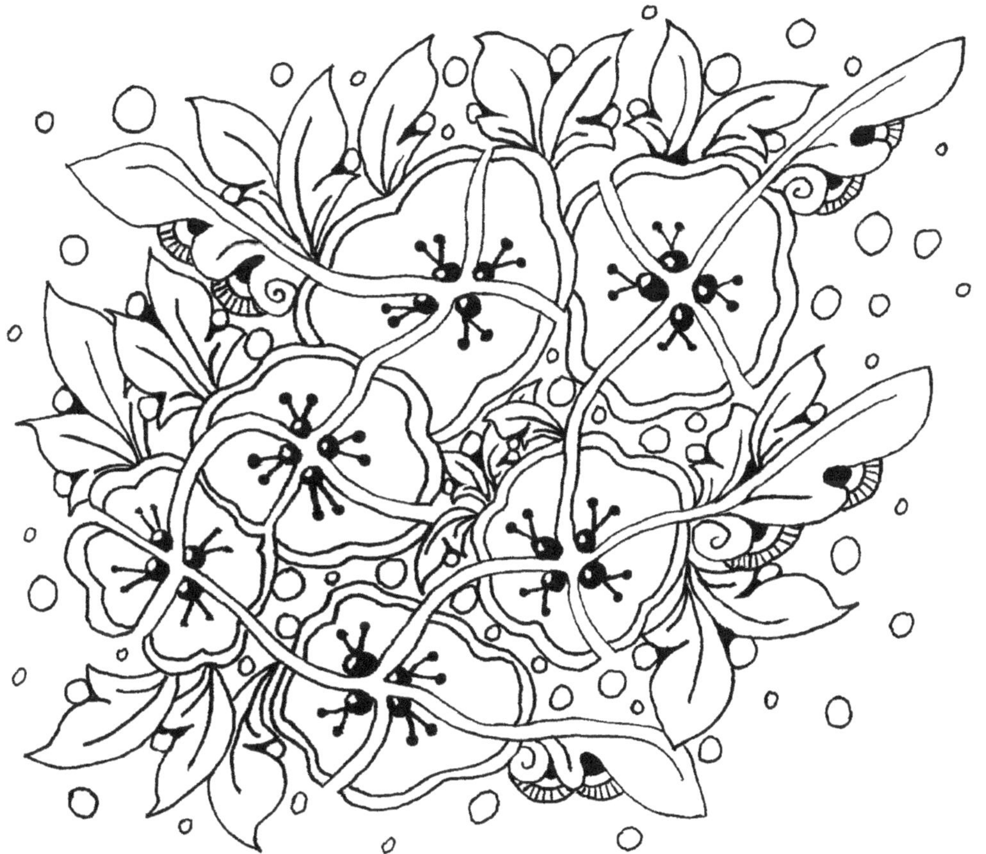

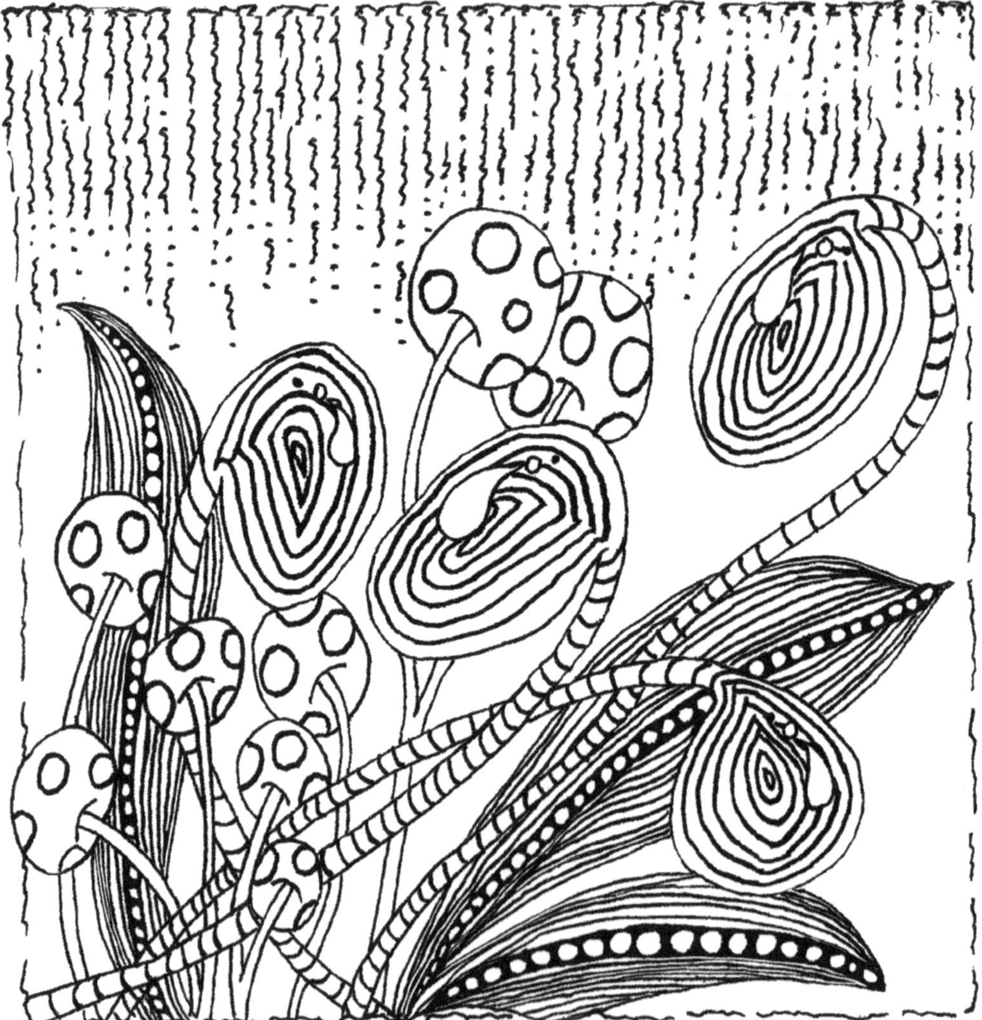

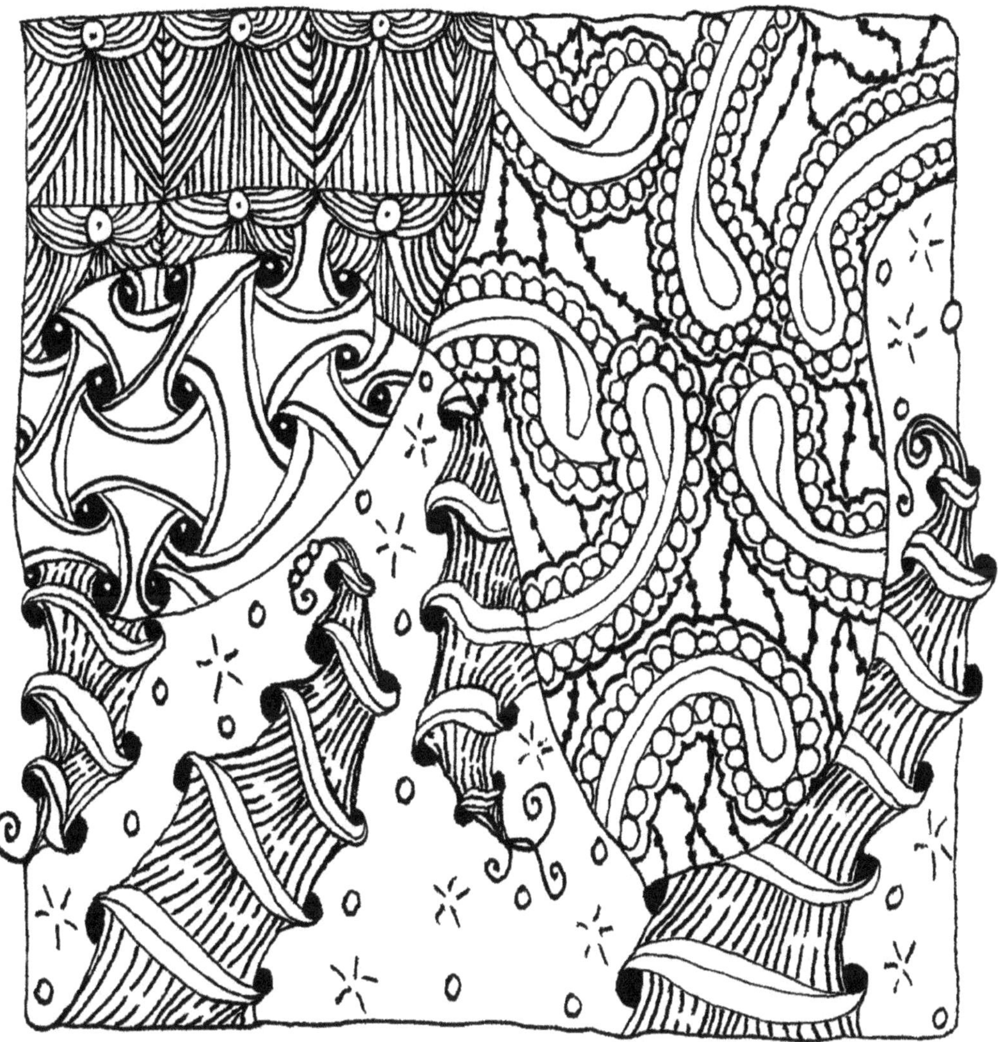

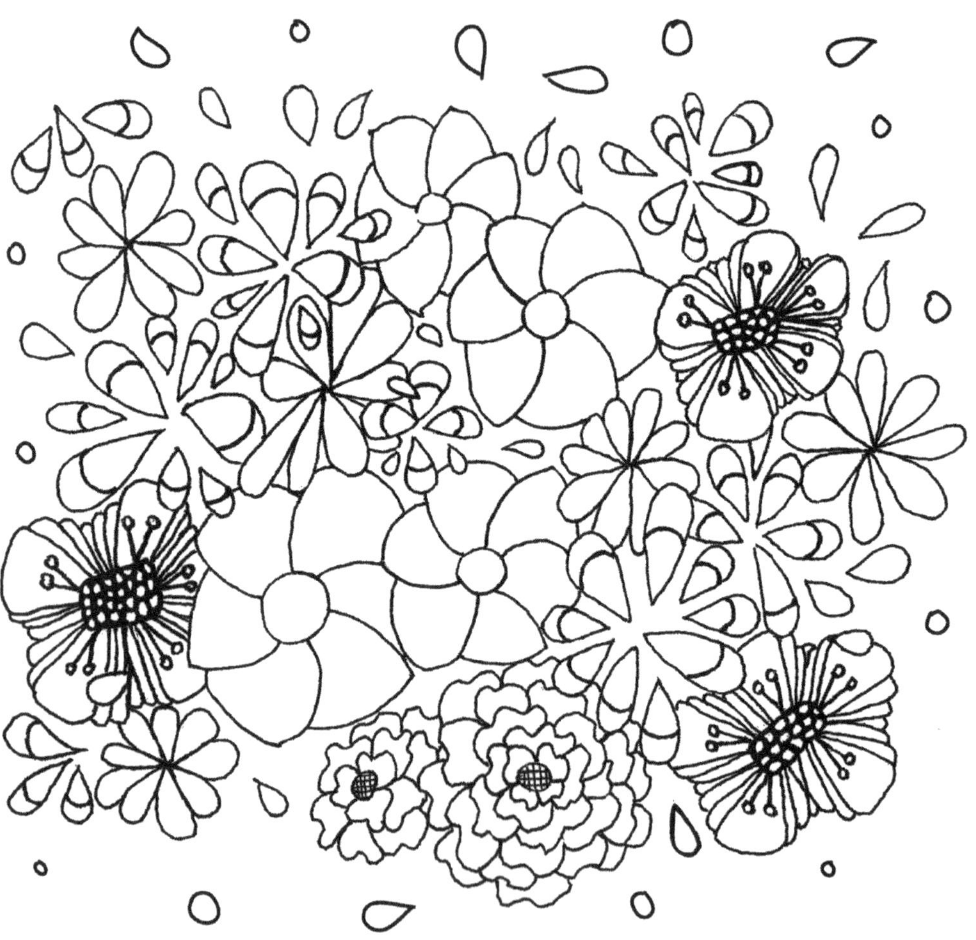

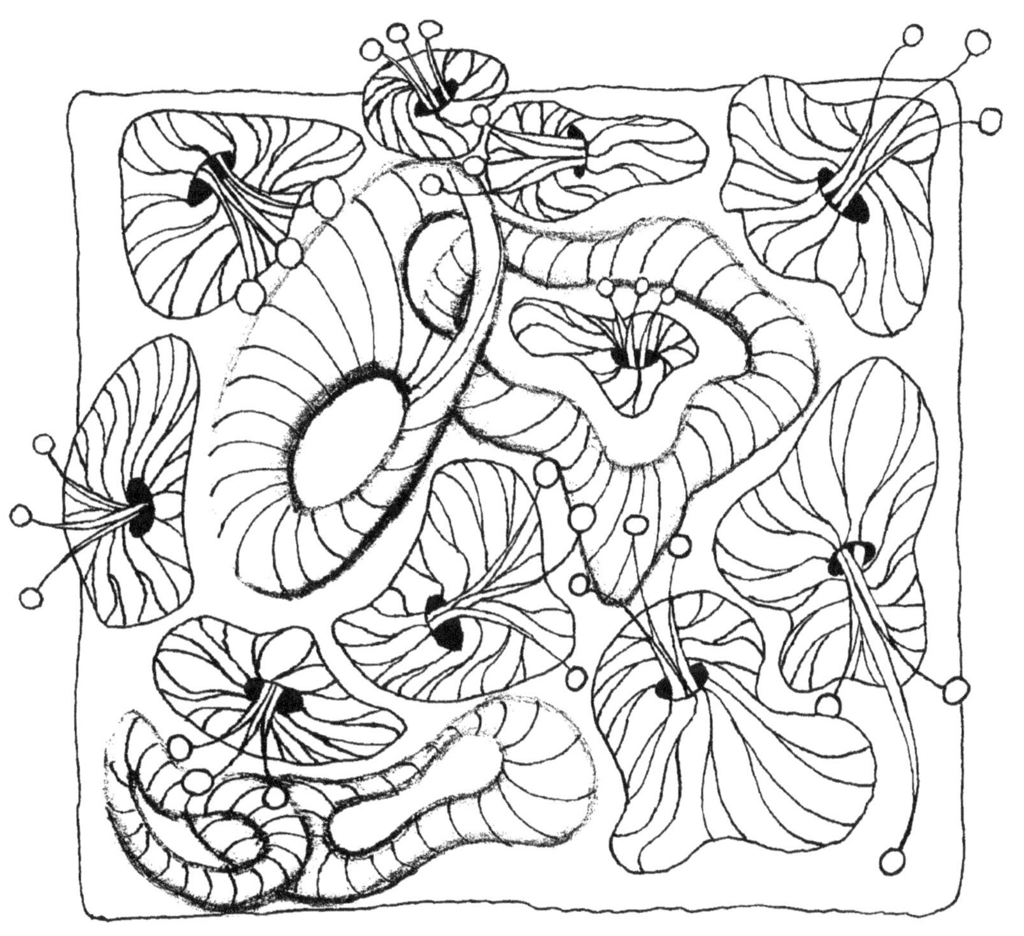

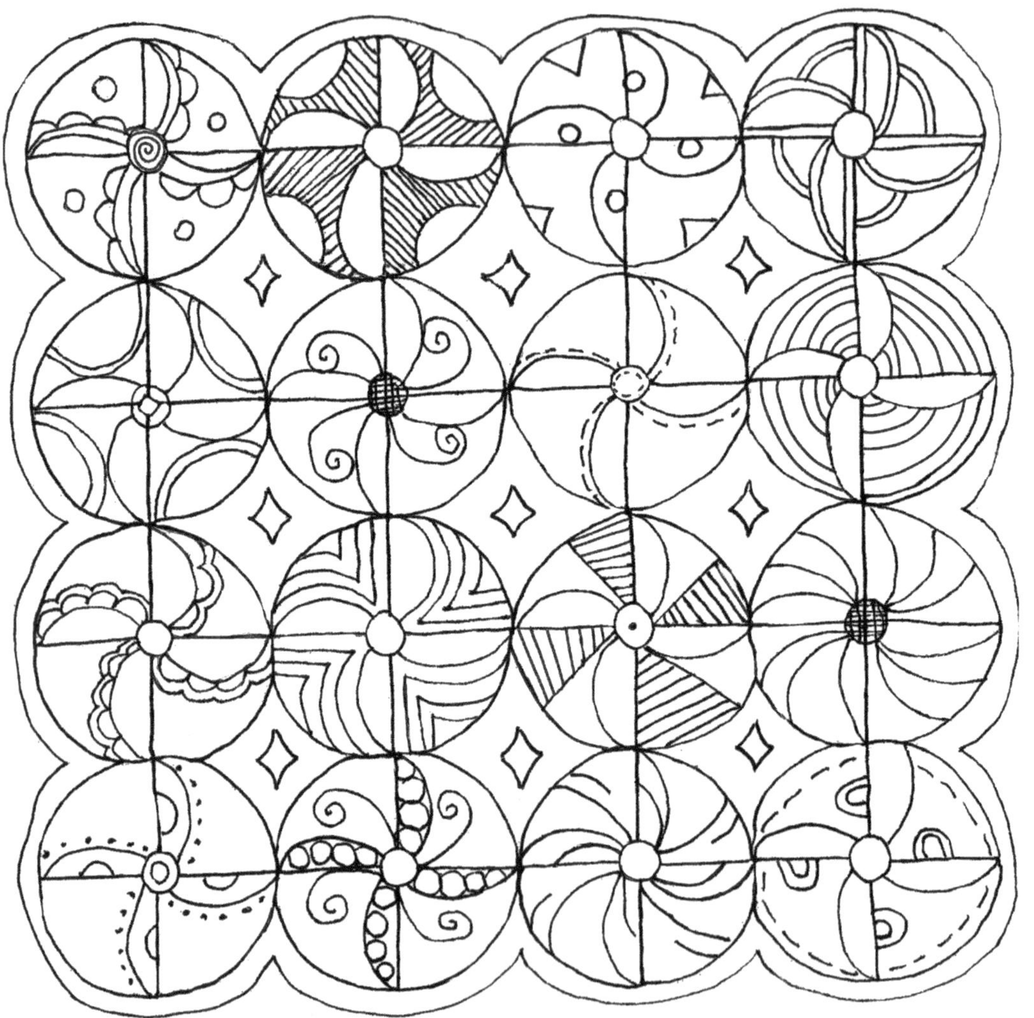

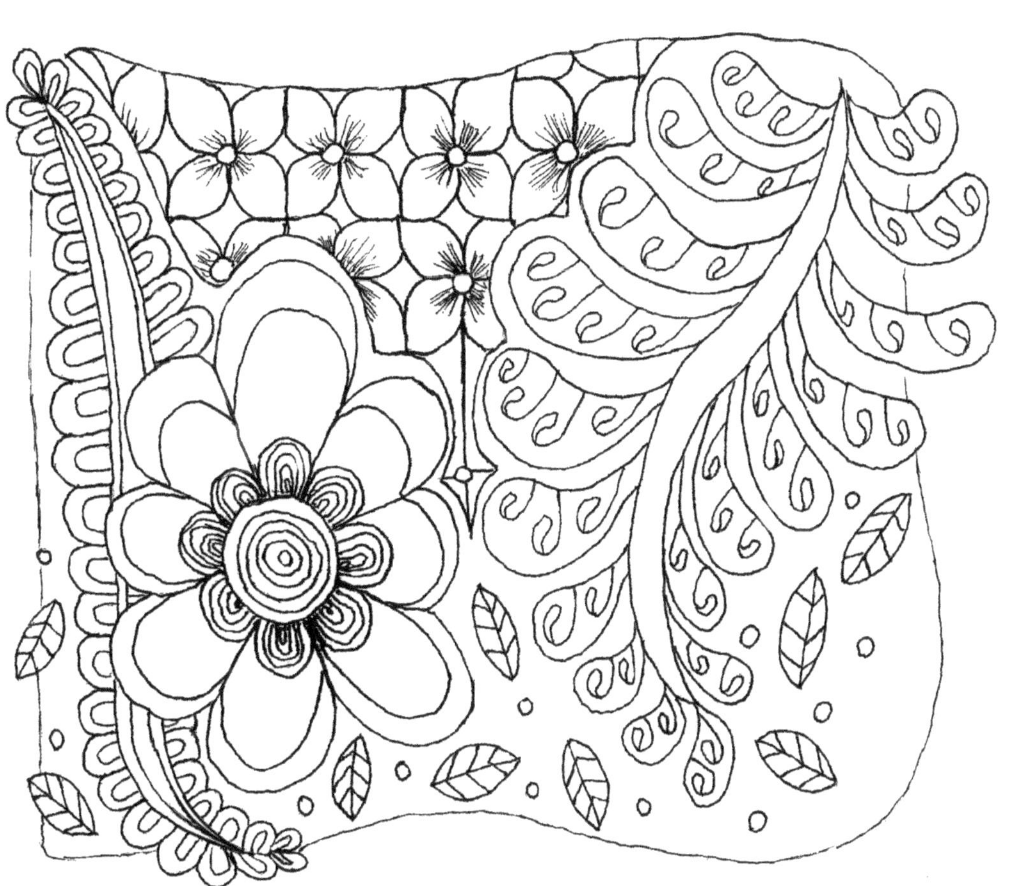

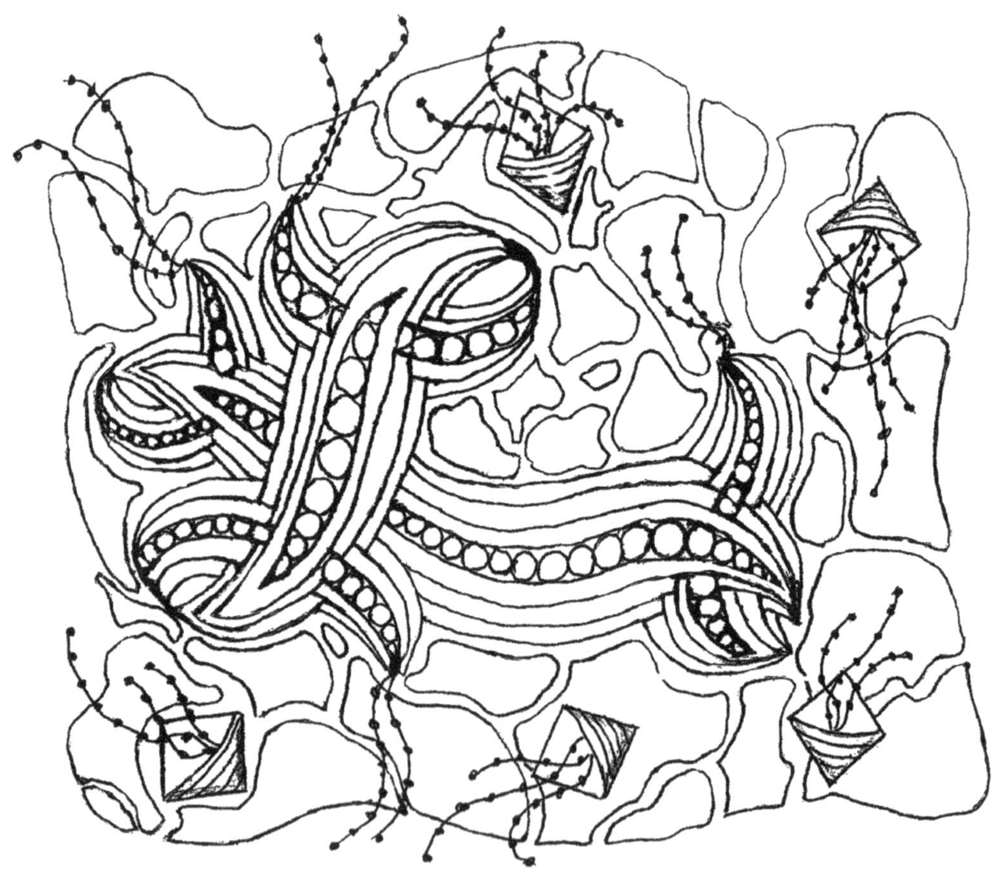

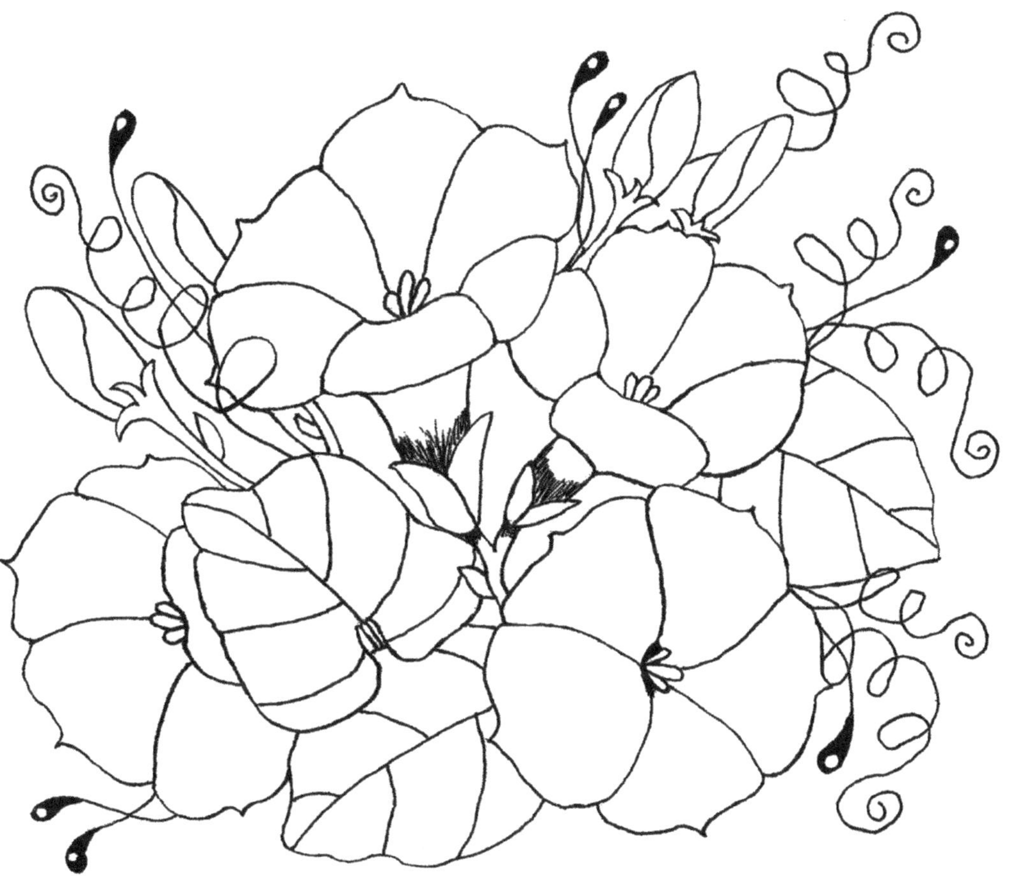

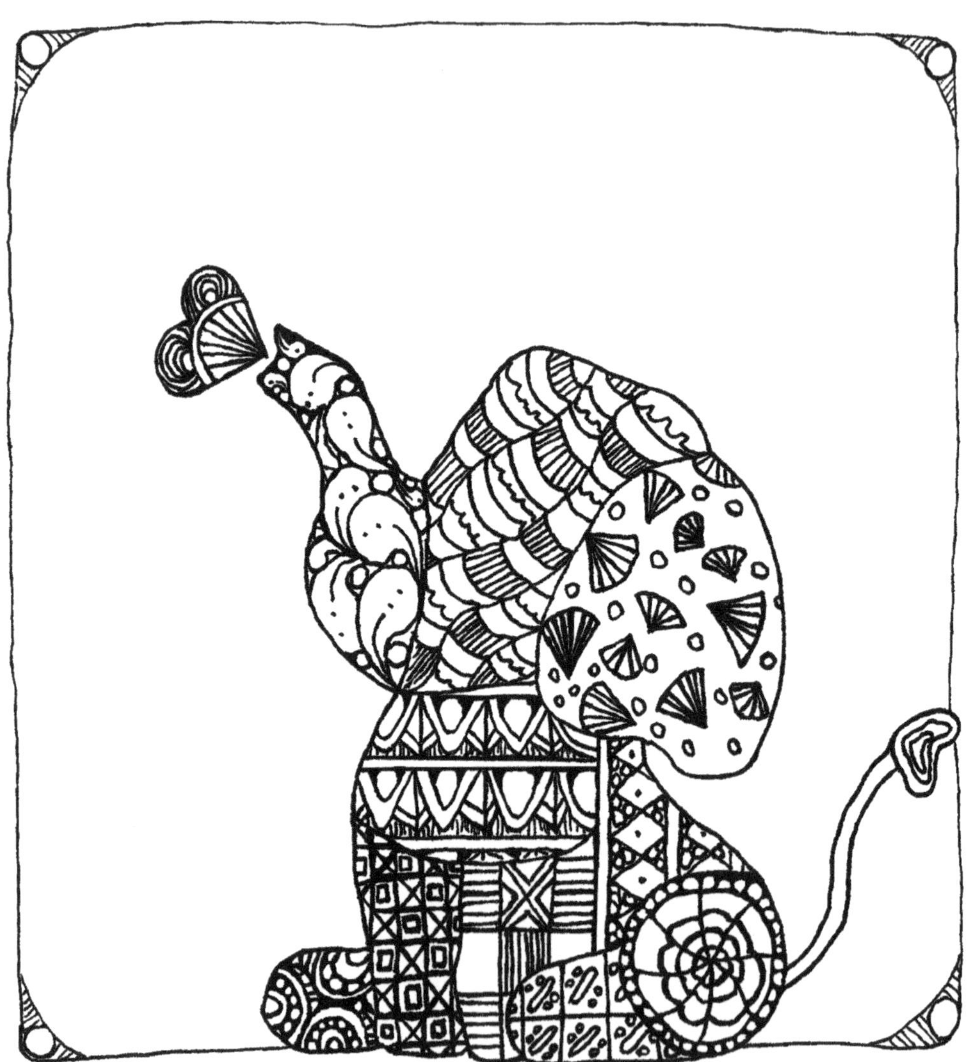

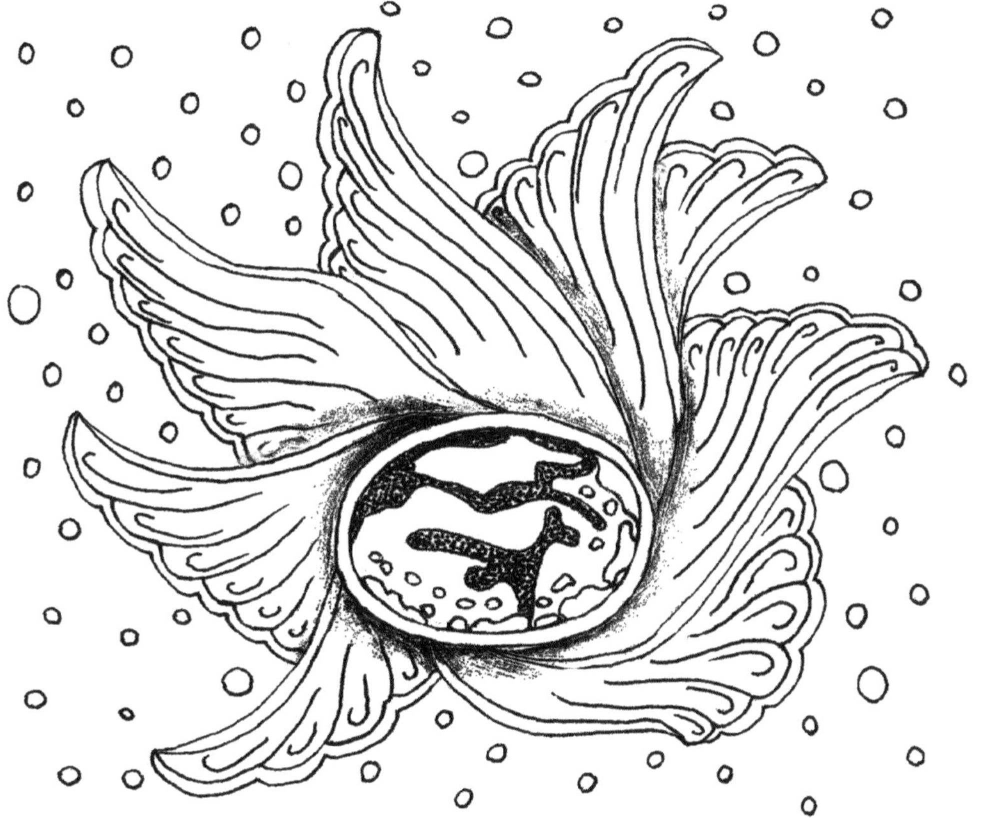

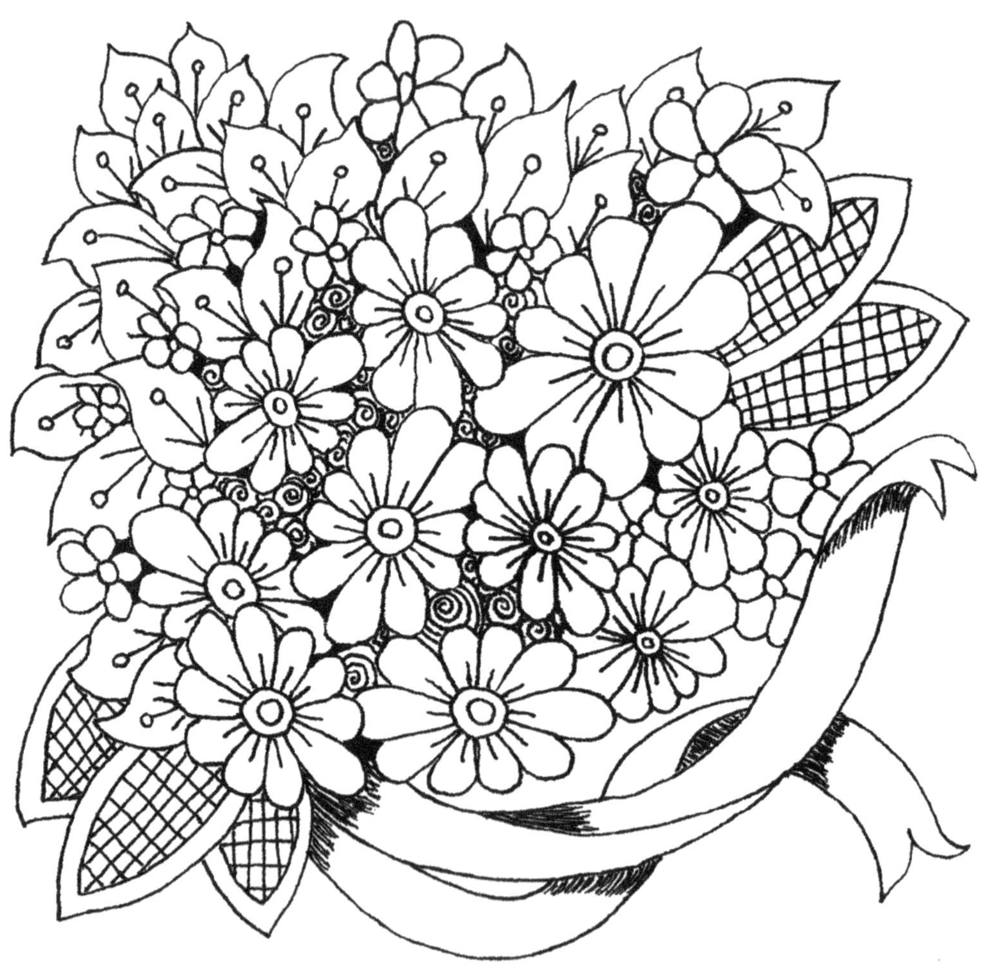

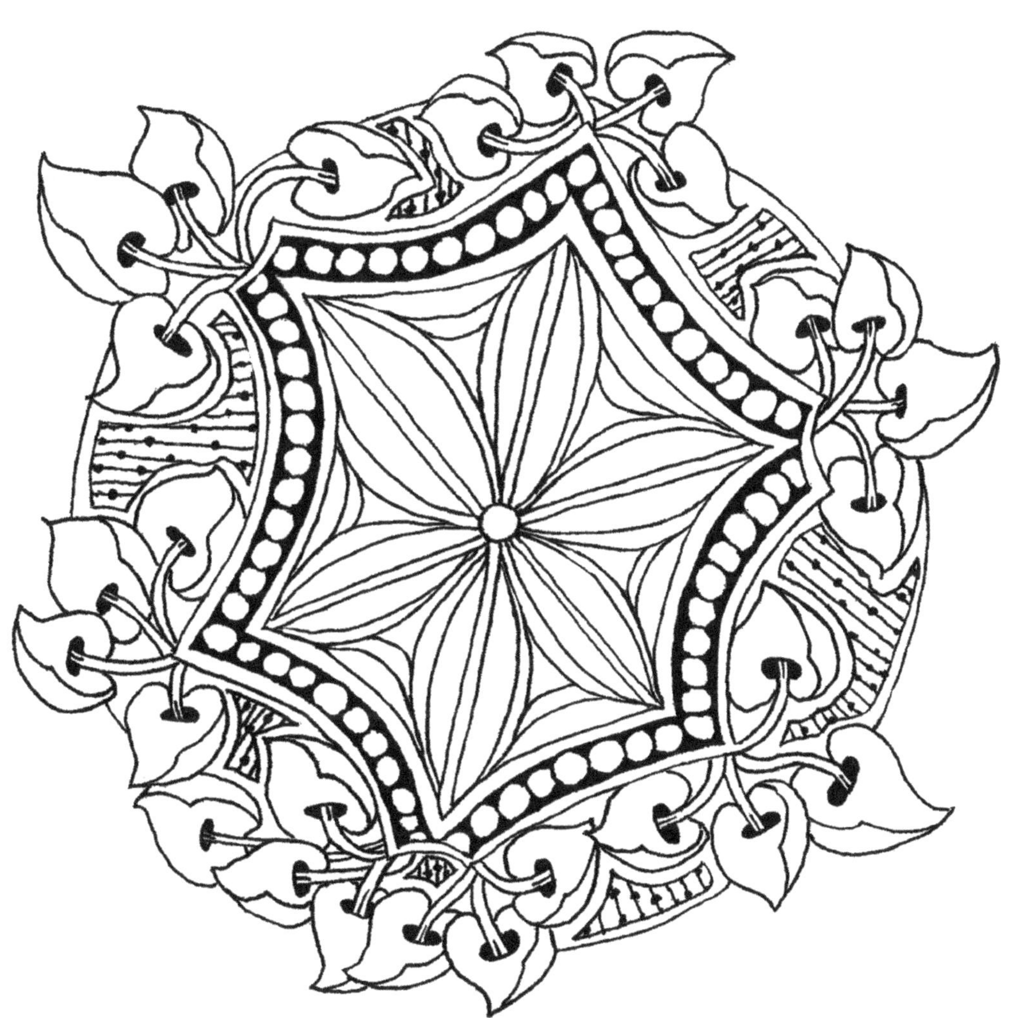

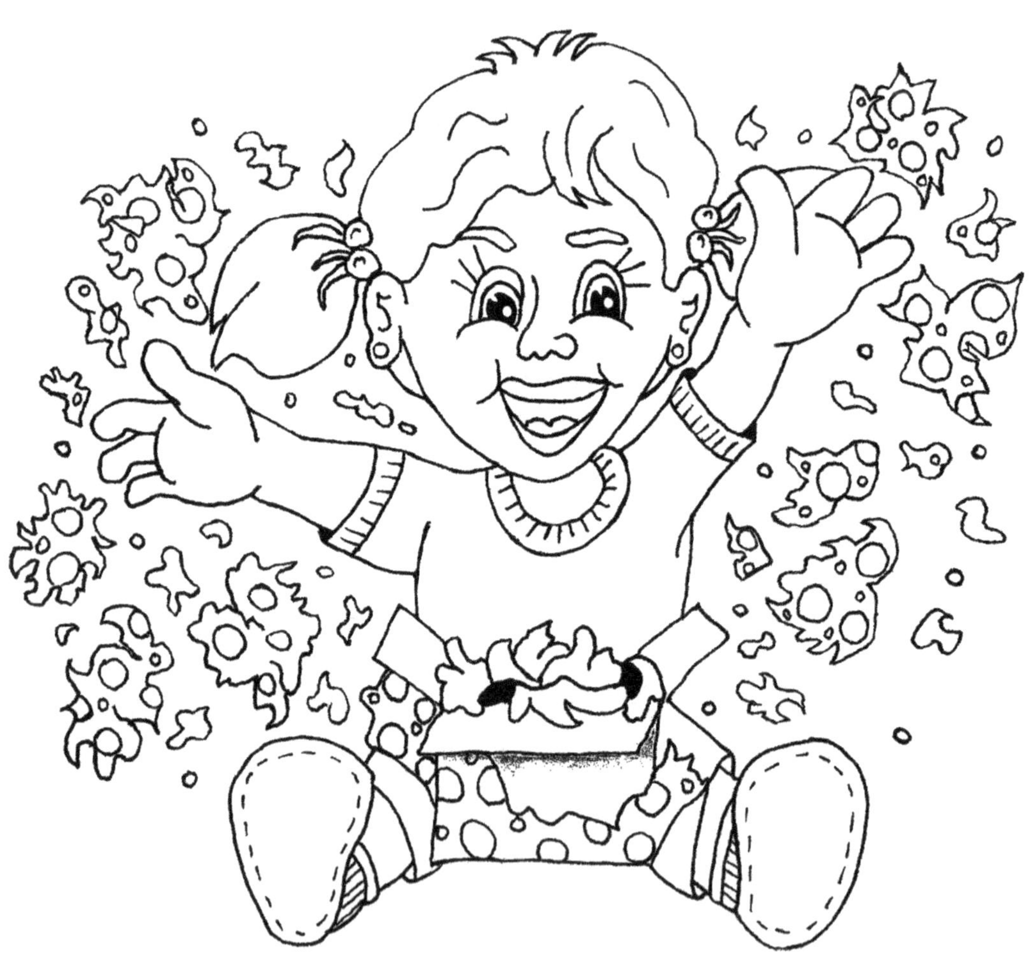

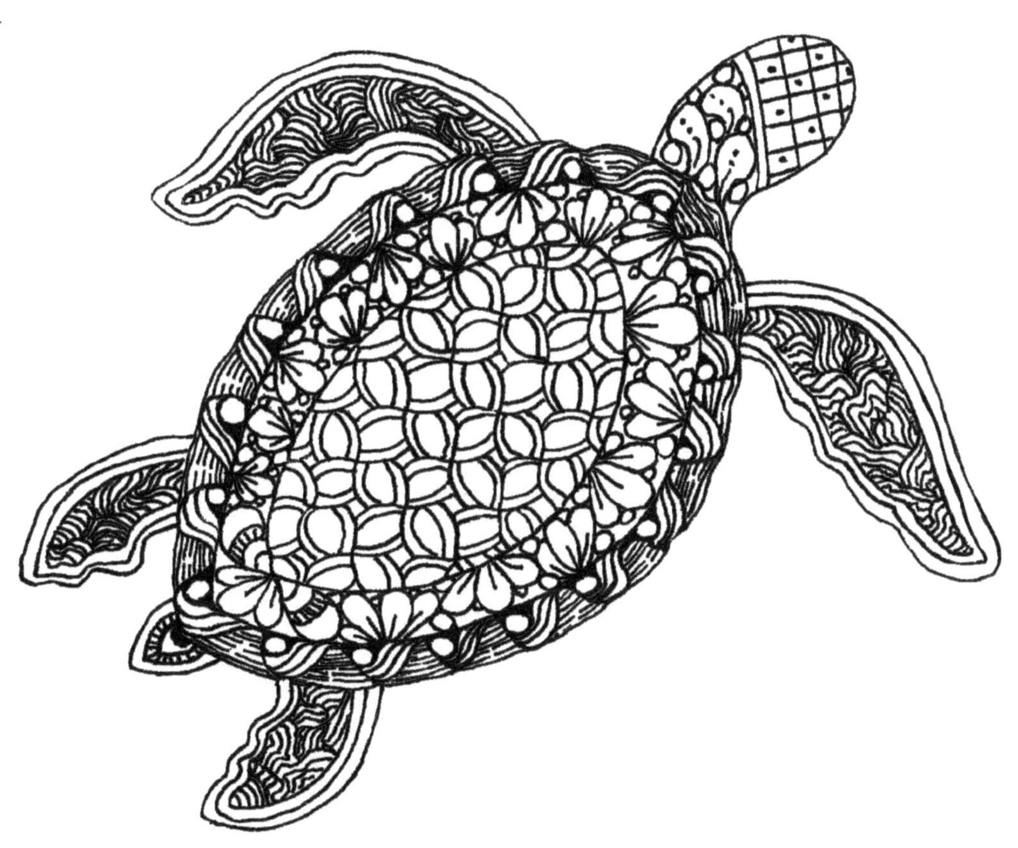

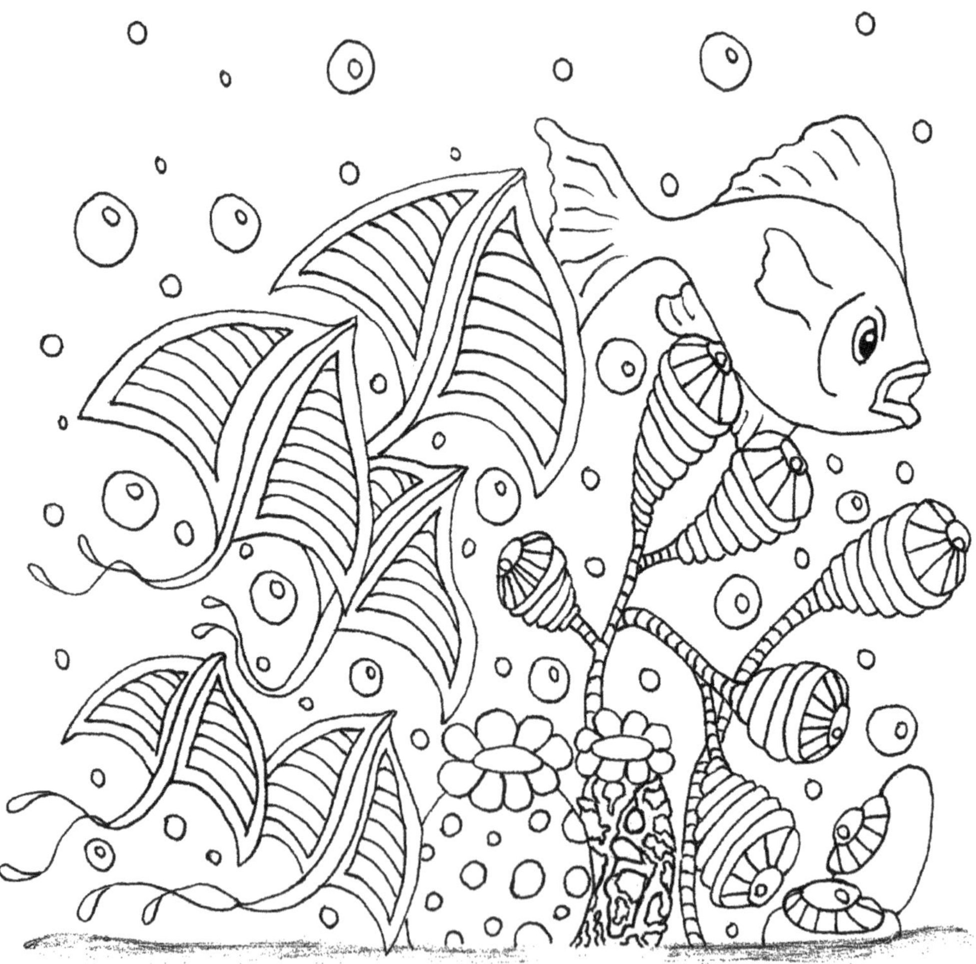

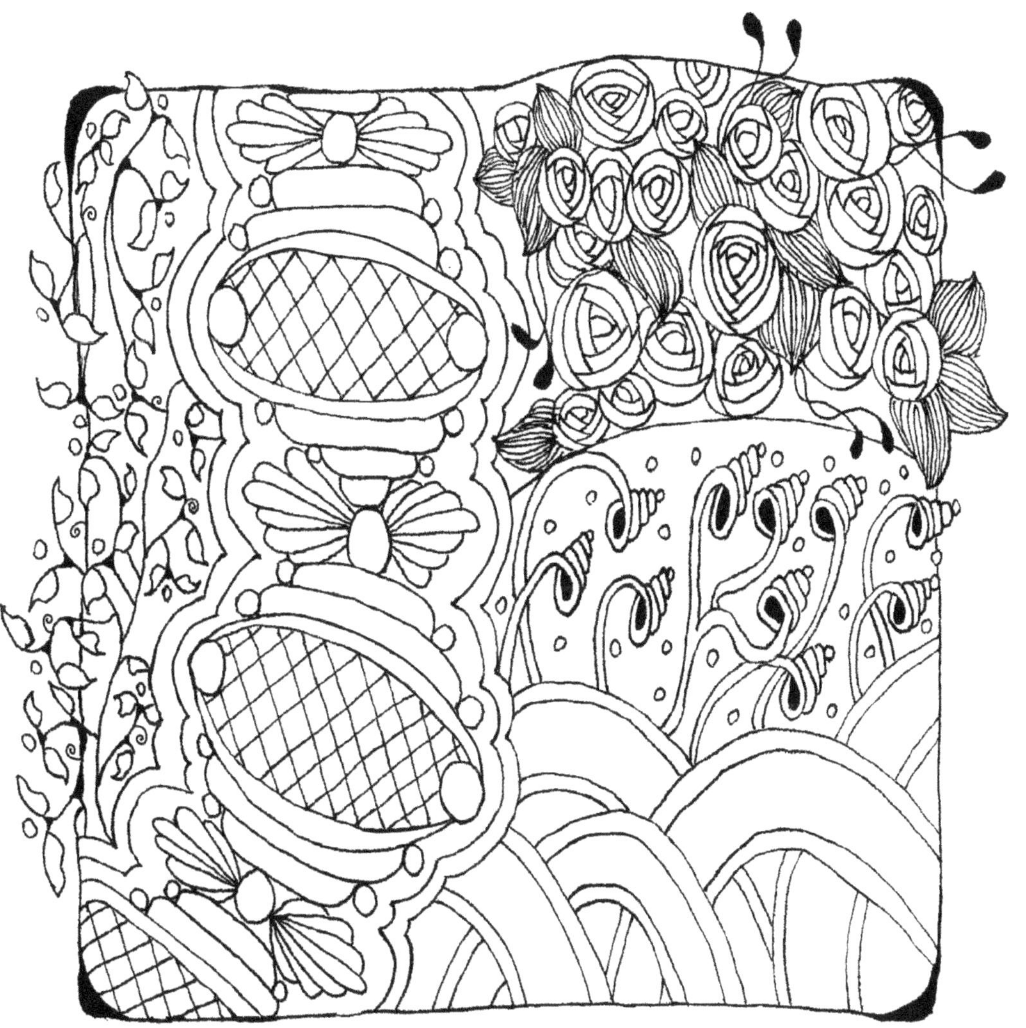

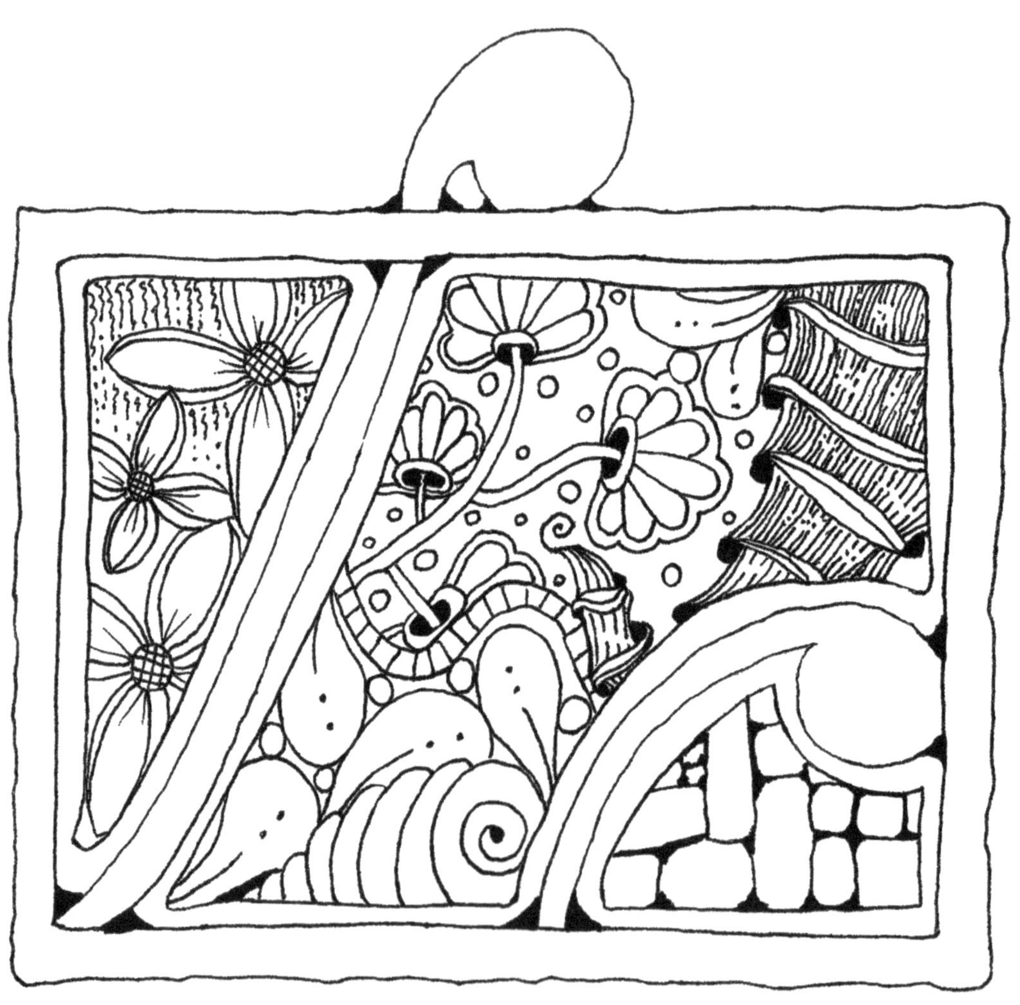

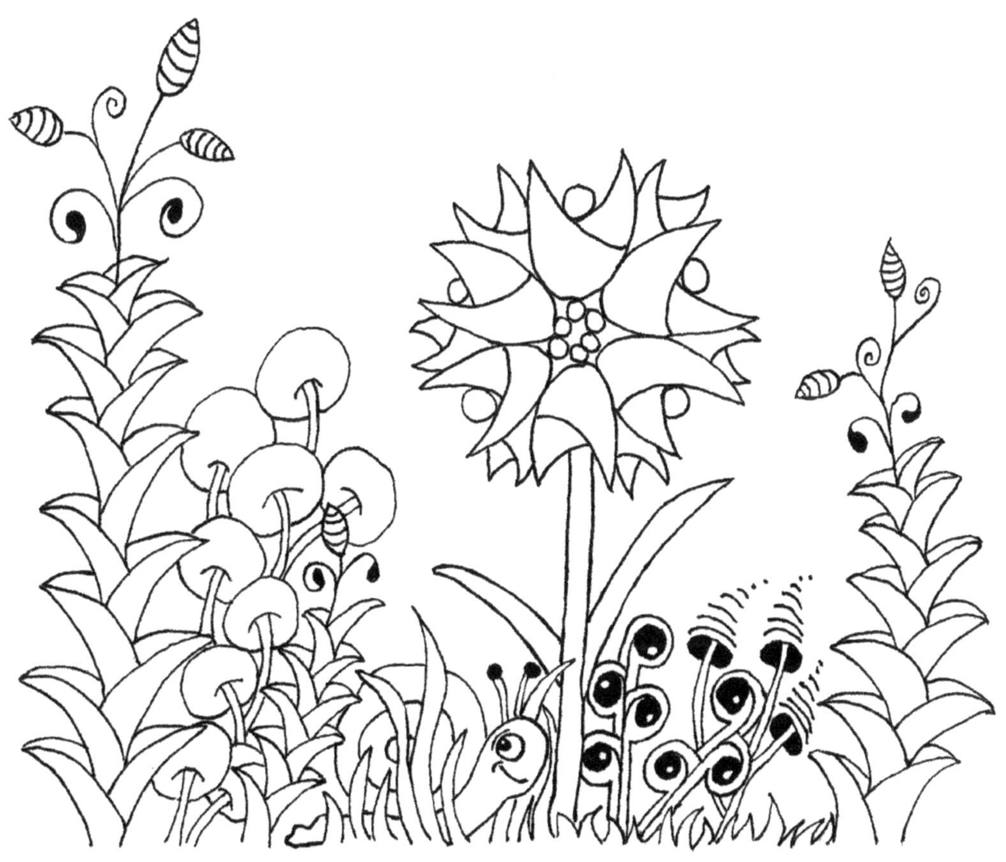

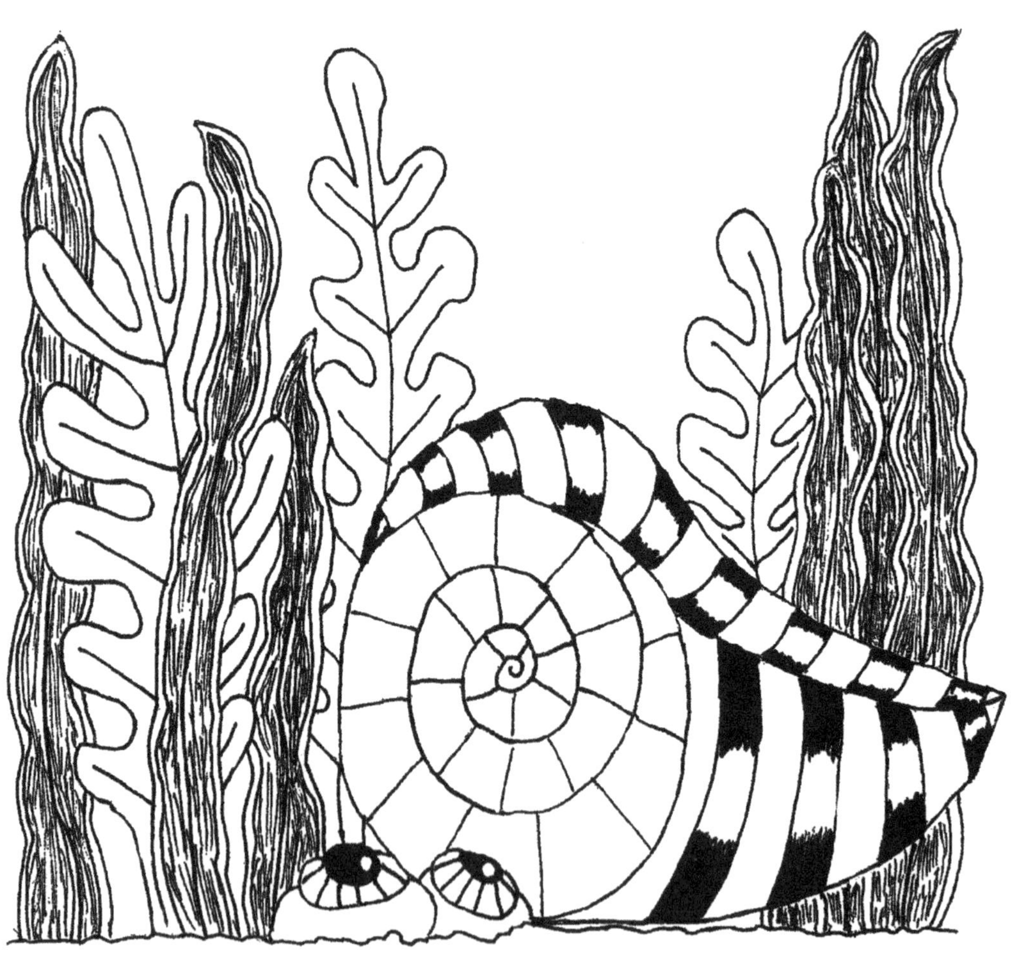

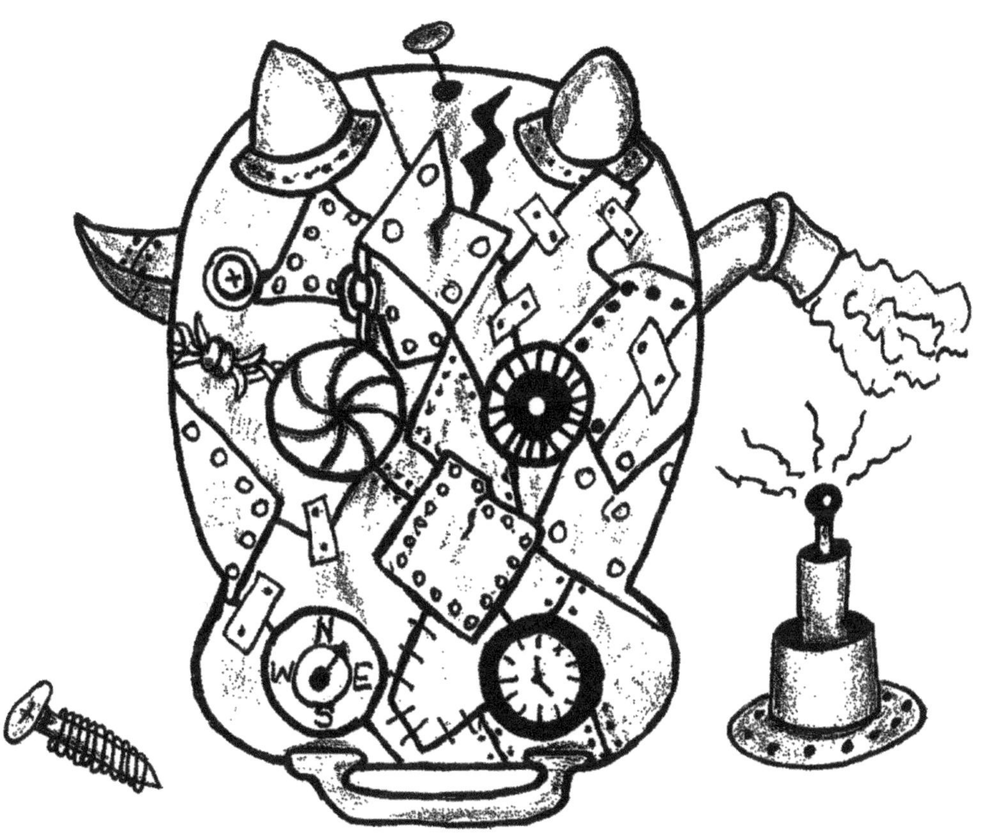
N
W
E
S

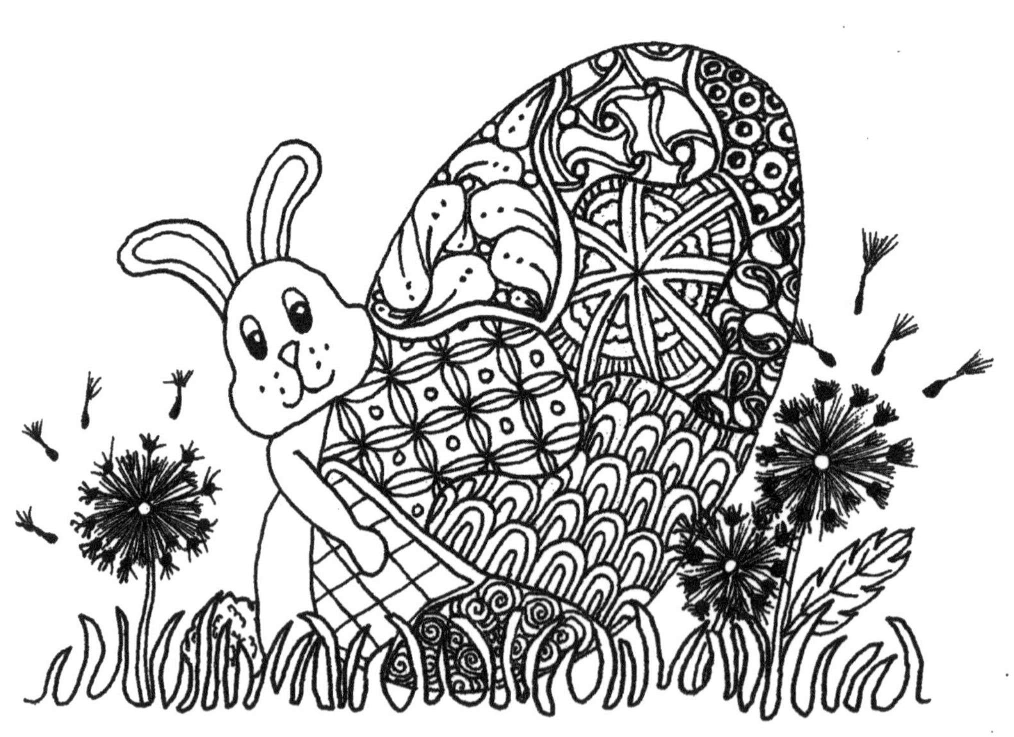

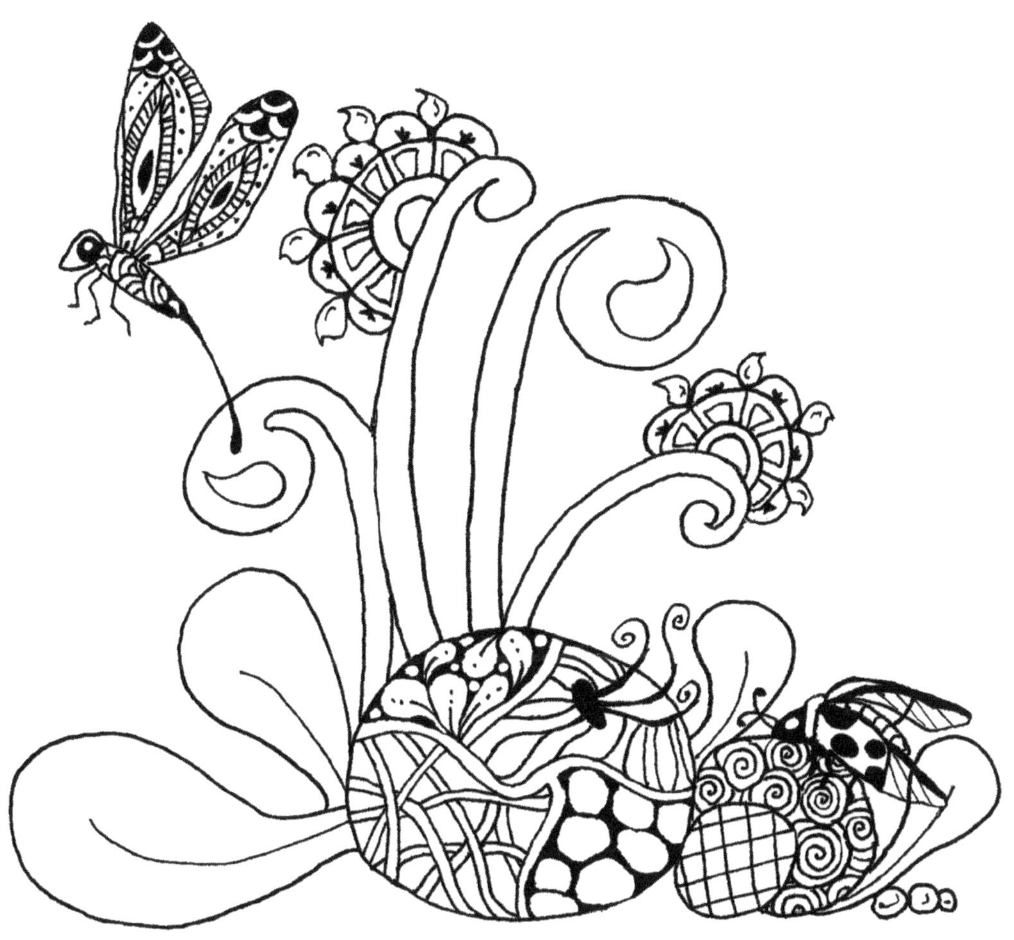

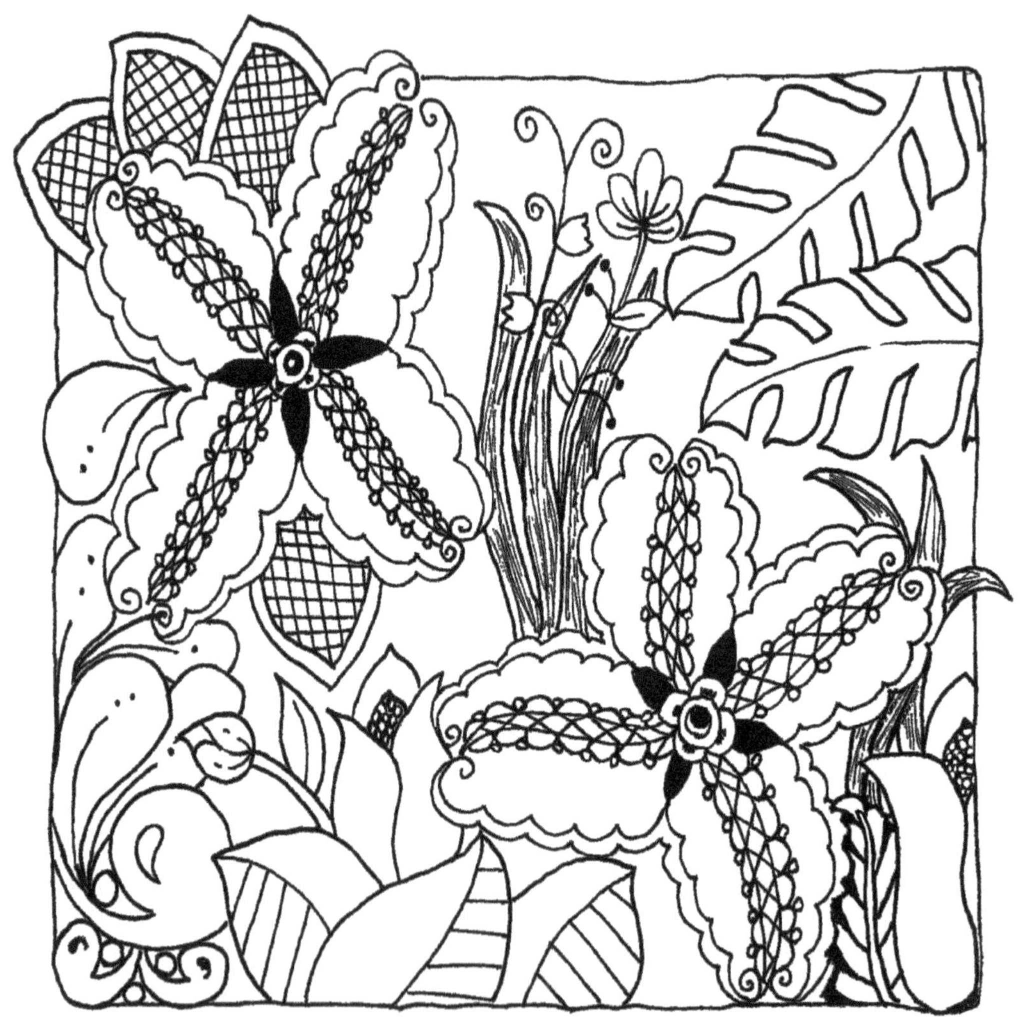

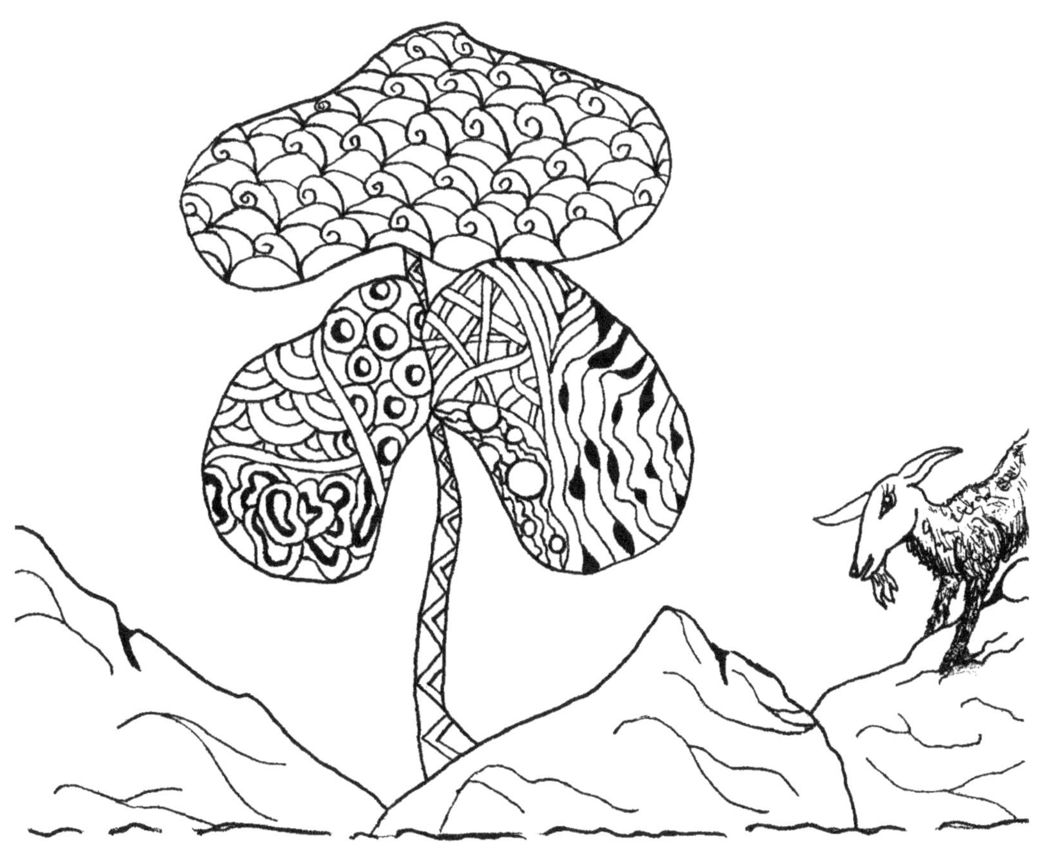

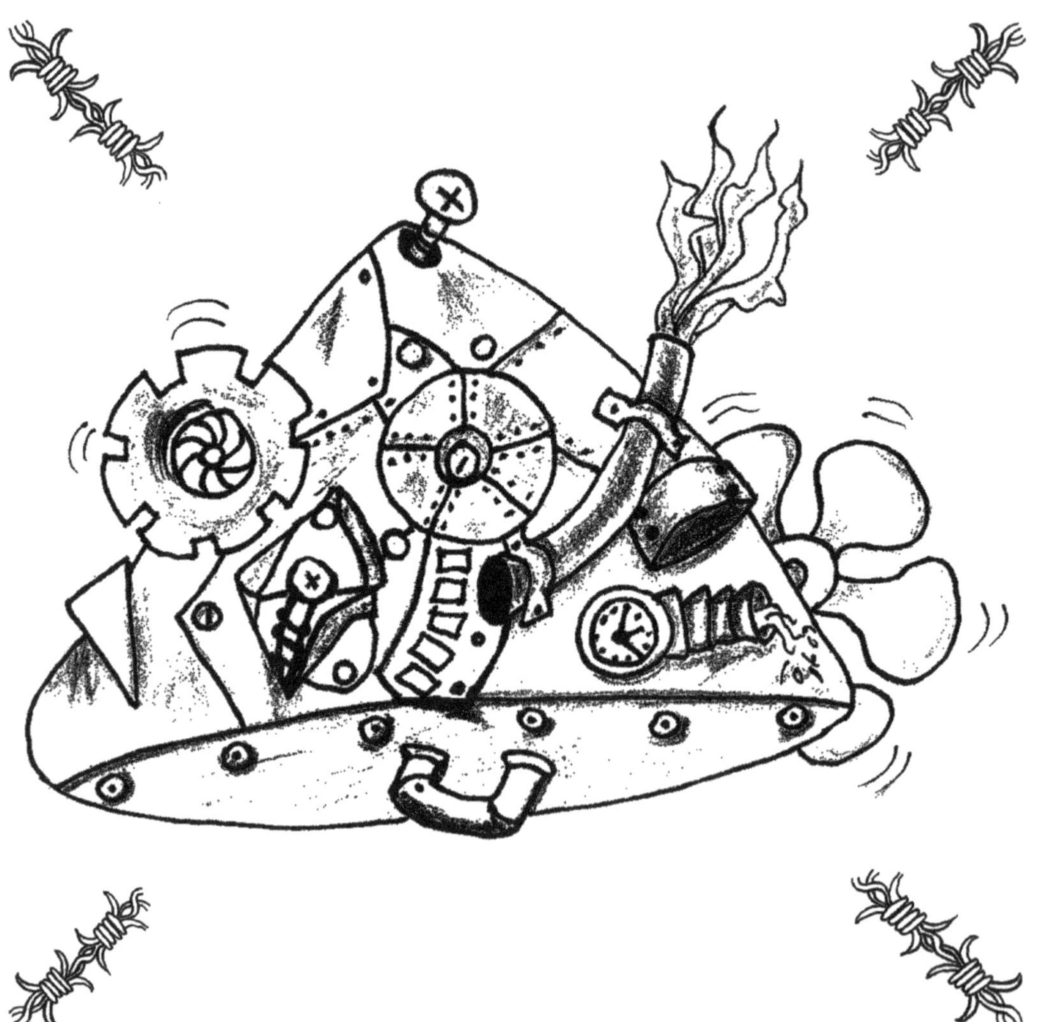

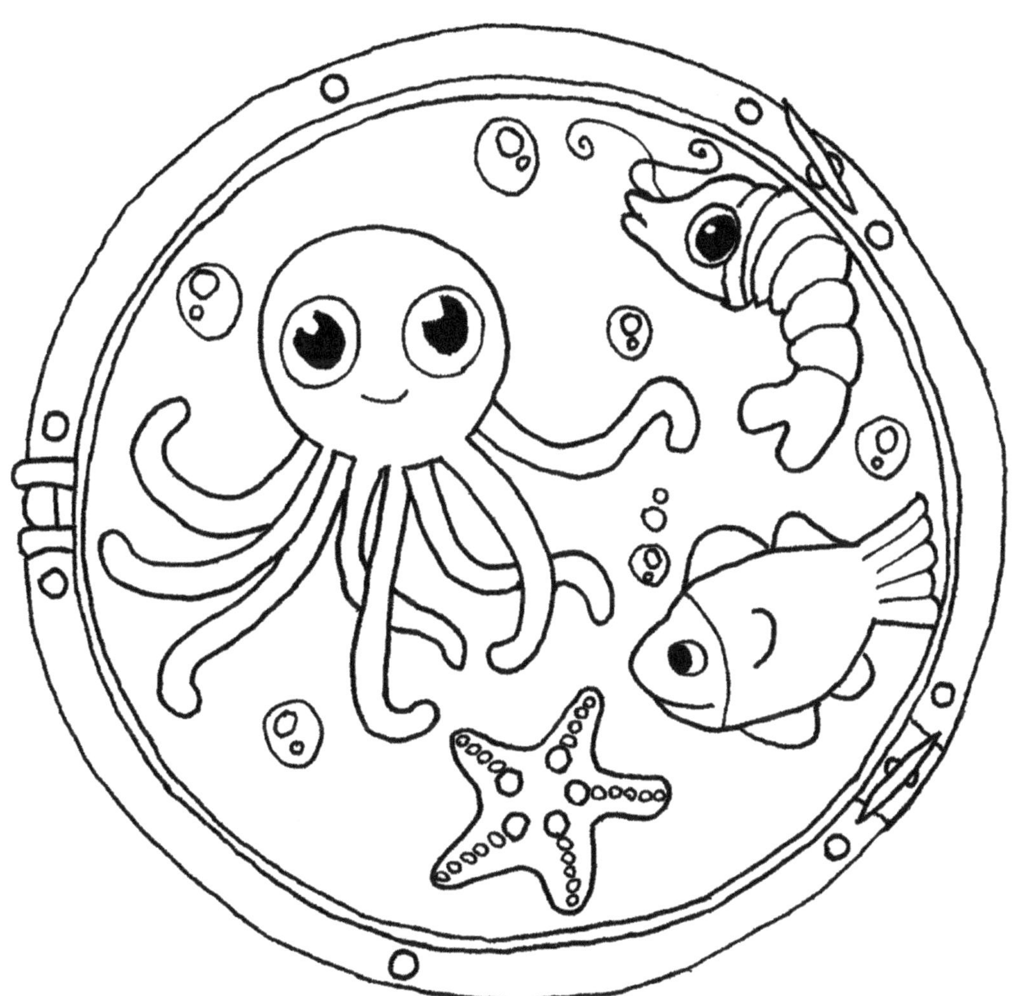

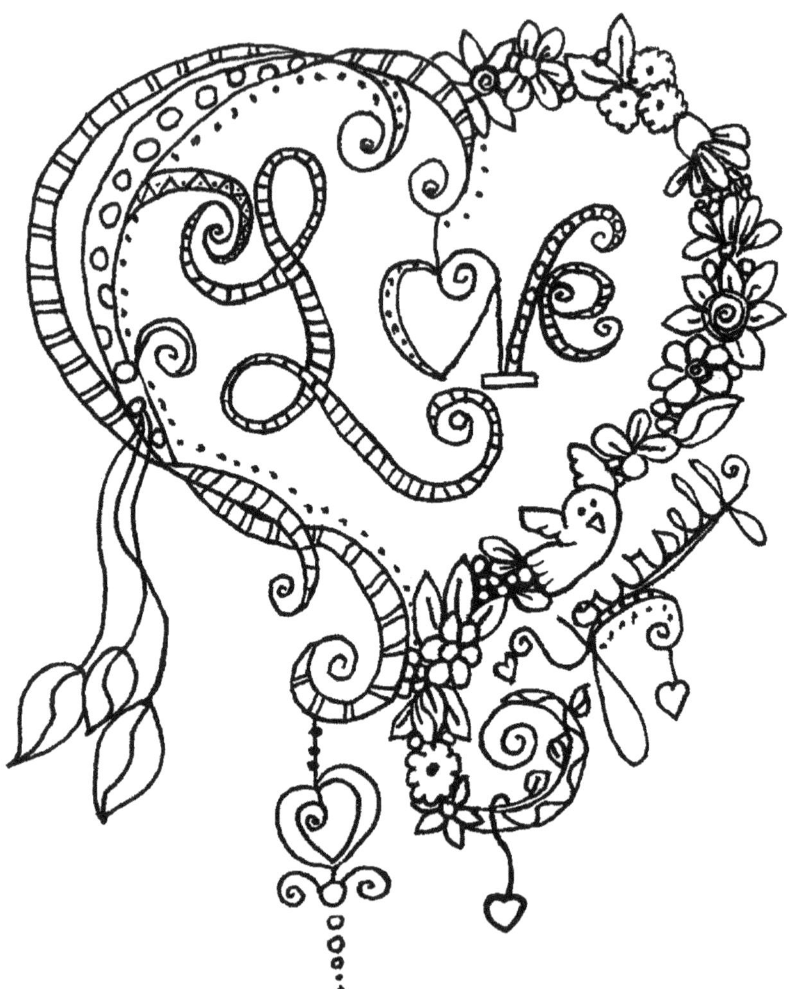
Love
yourself

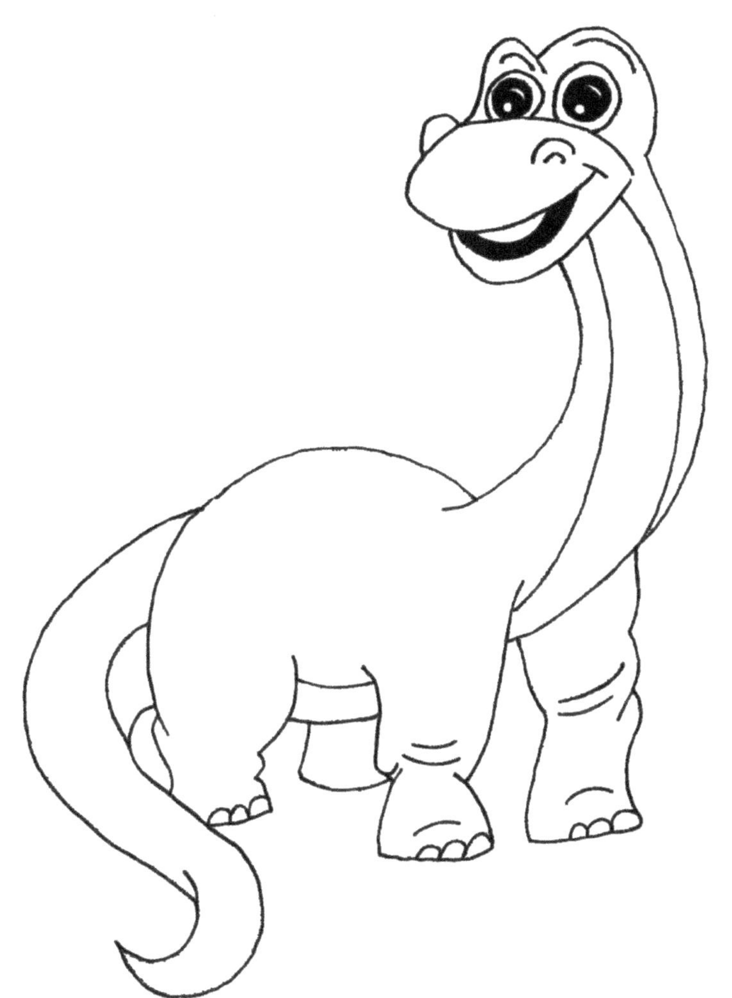

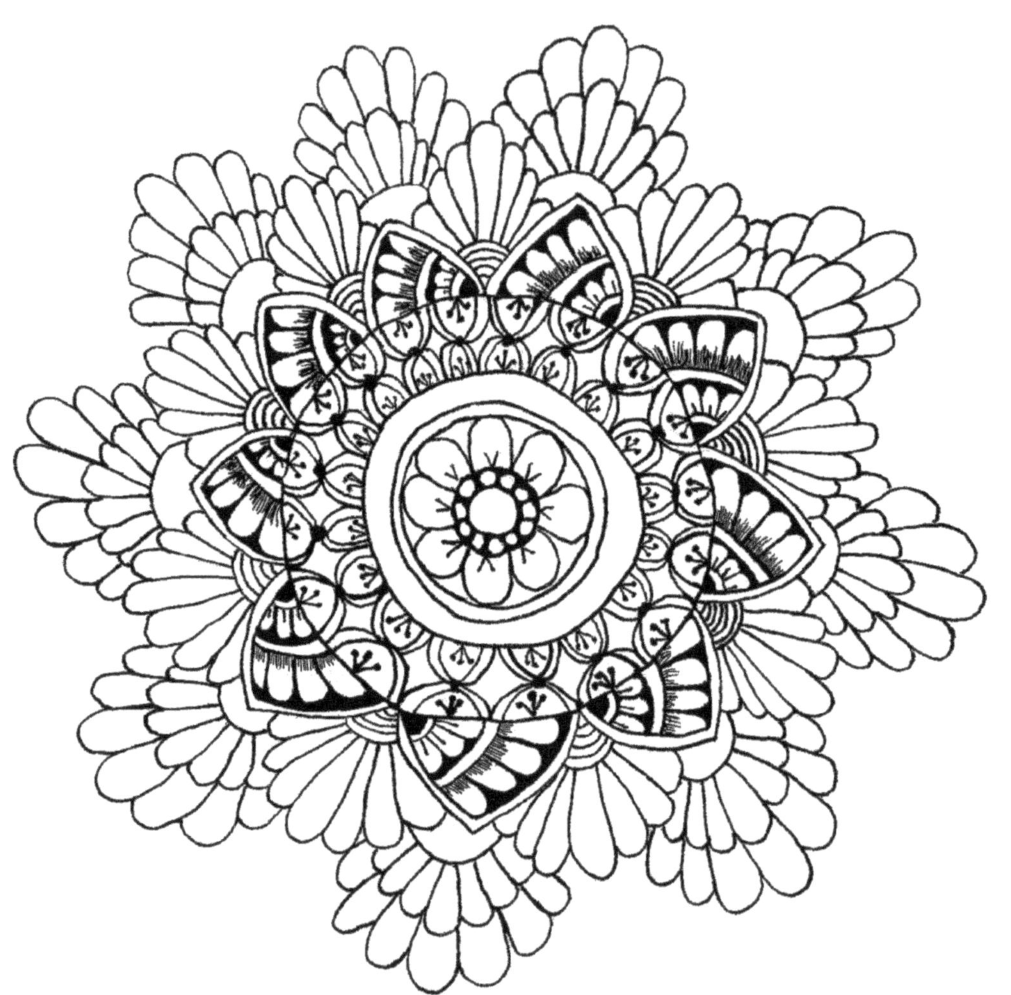

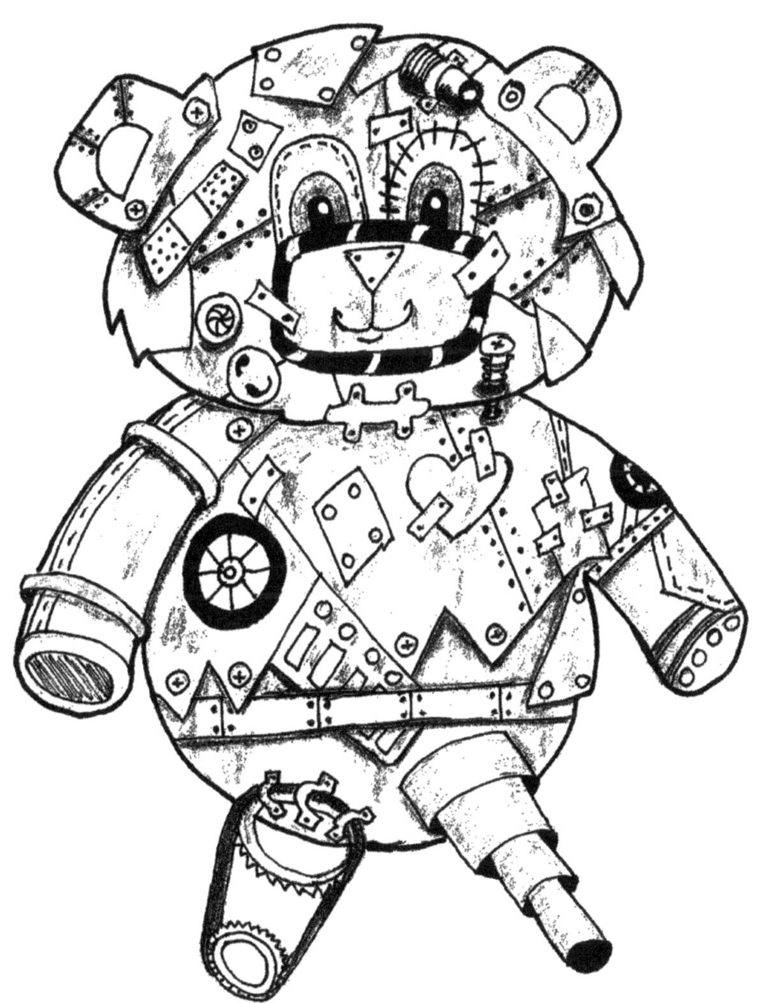

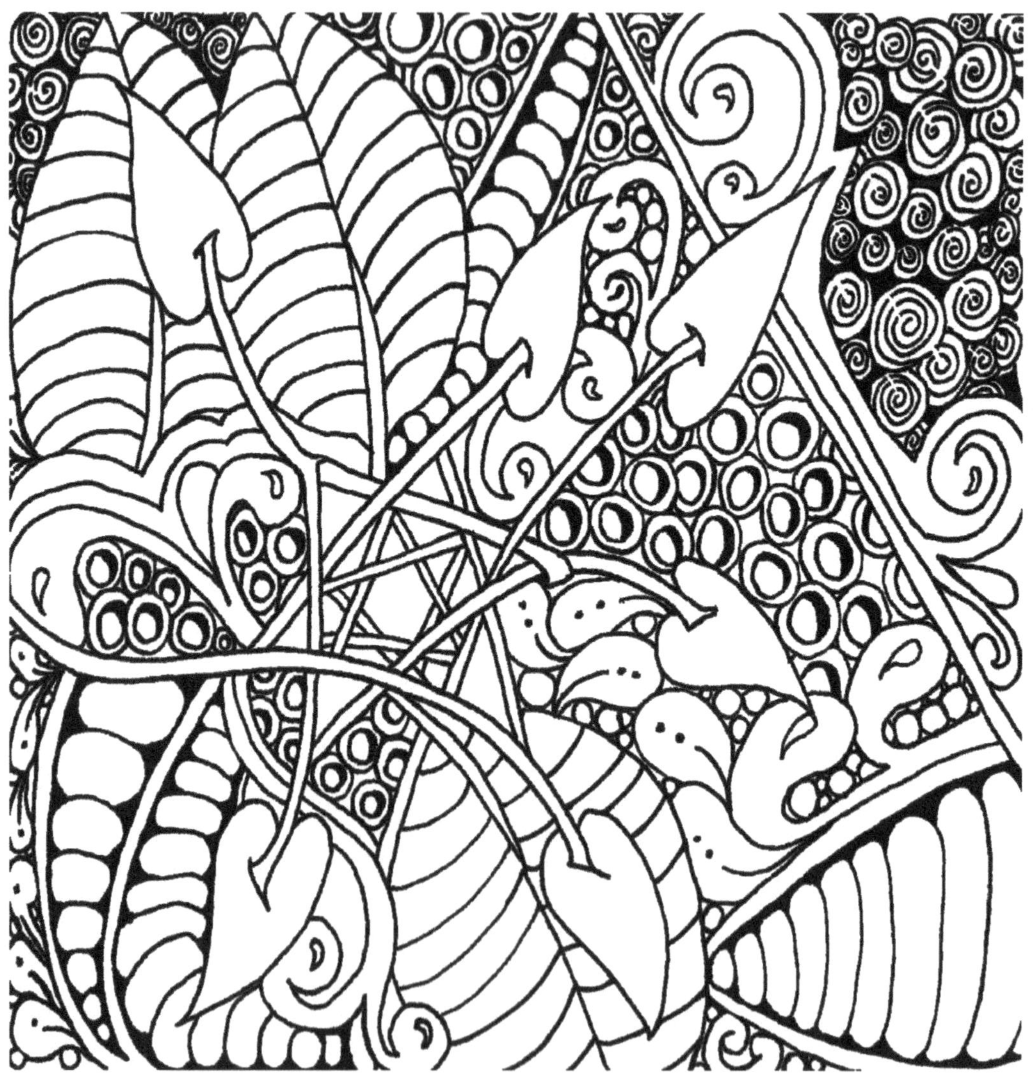

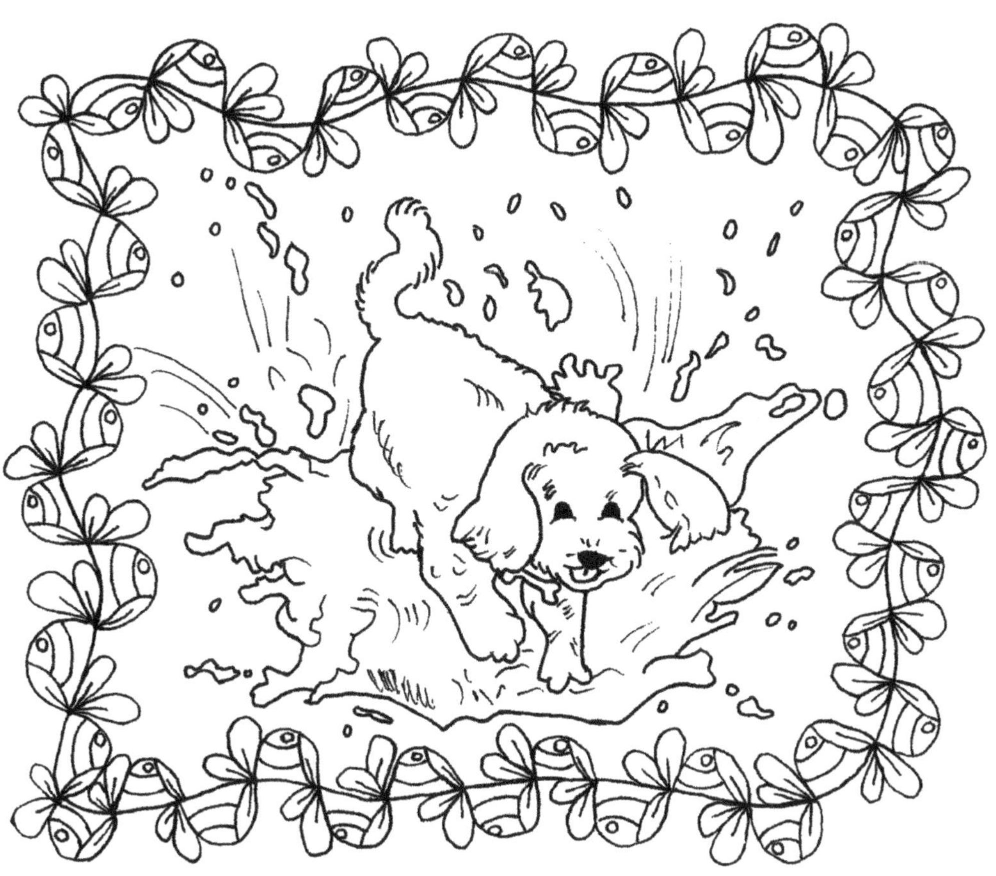

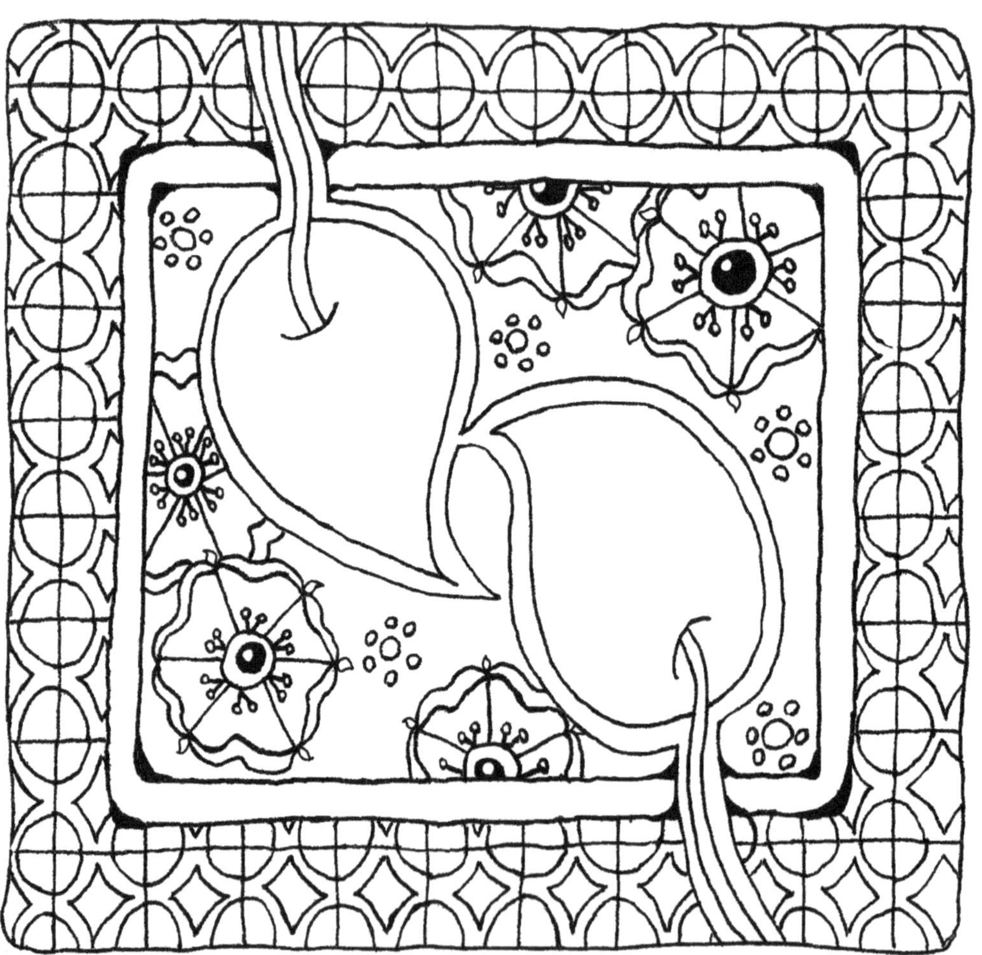

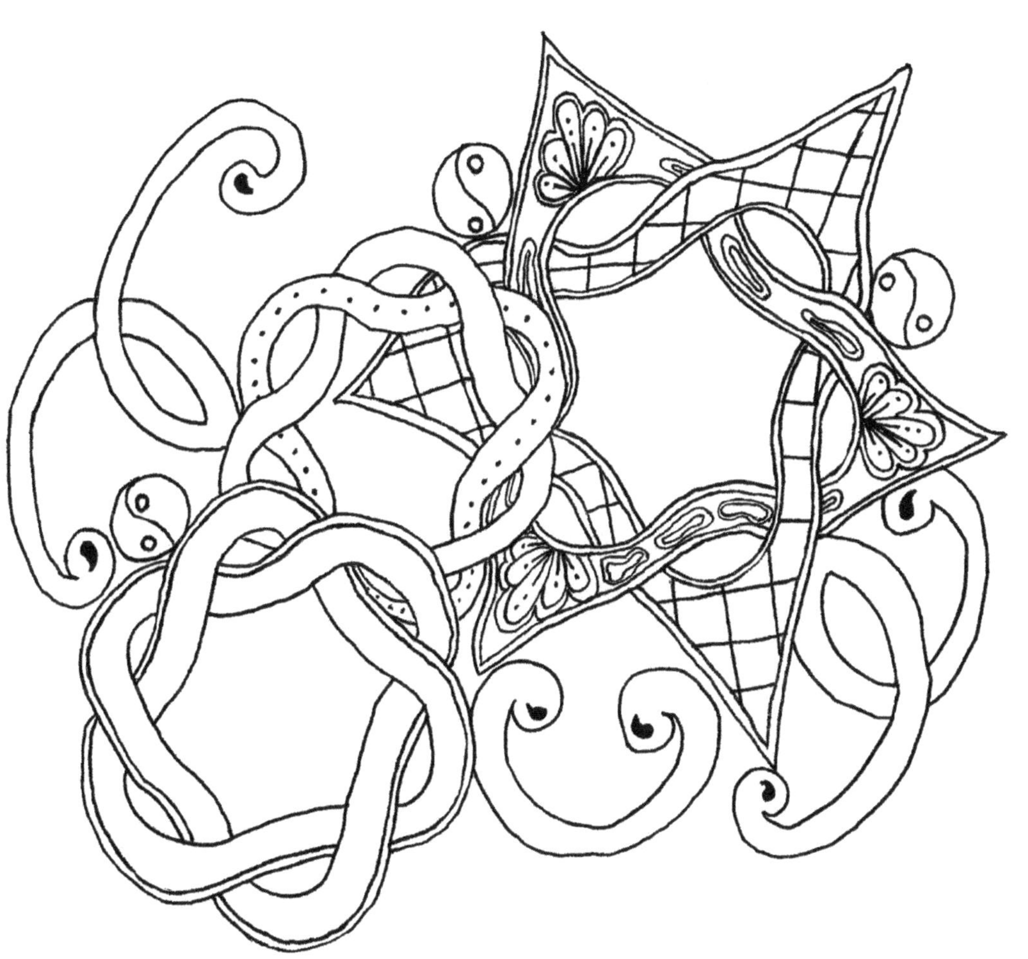

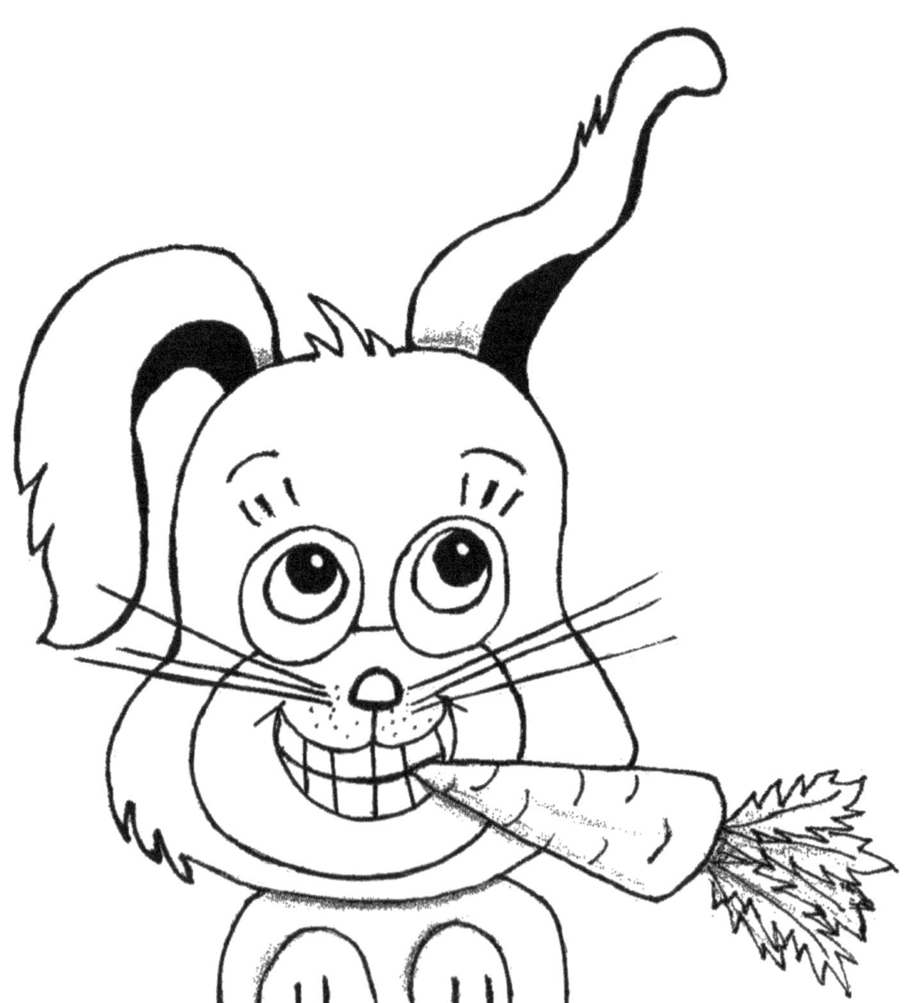

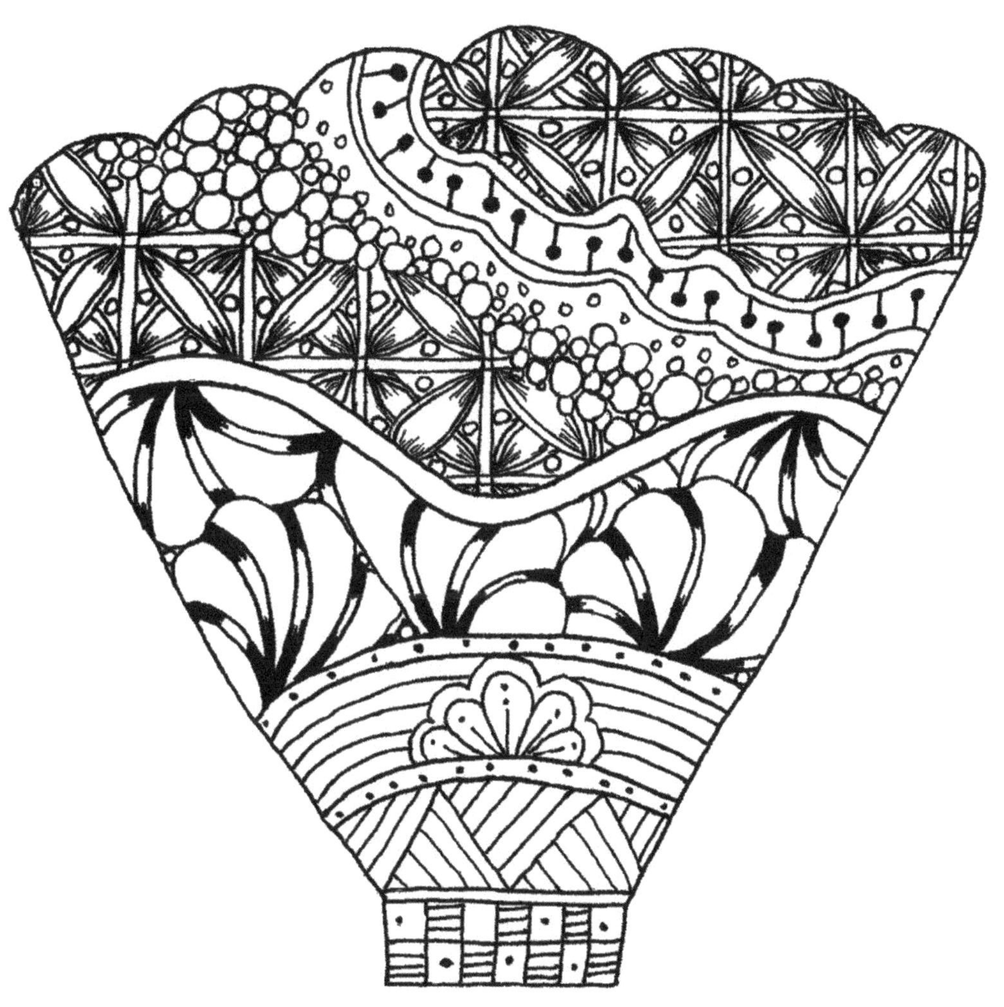

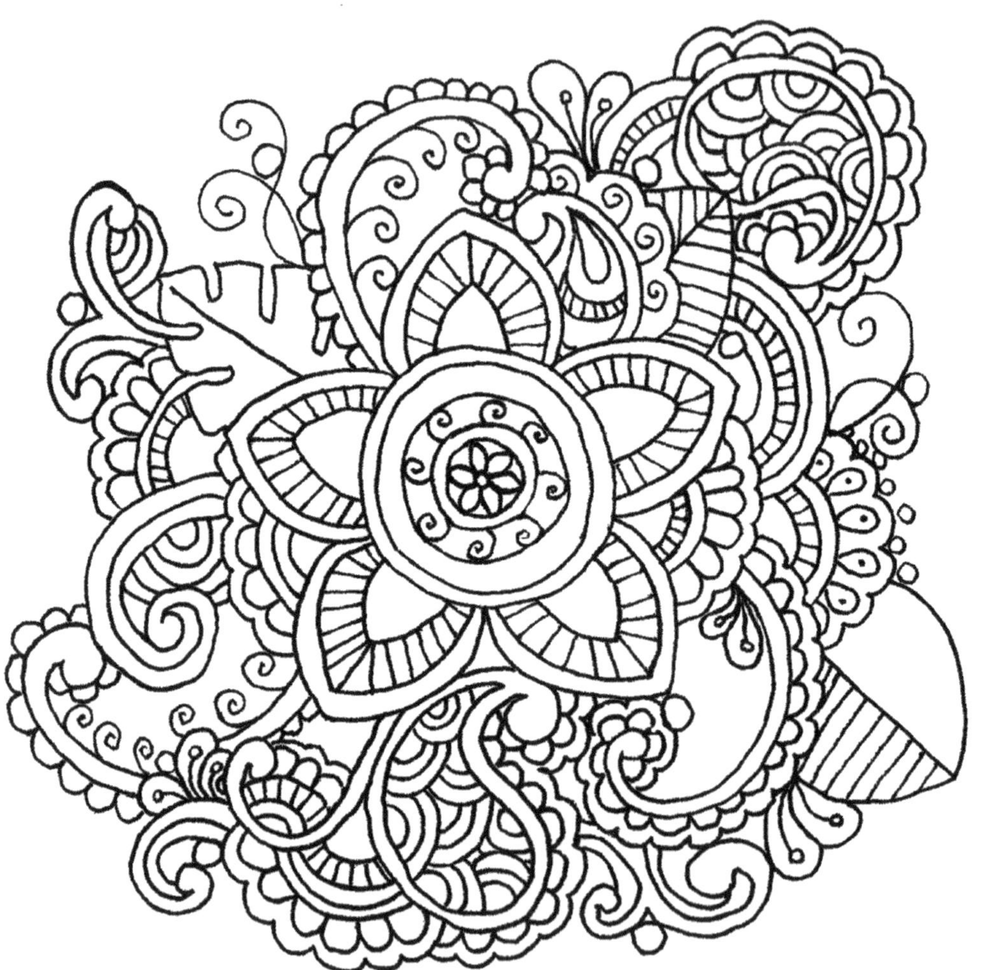

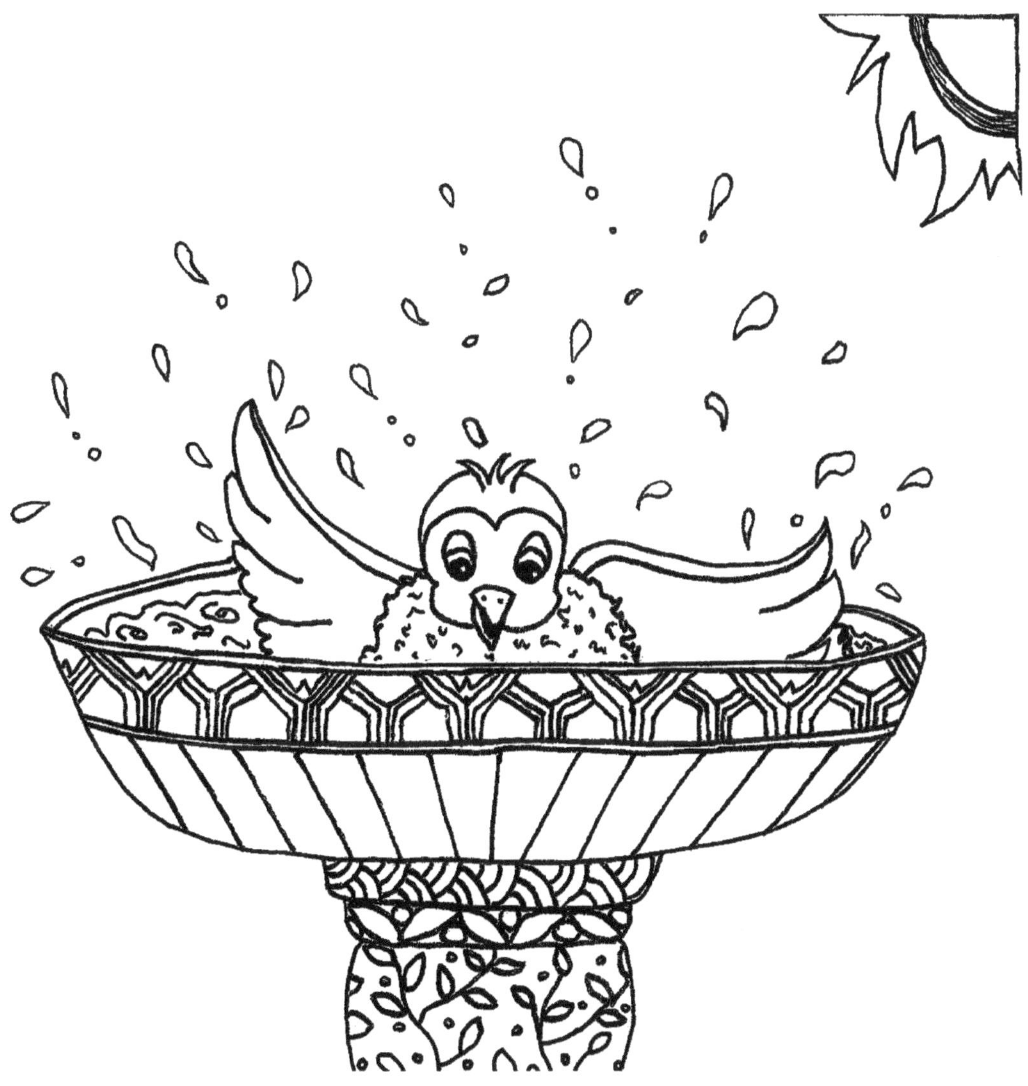

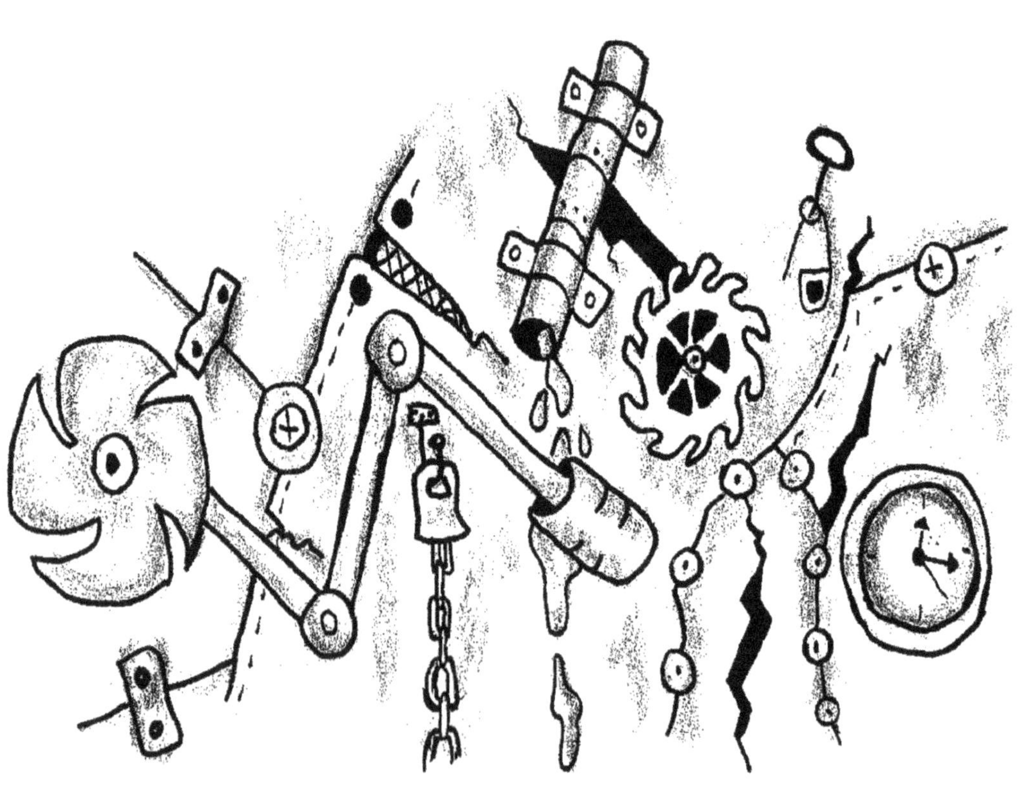

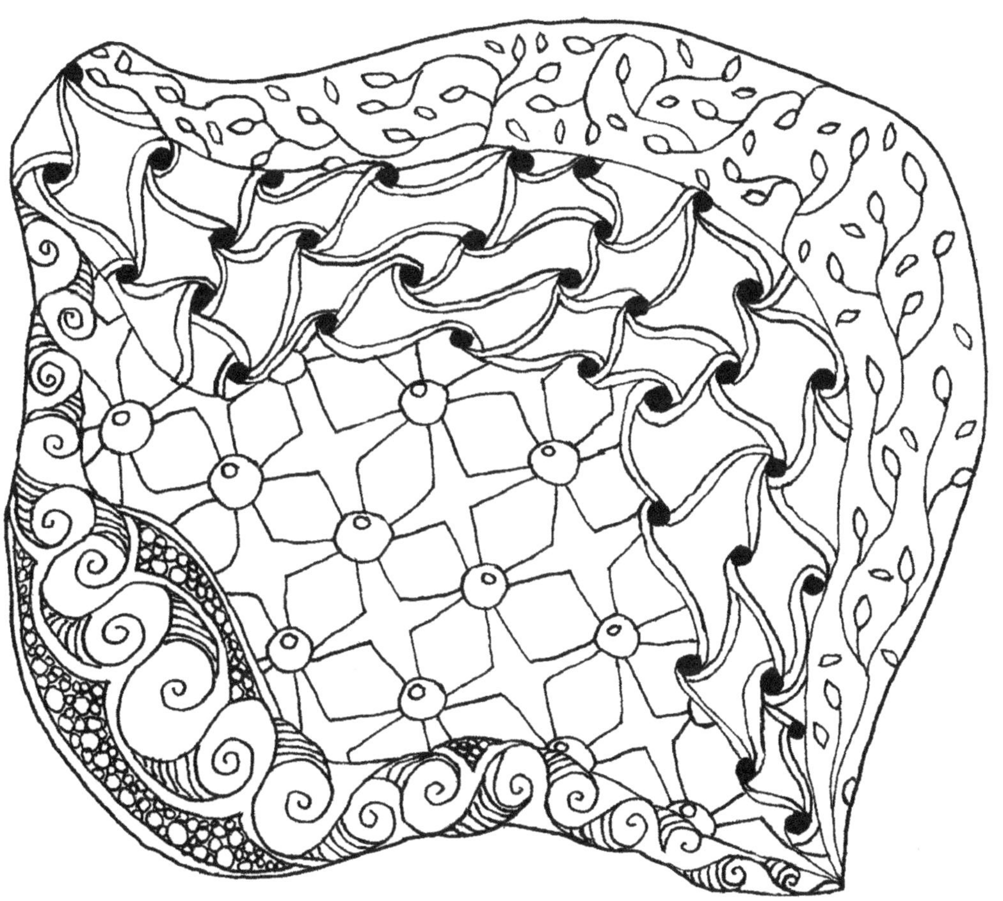

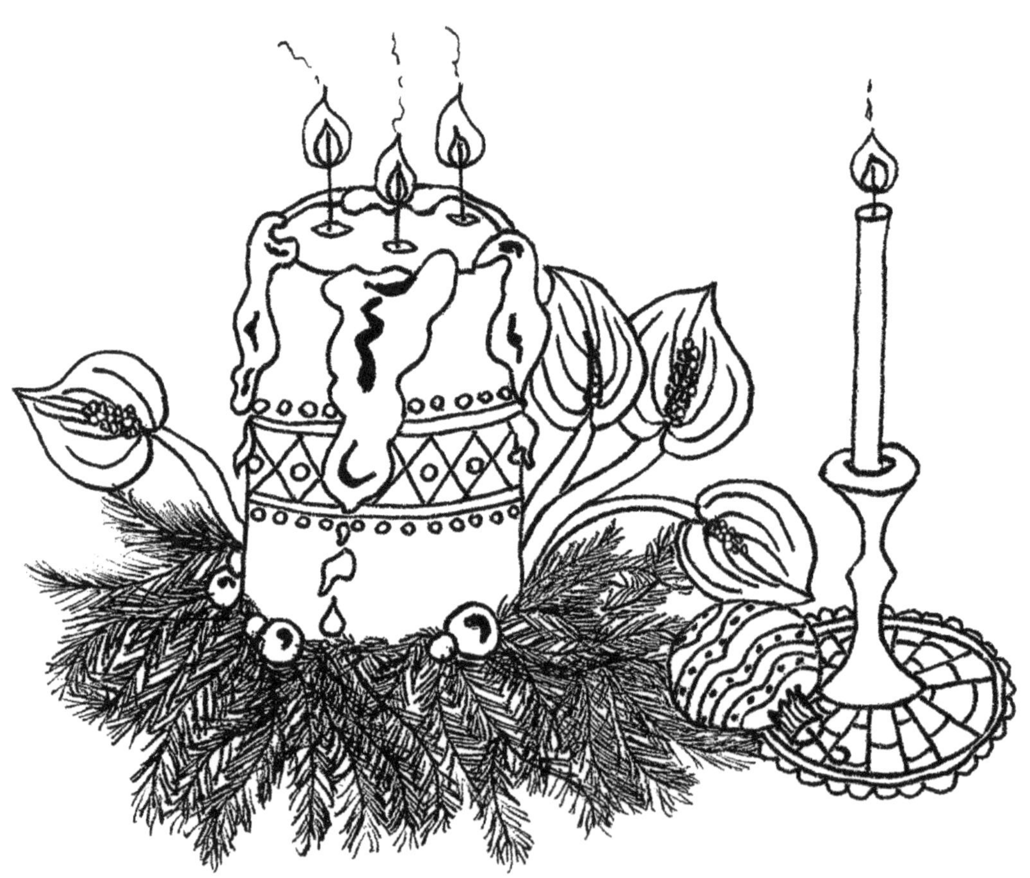

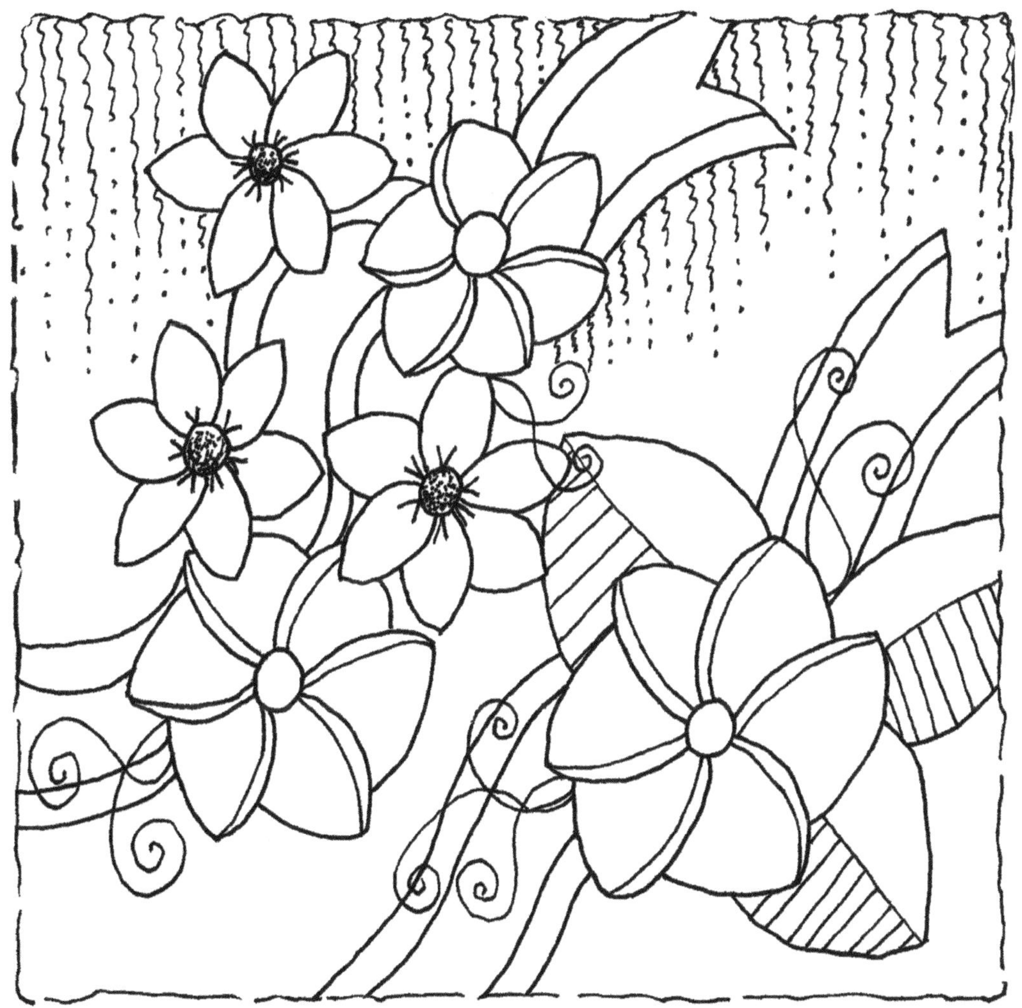

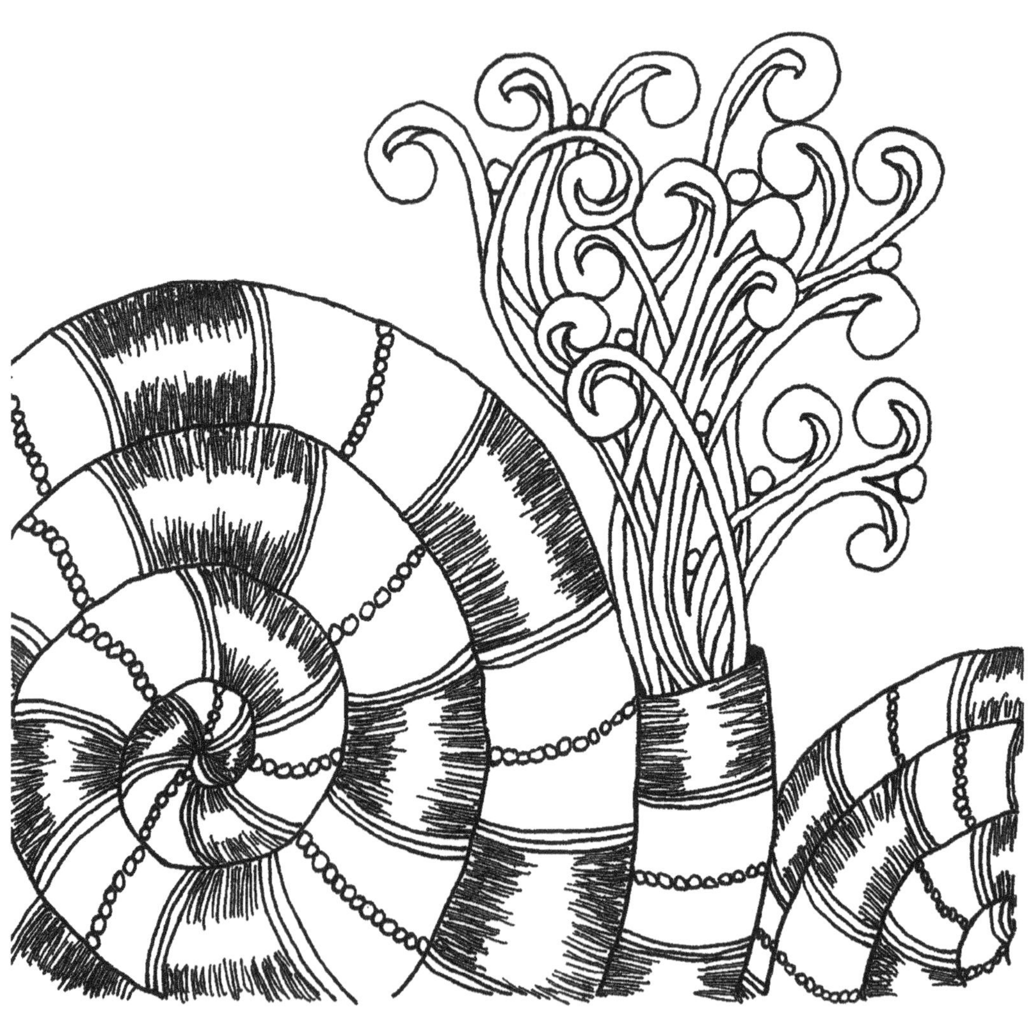

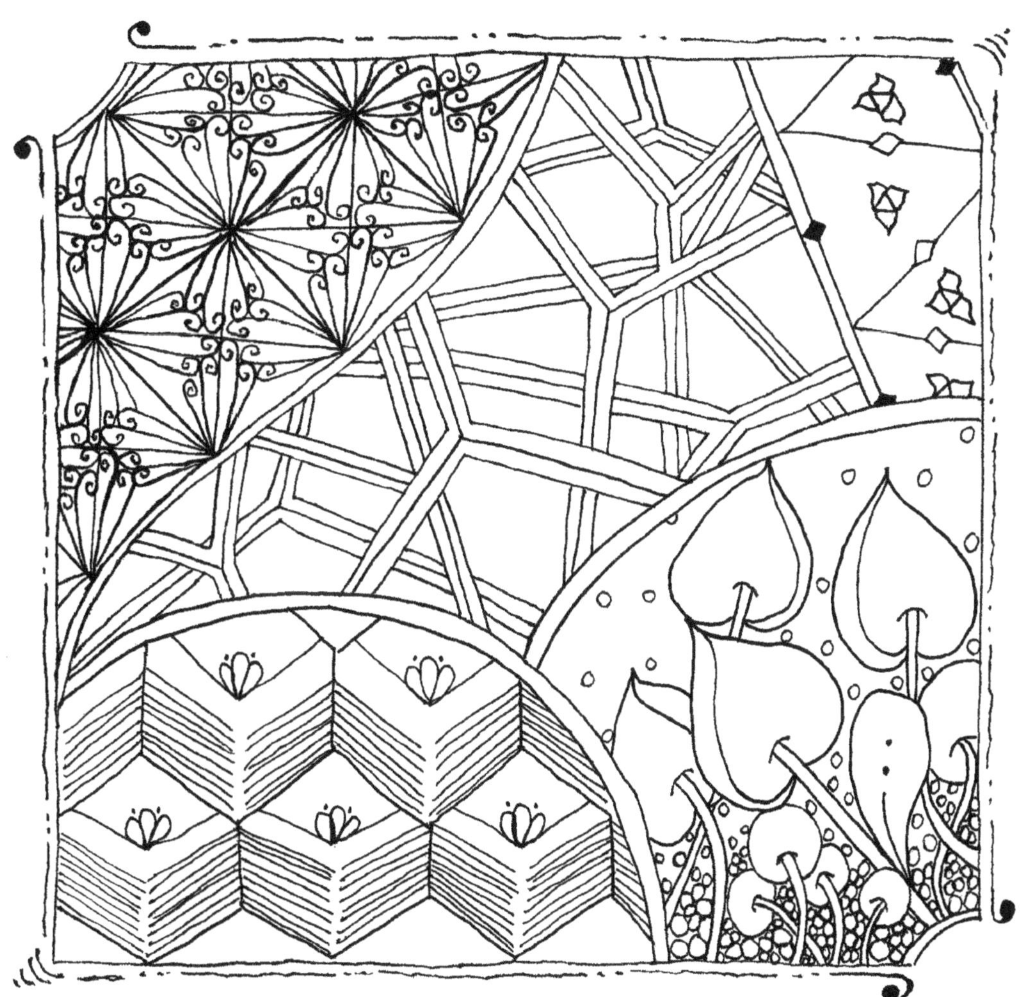

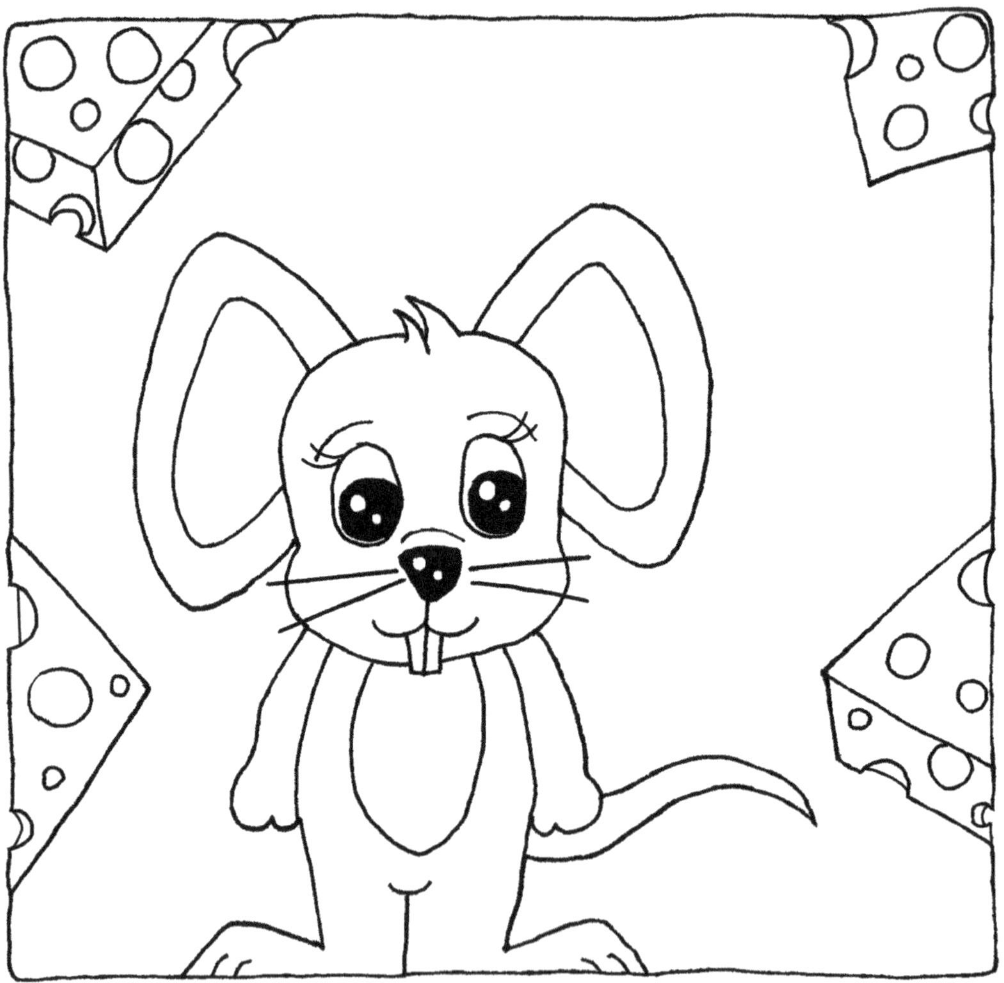

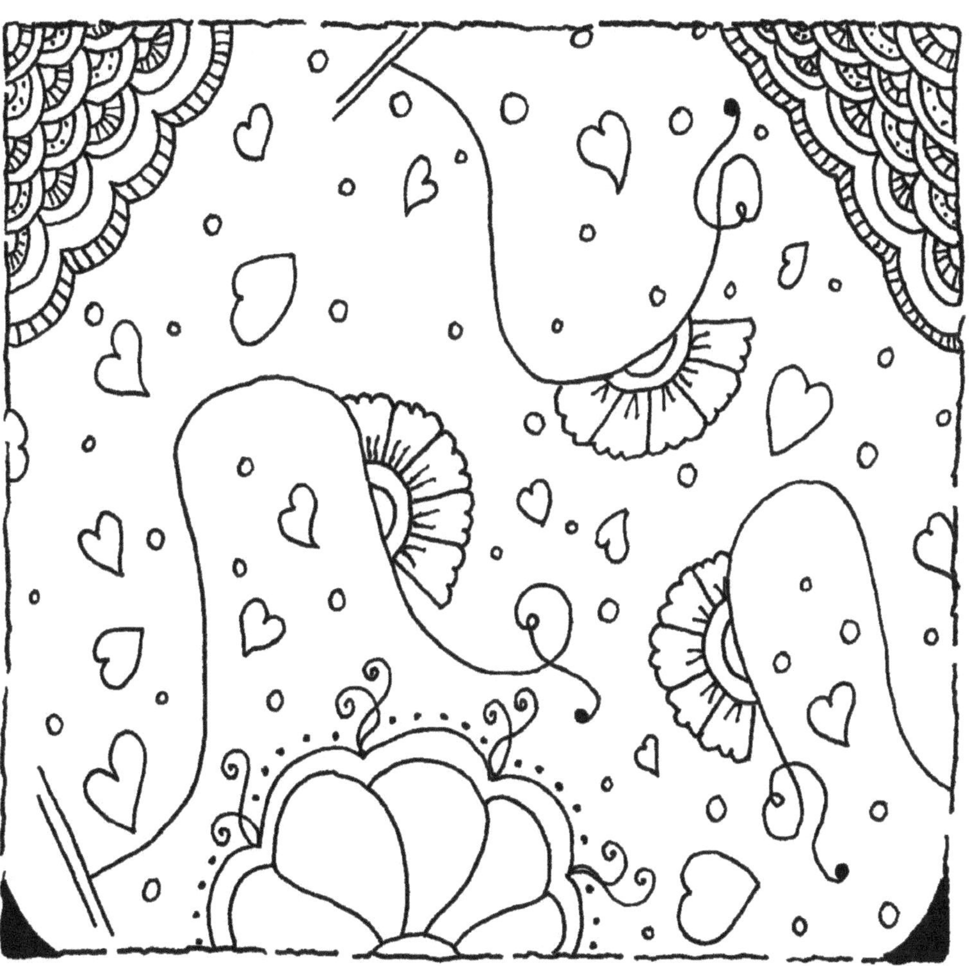

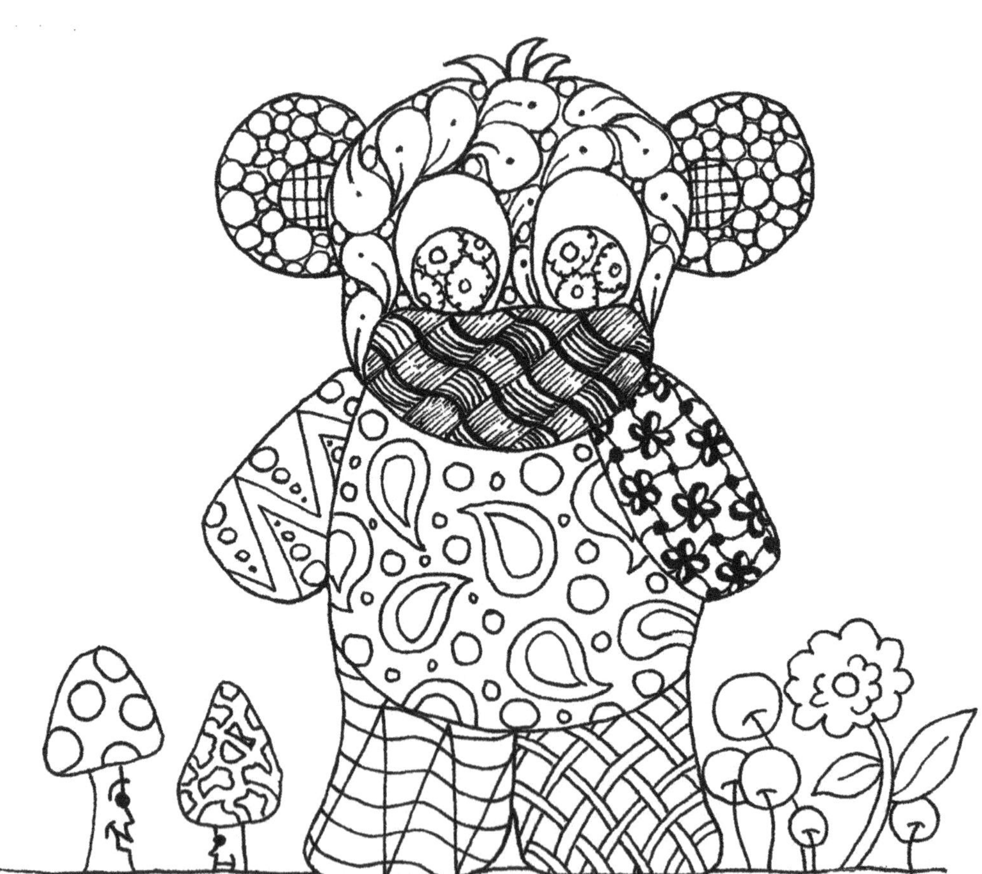

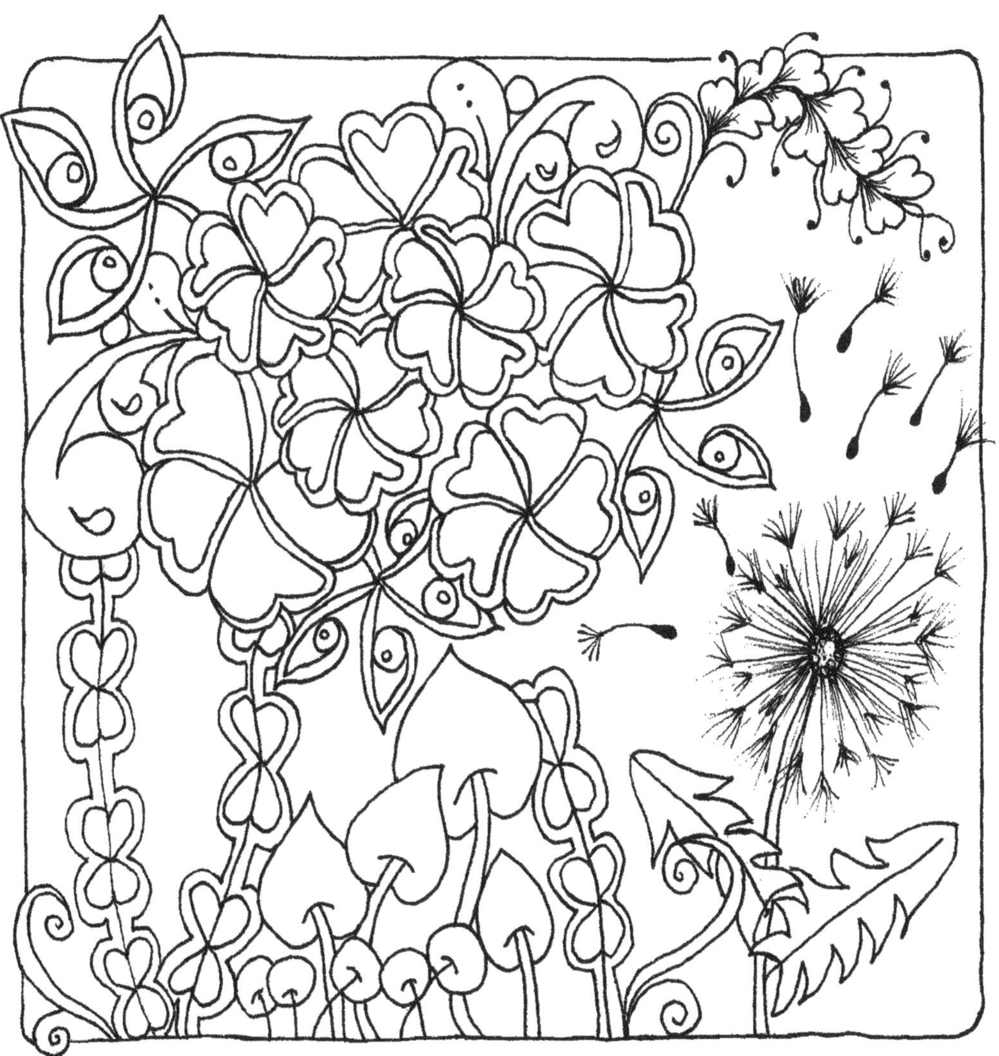

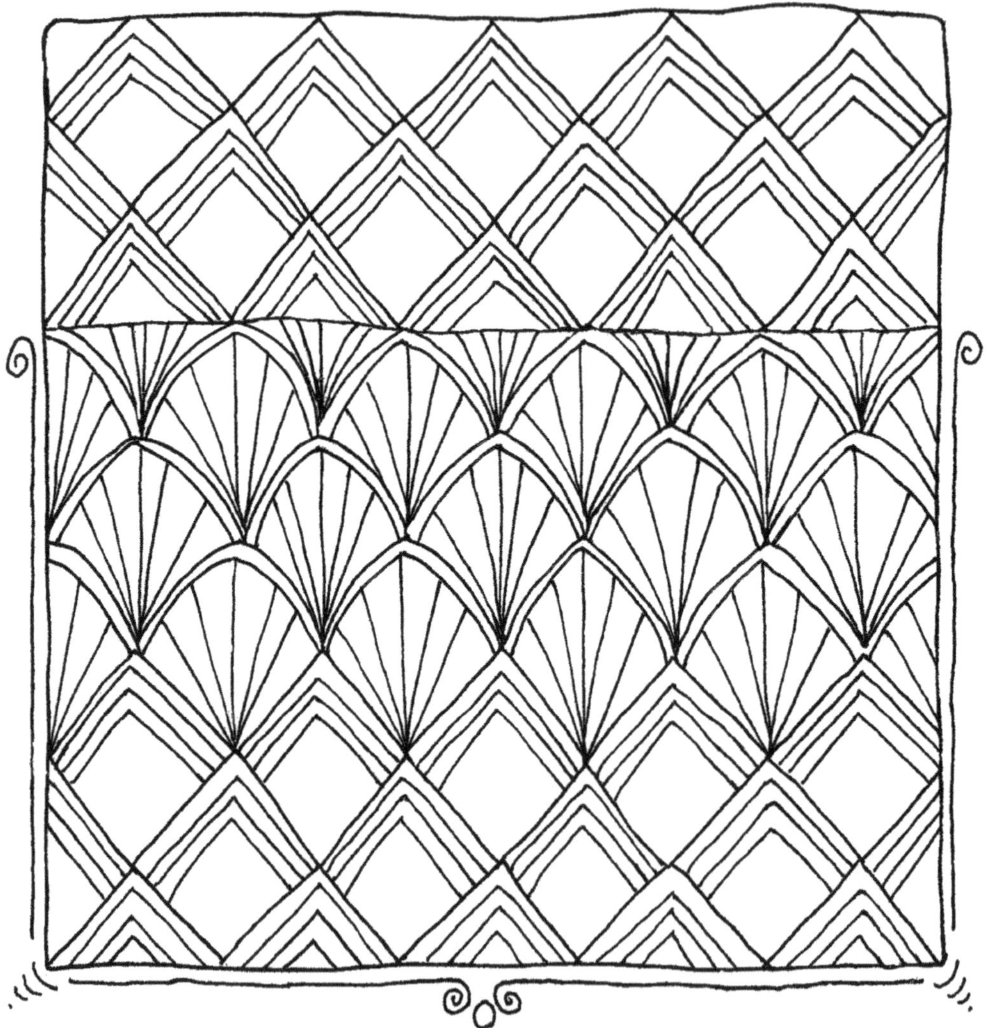

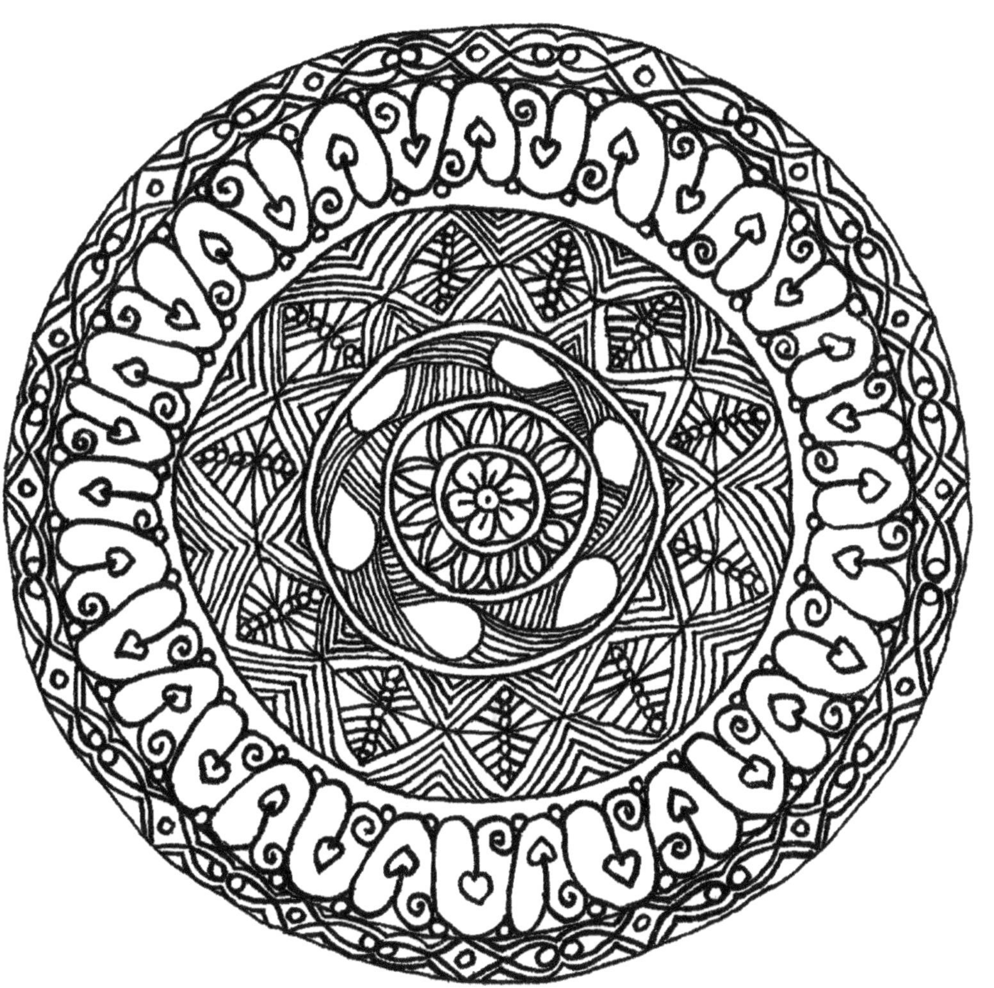

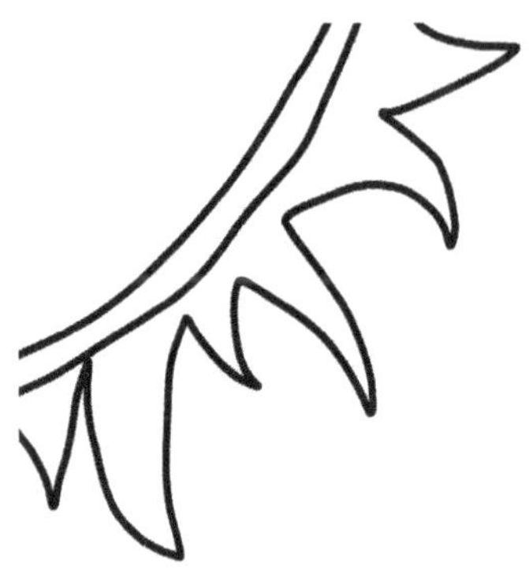

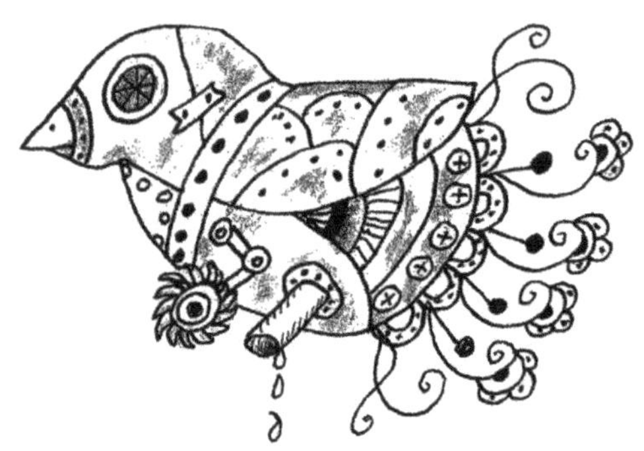

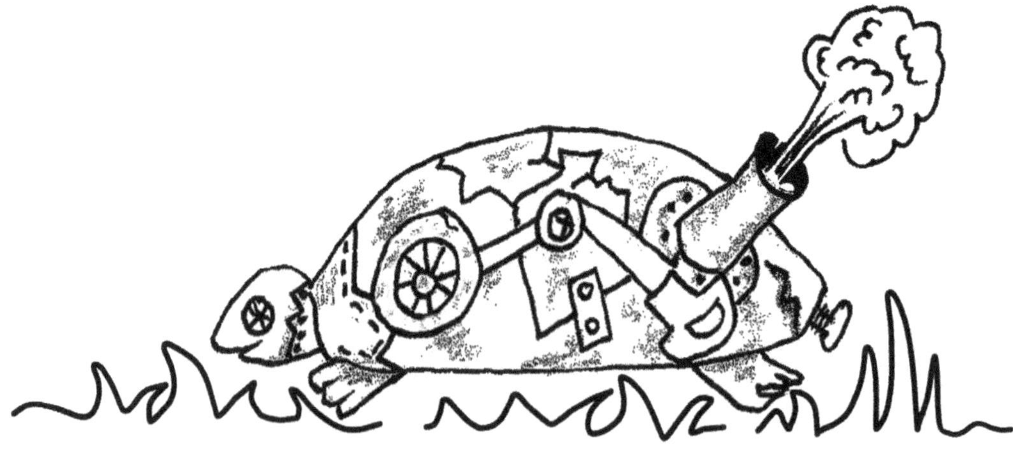

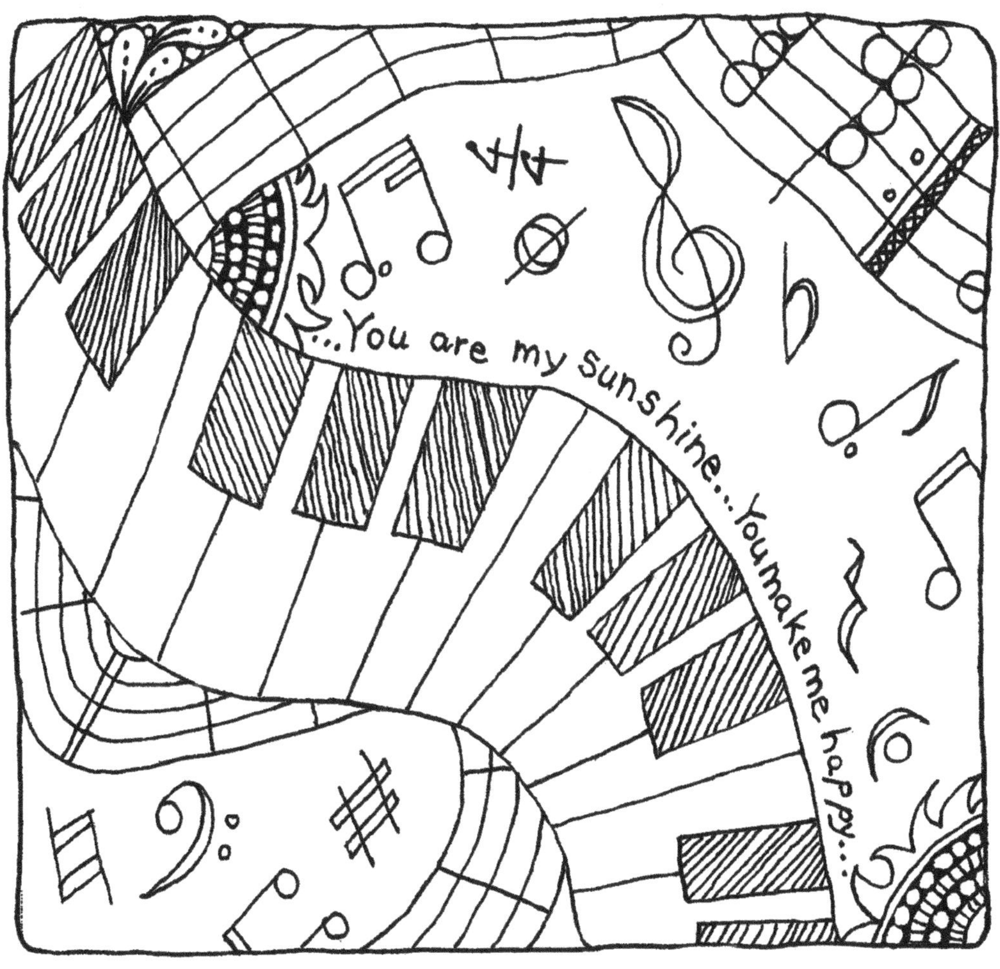
...You are my sunshine...You make me happy...

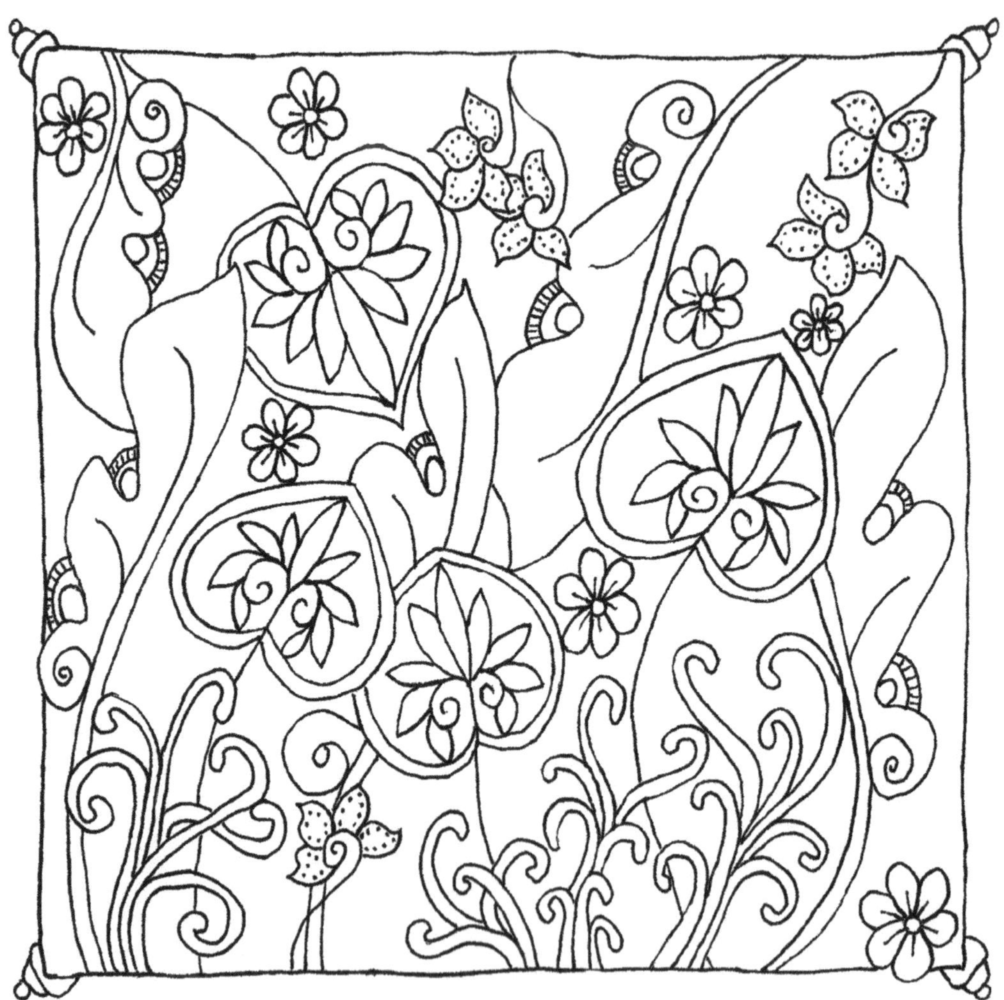

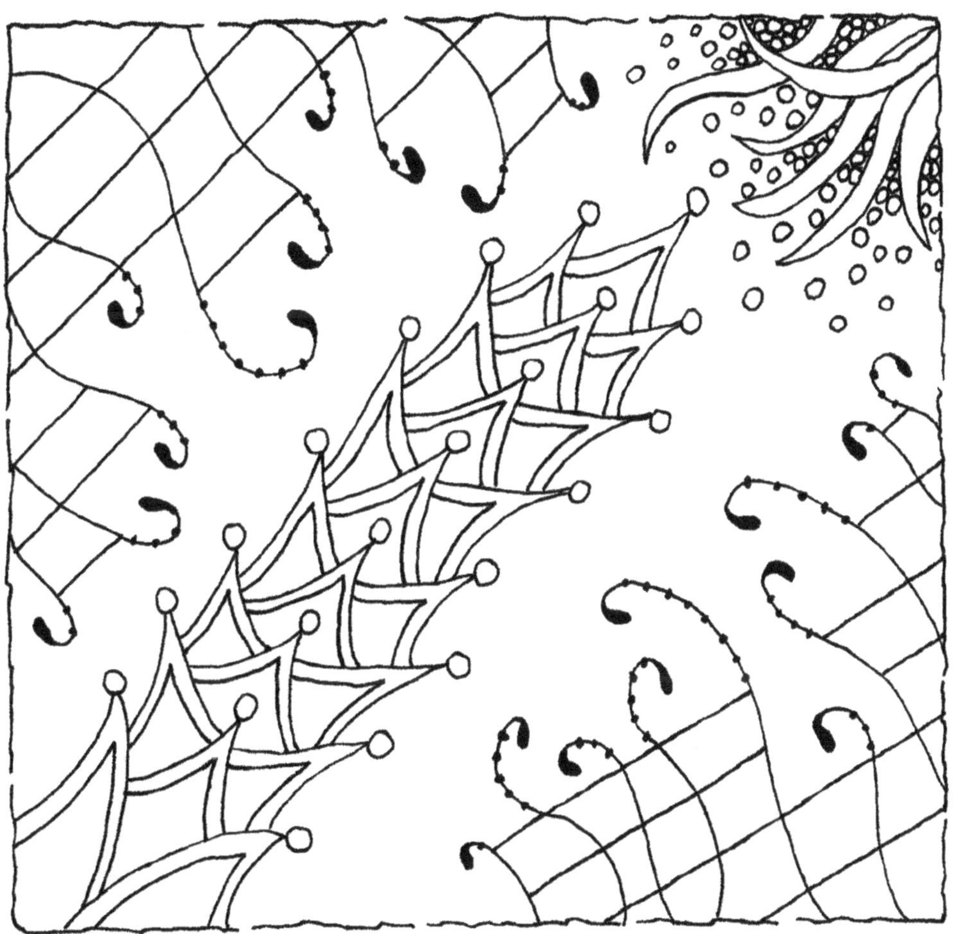

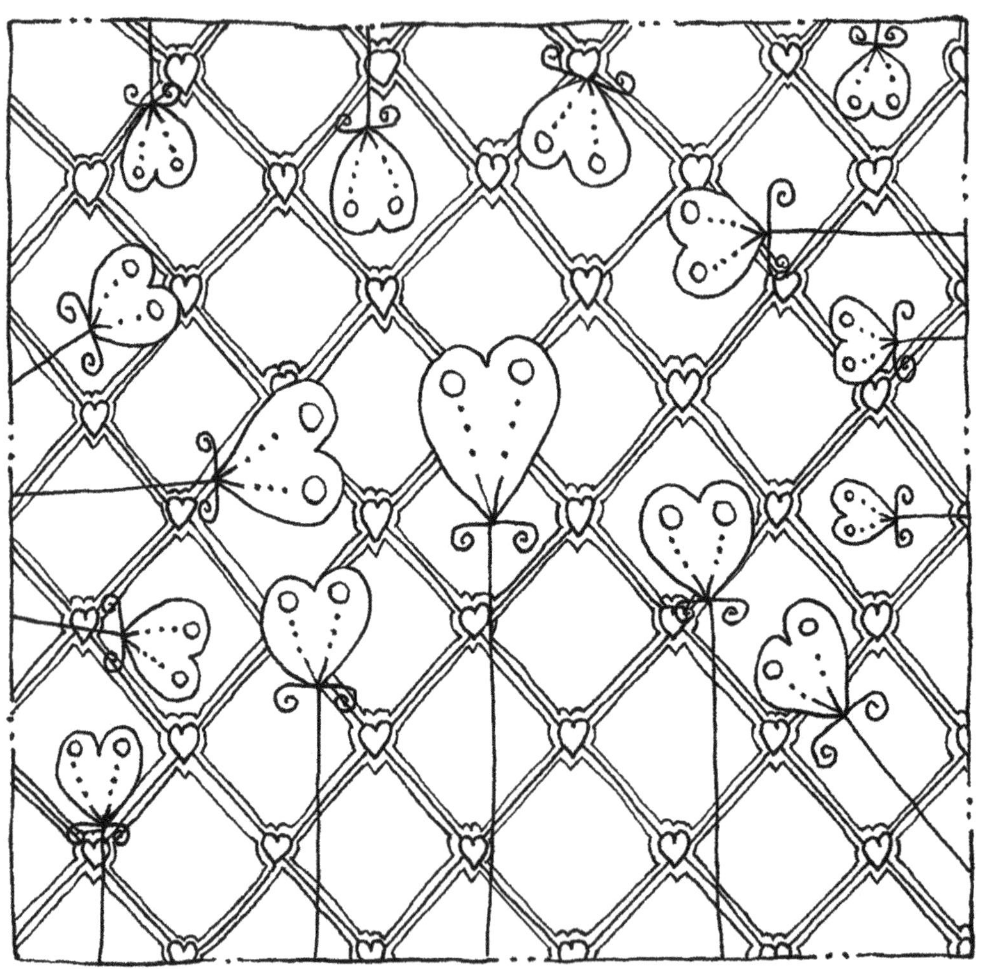

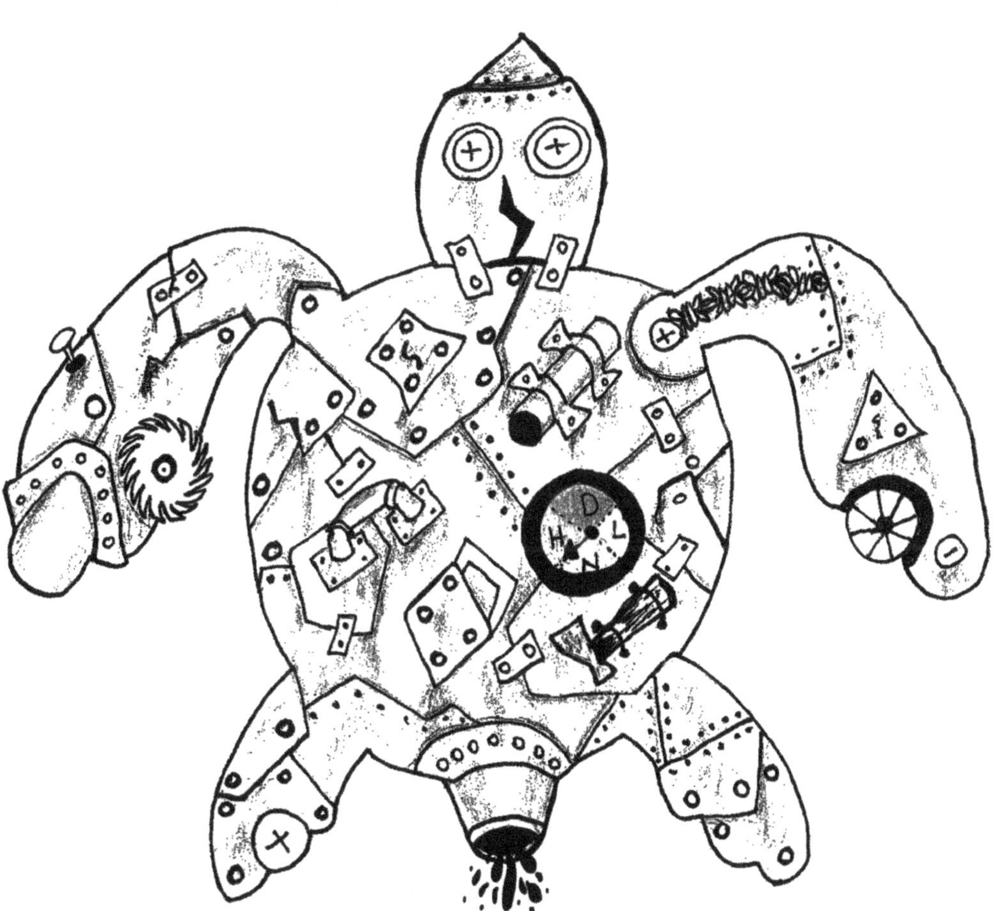

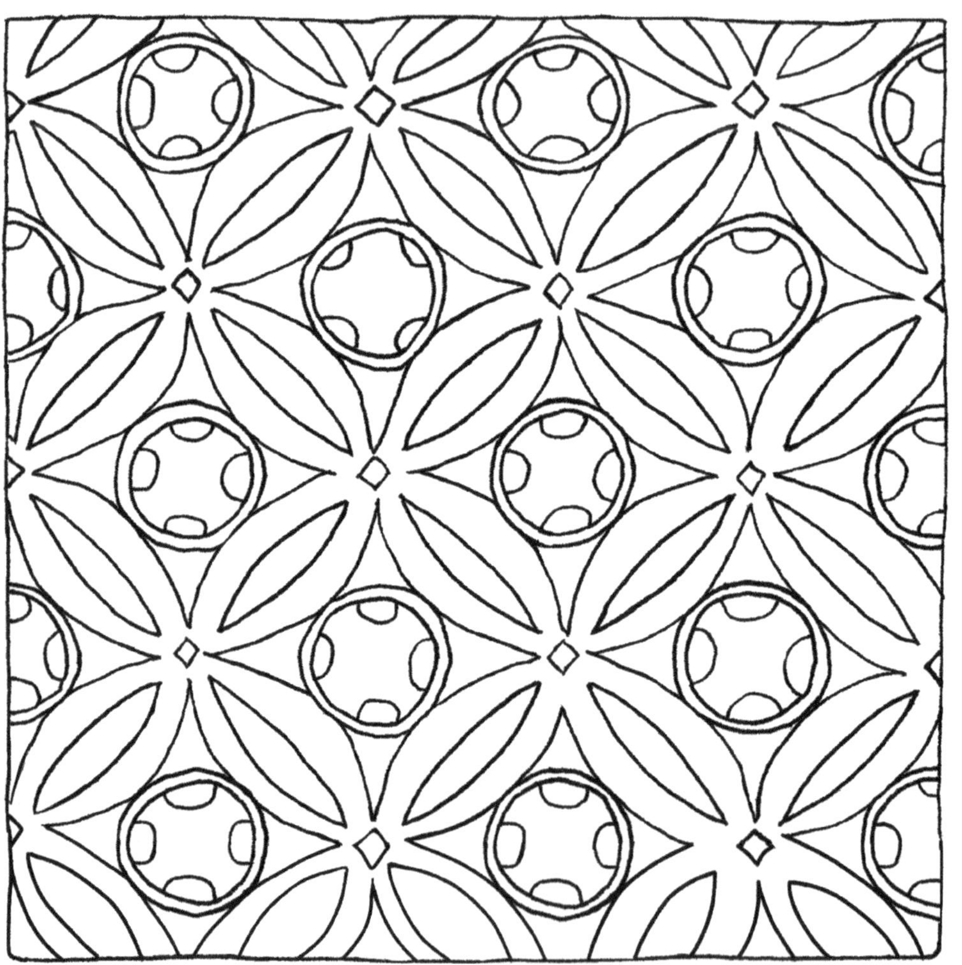

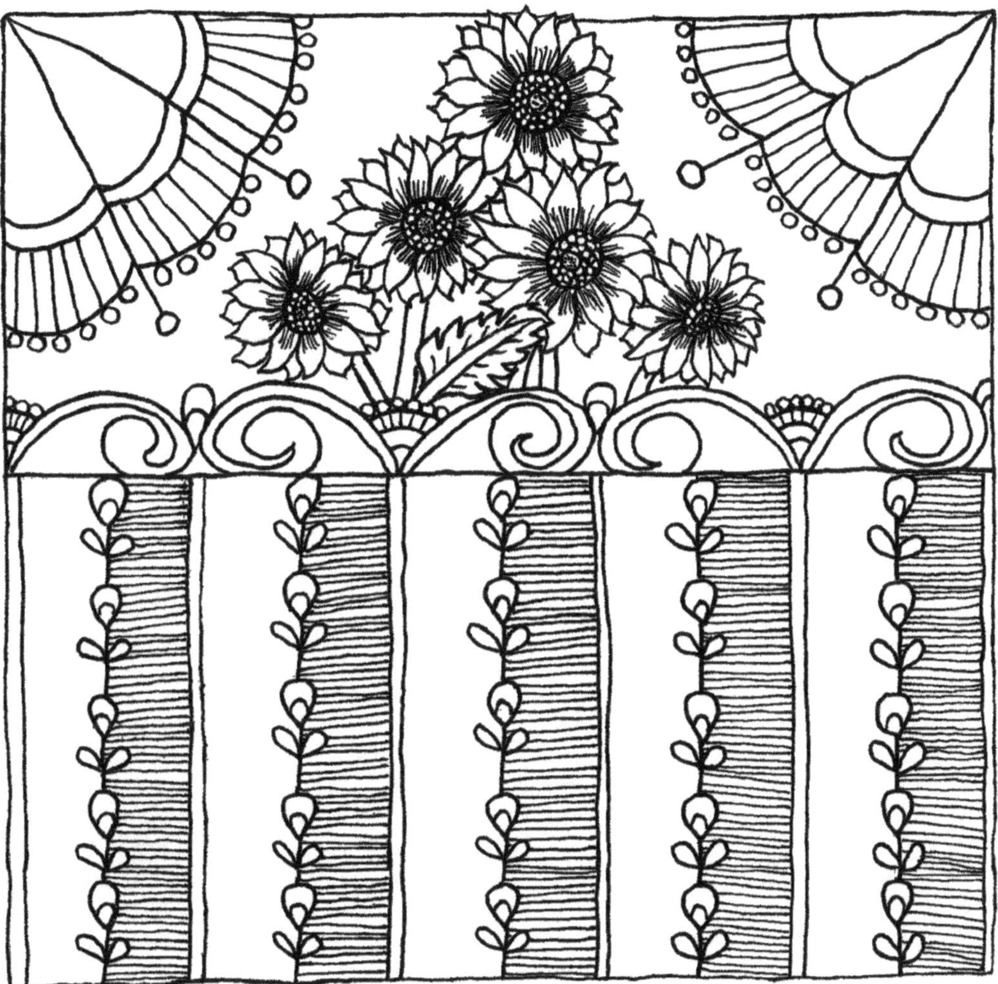

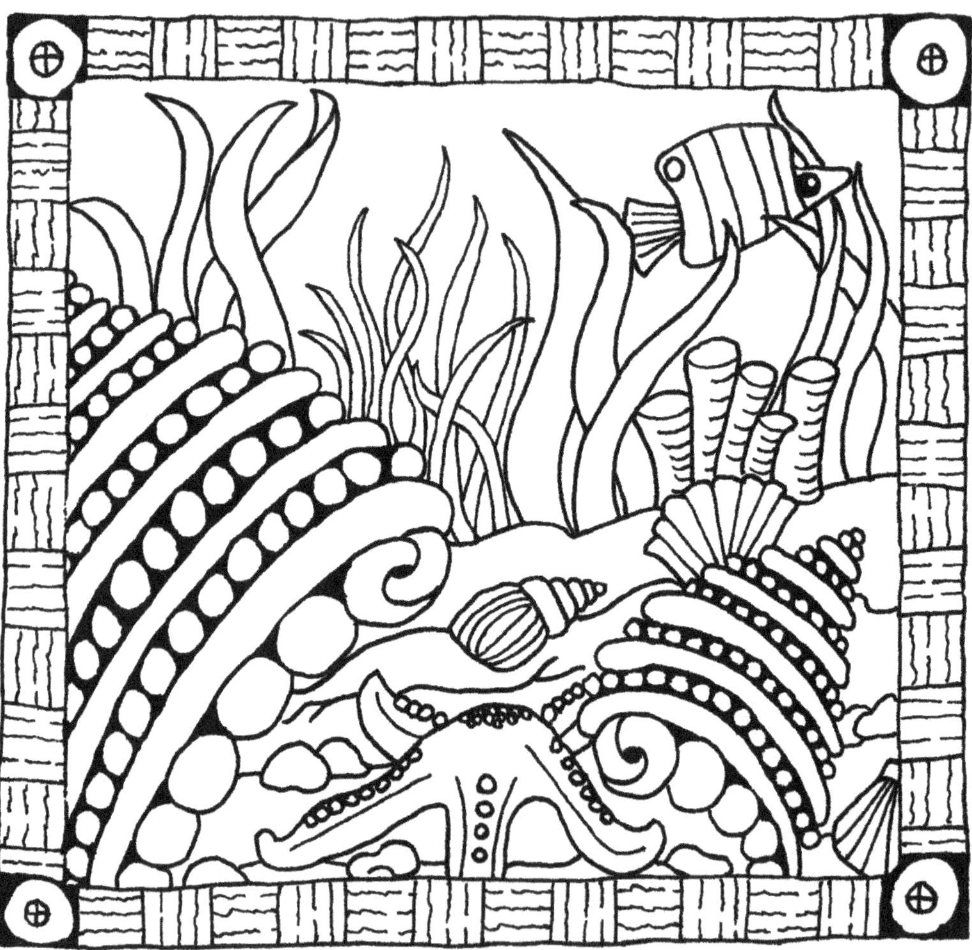

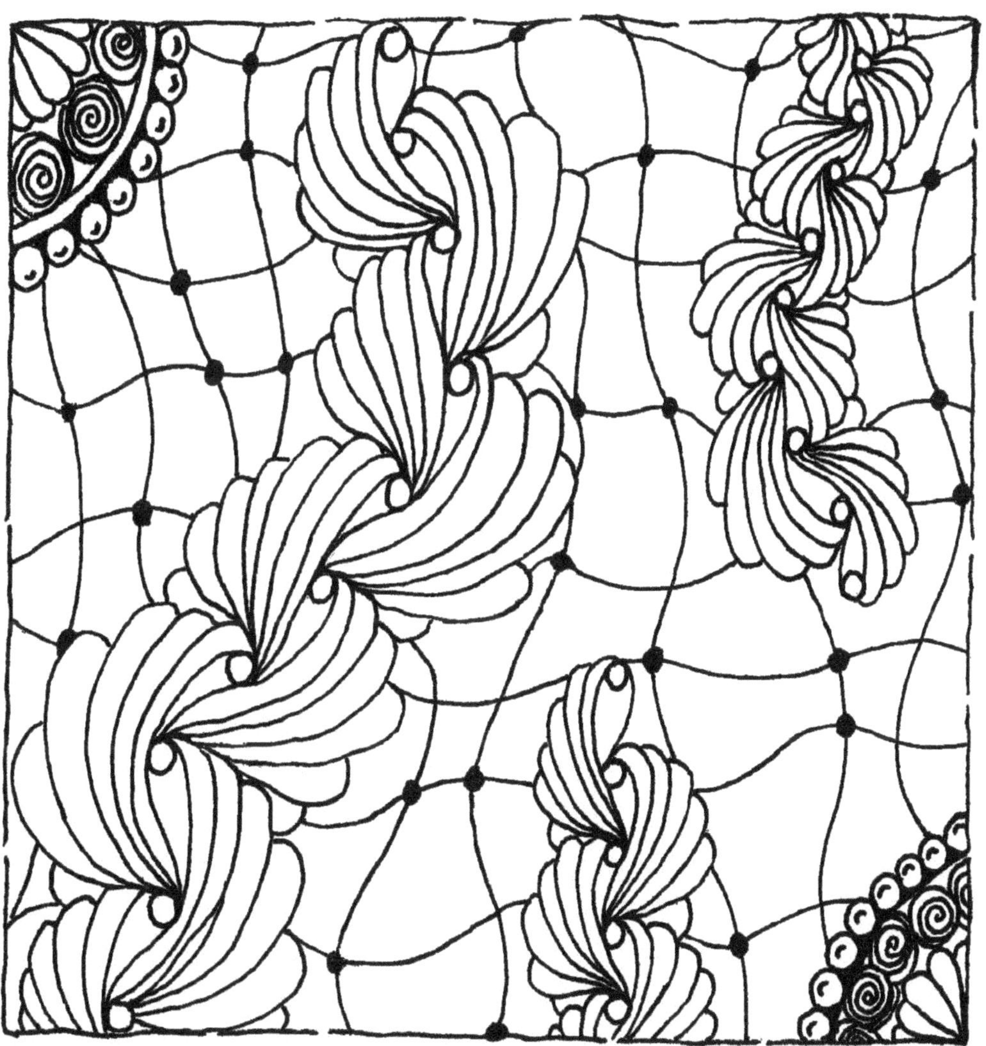

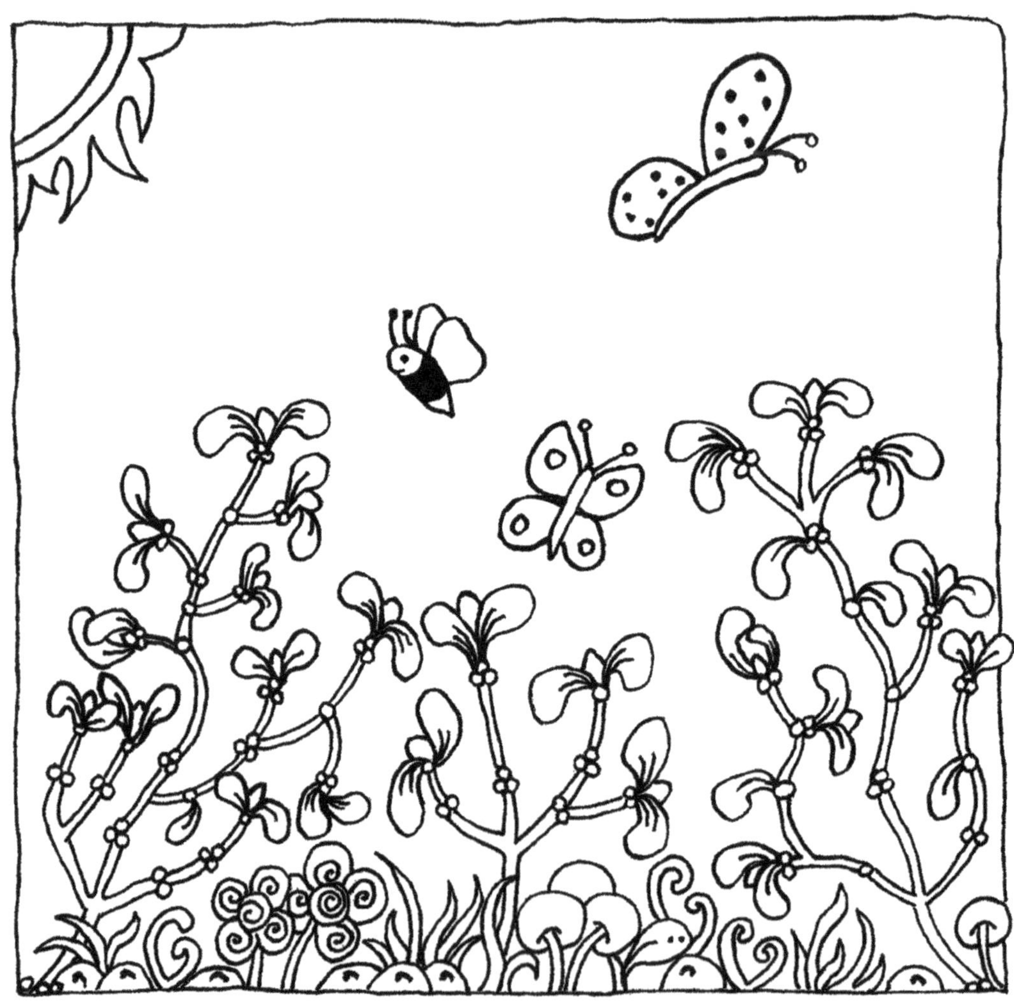

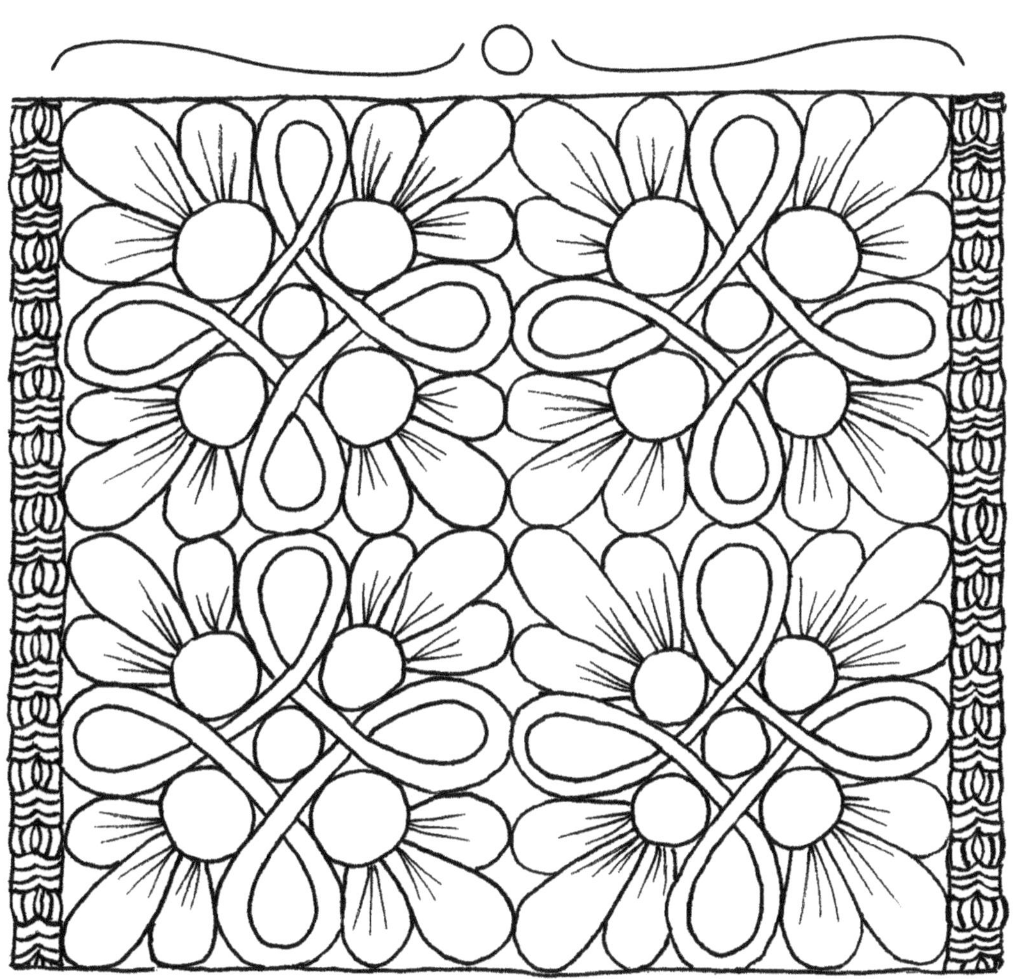

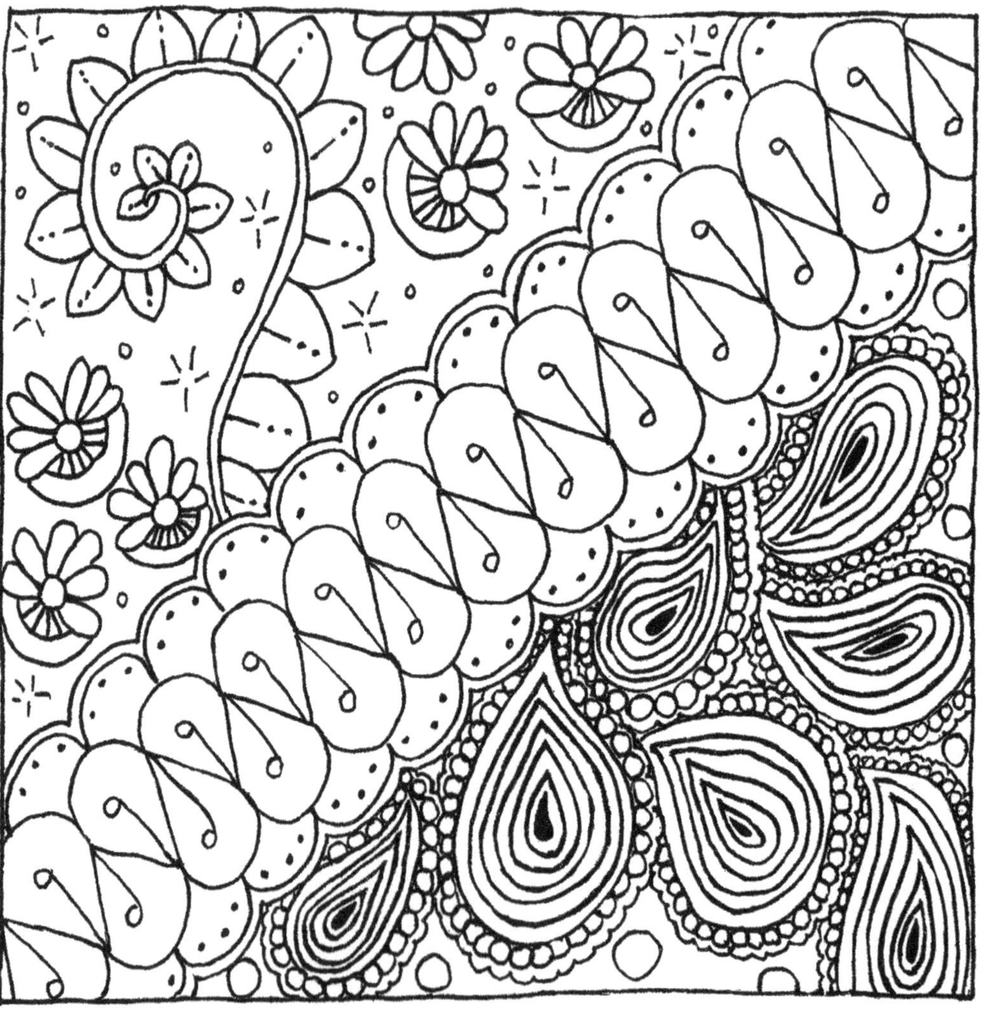

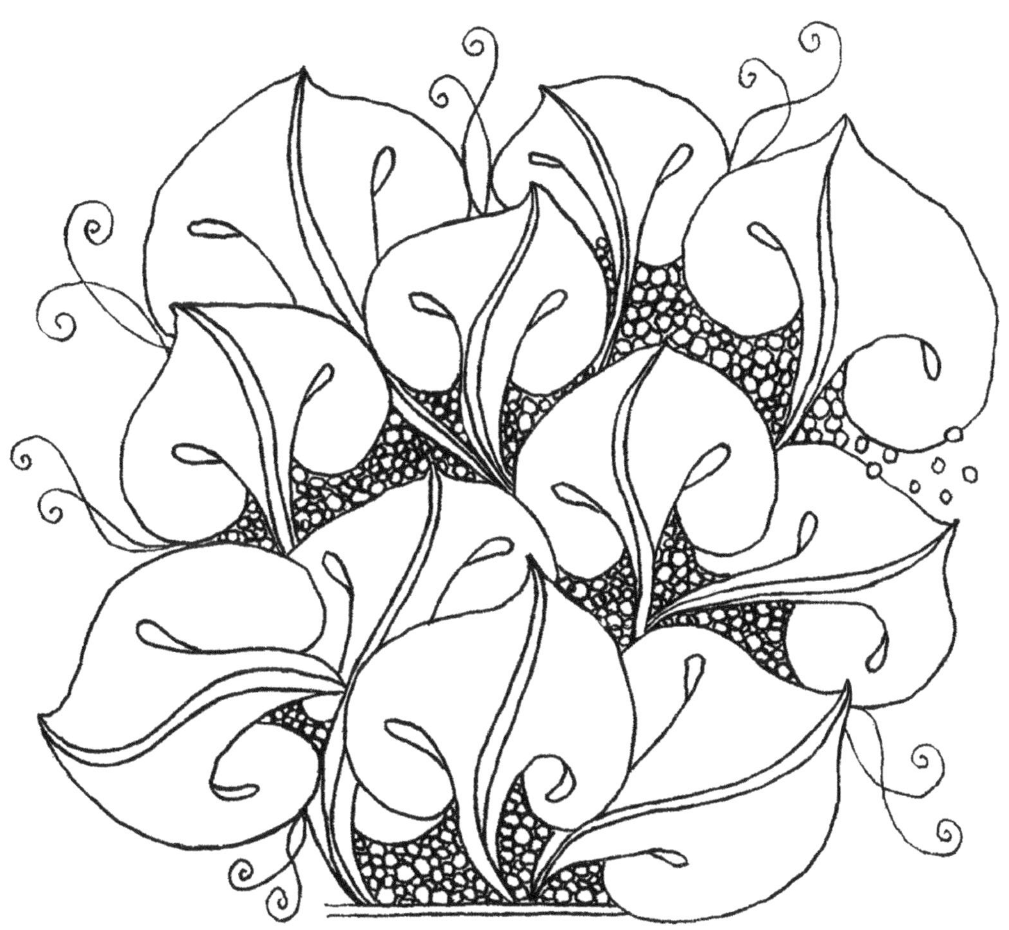

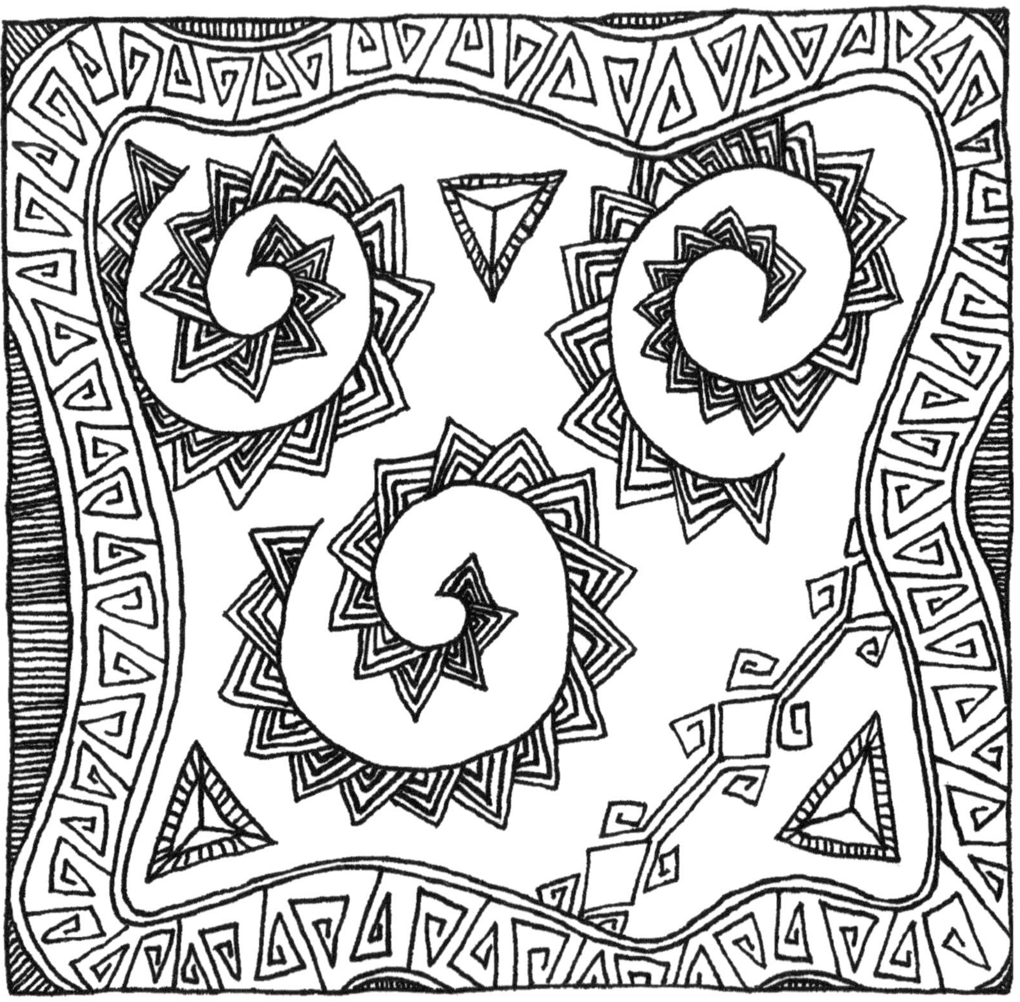

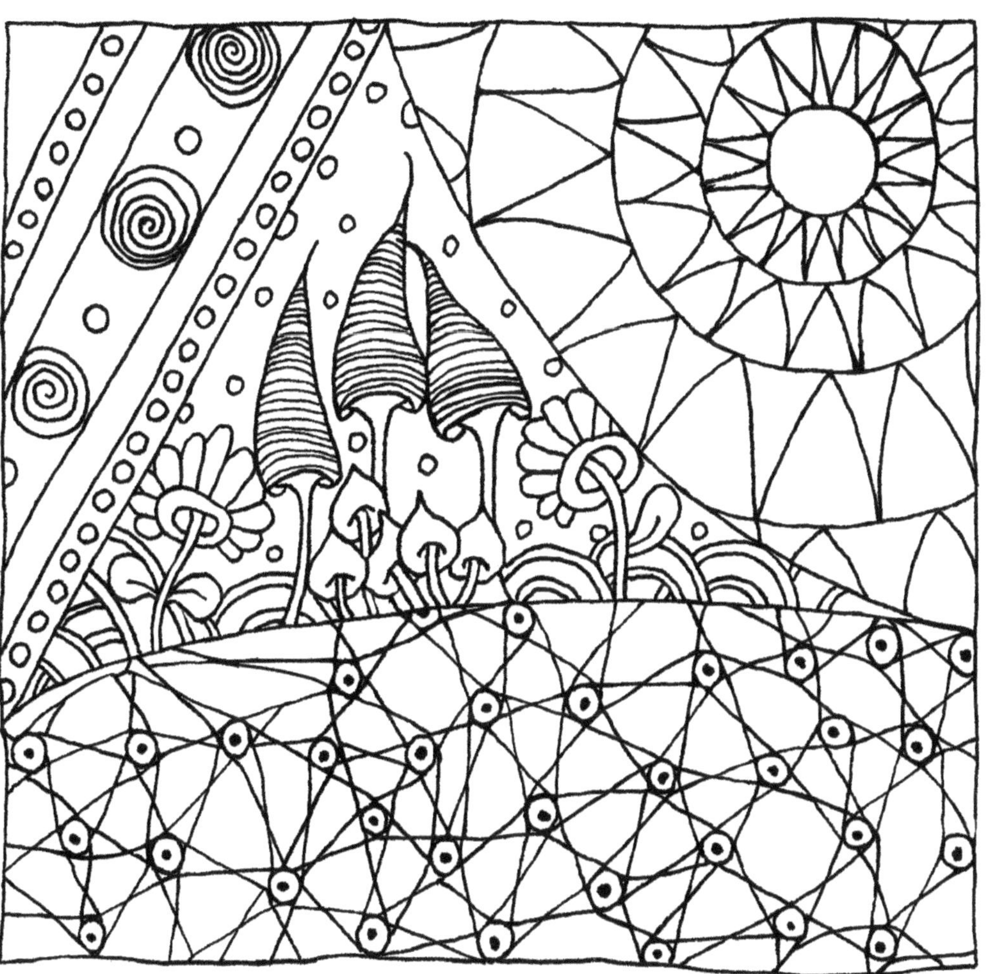

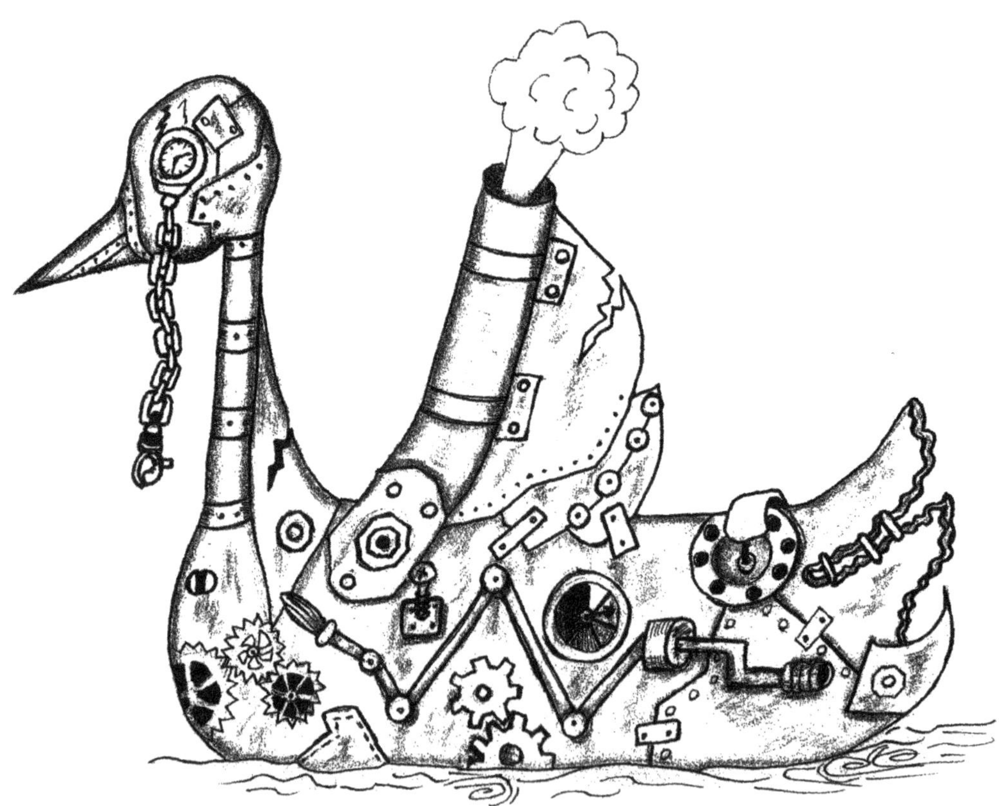

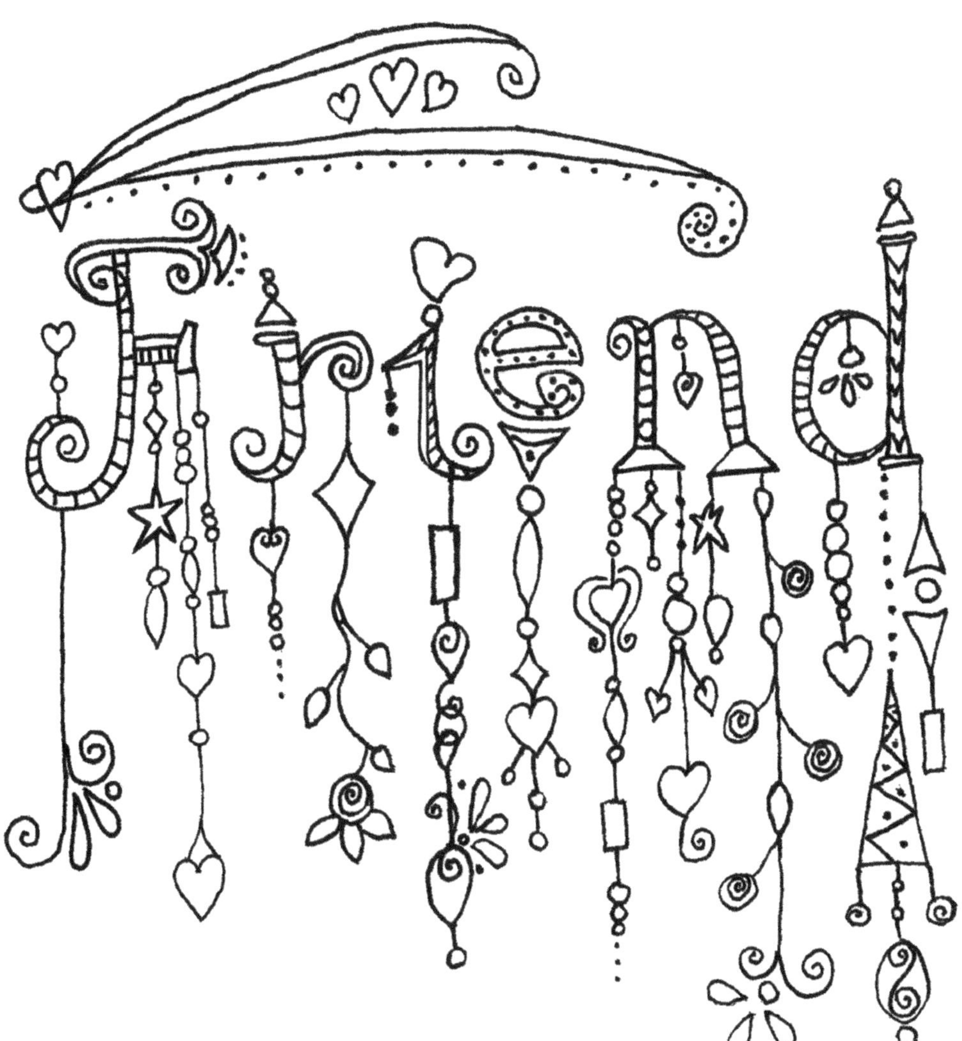
Friend

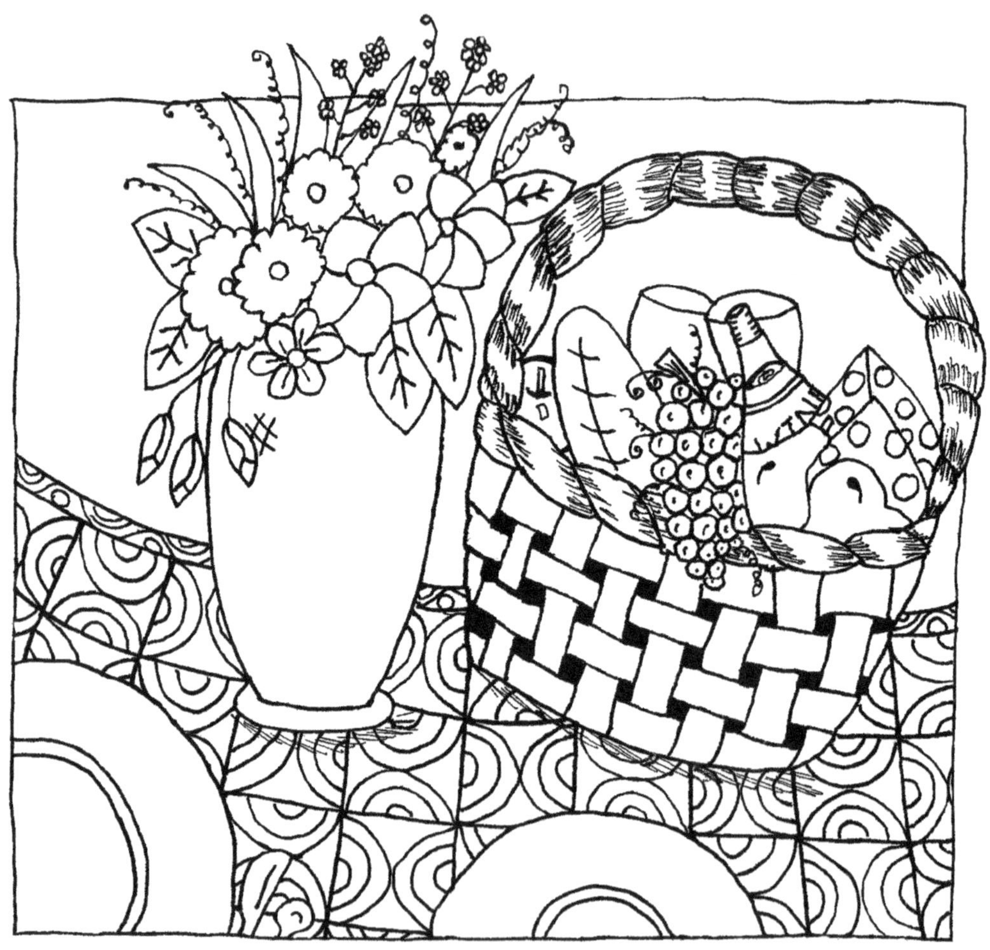

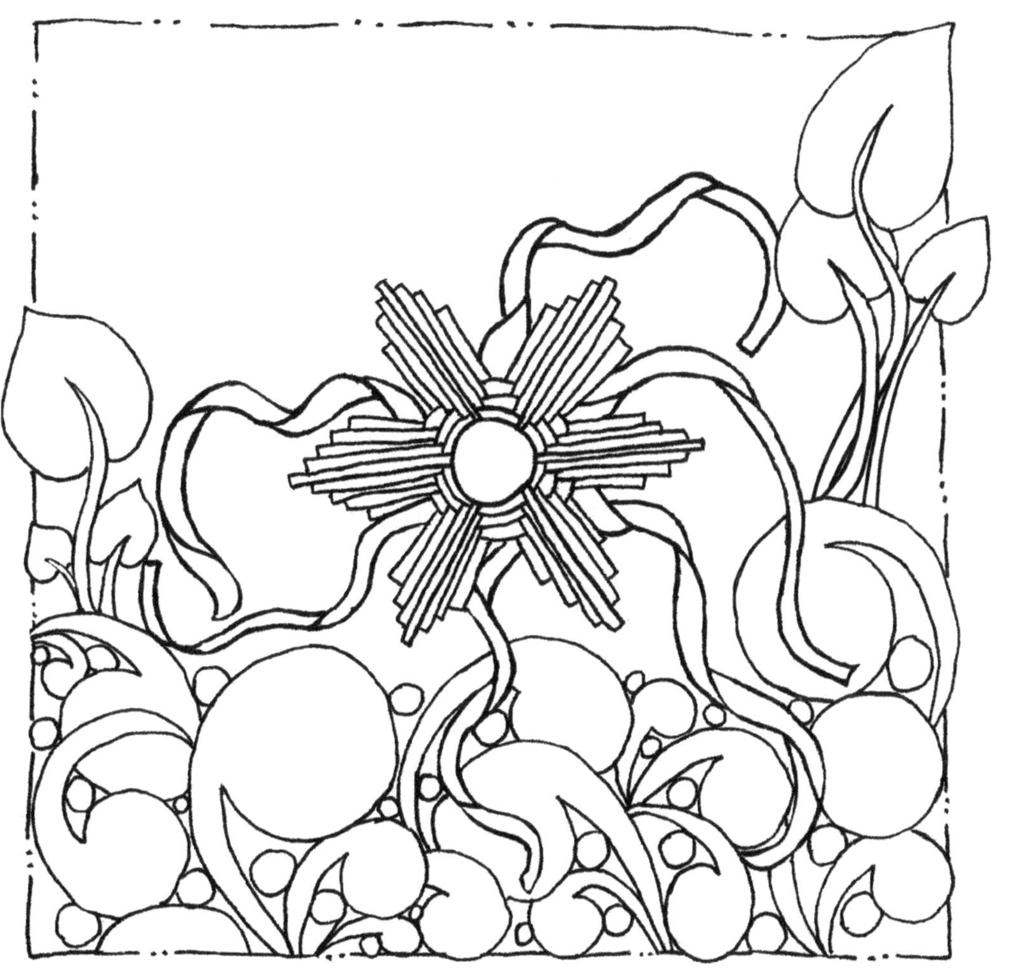

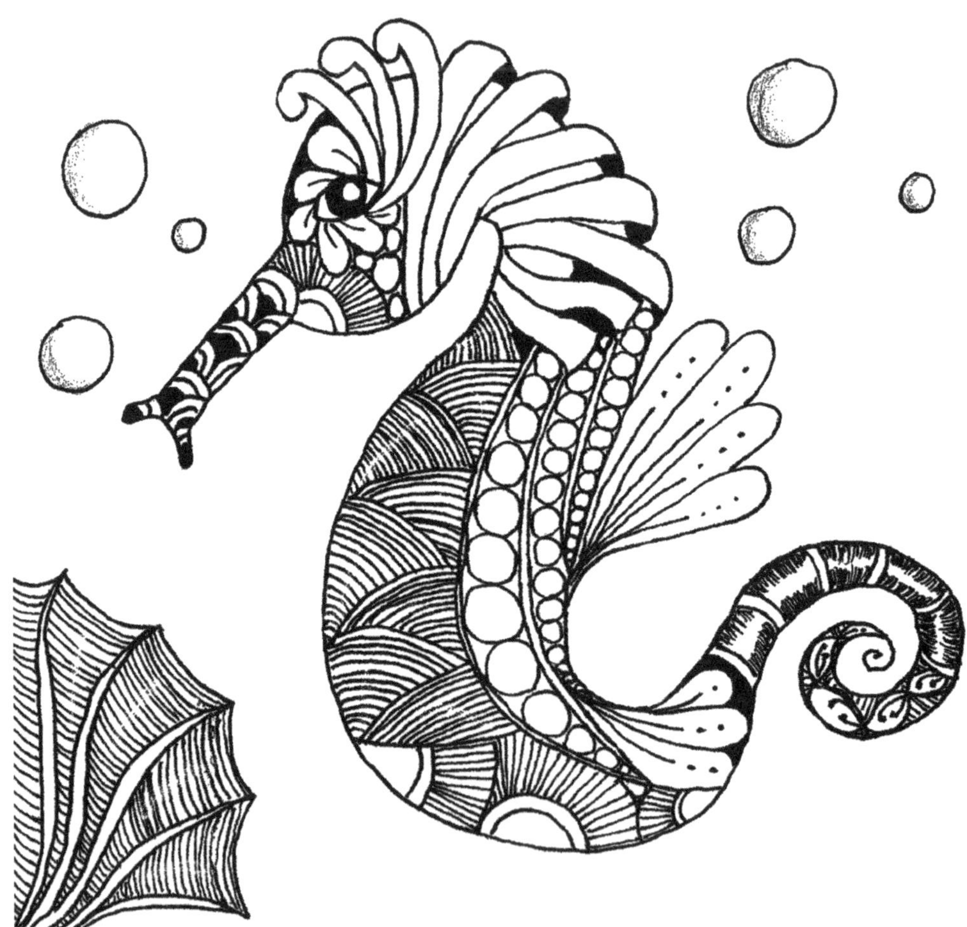

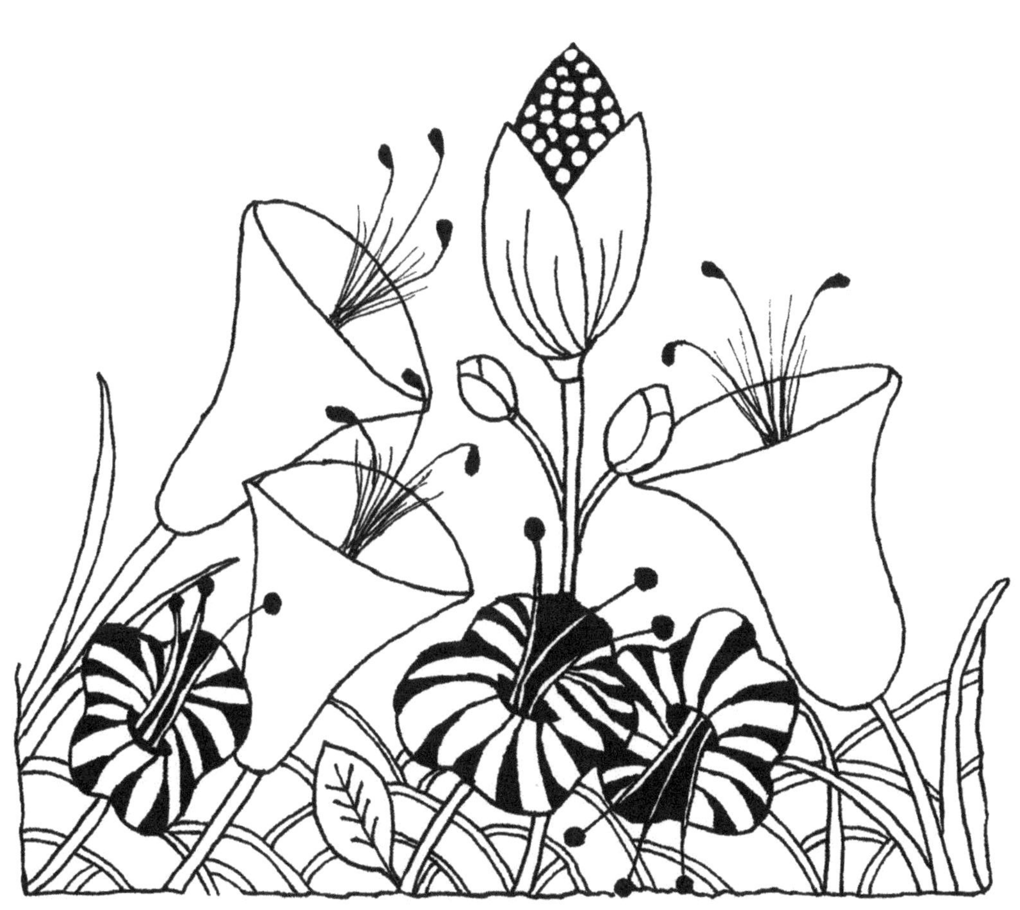

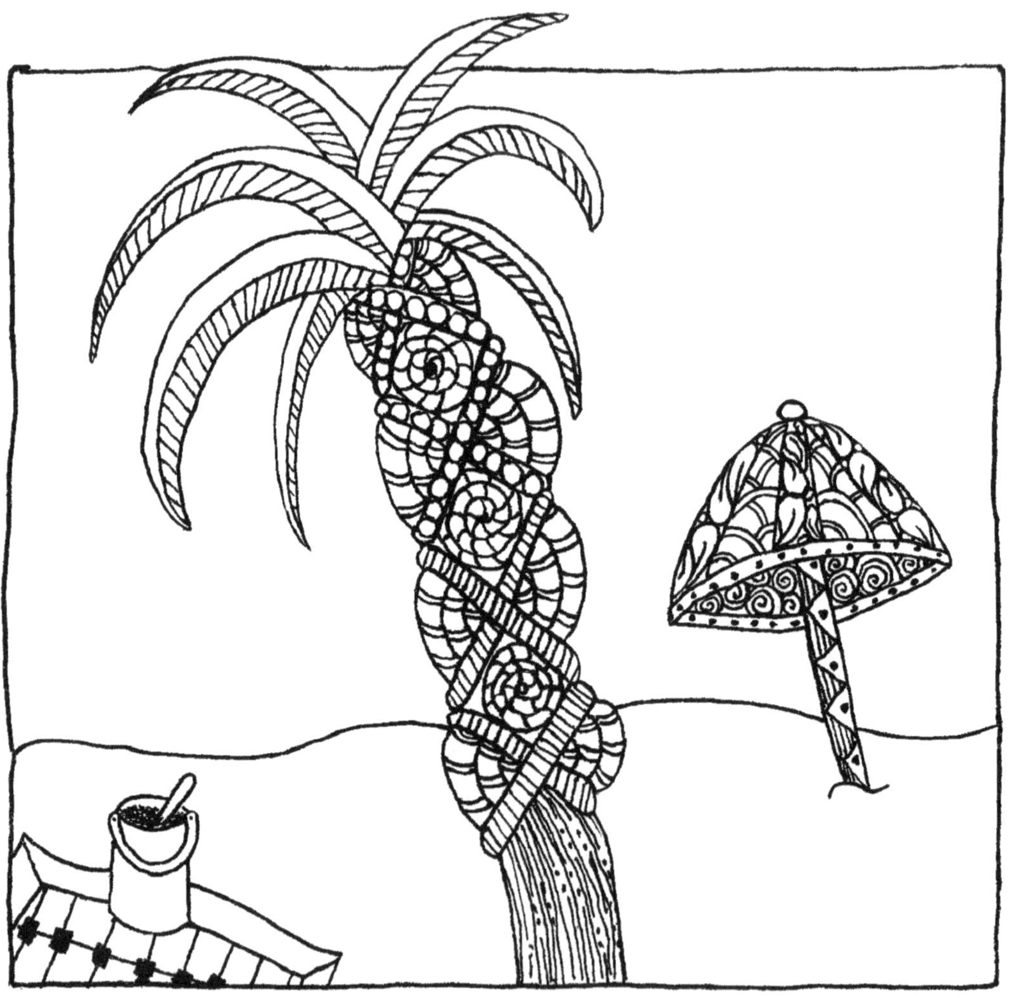

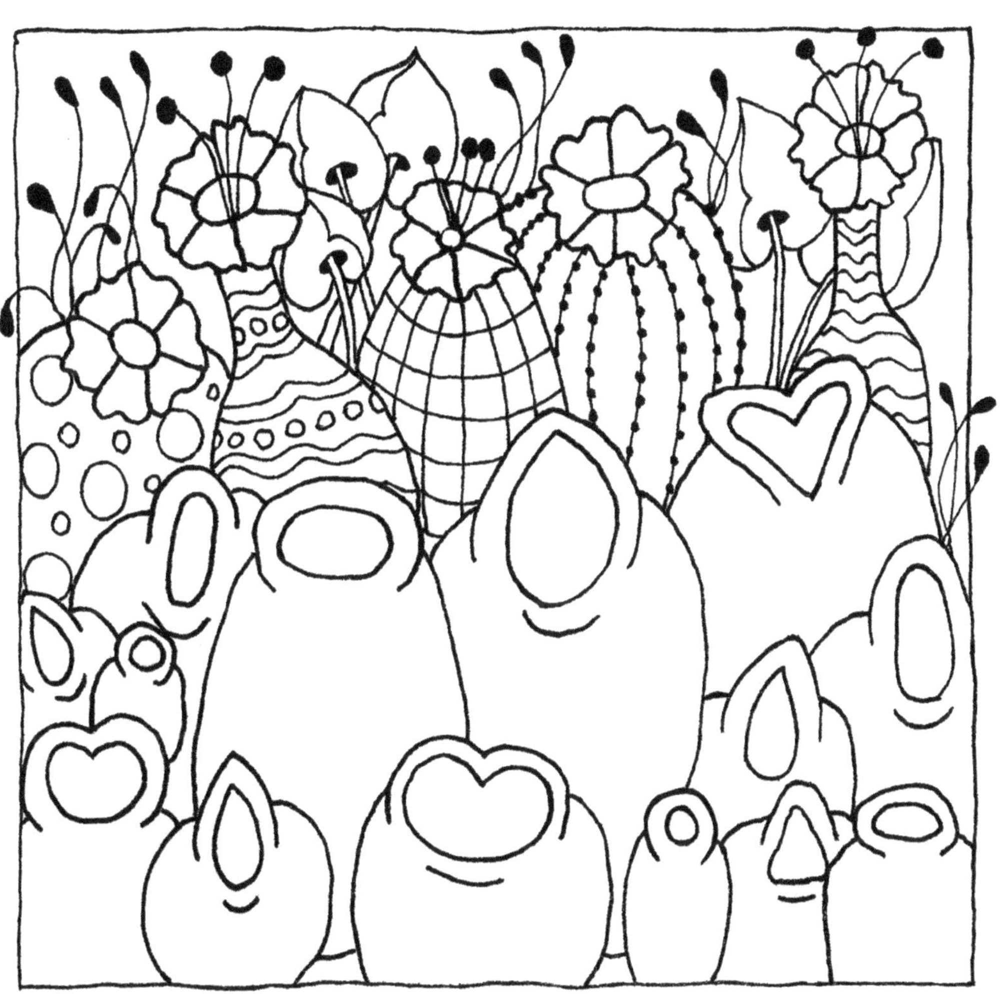

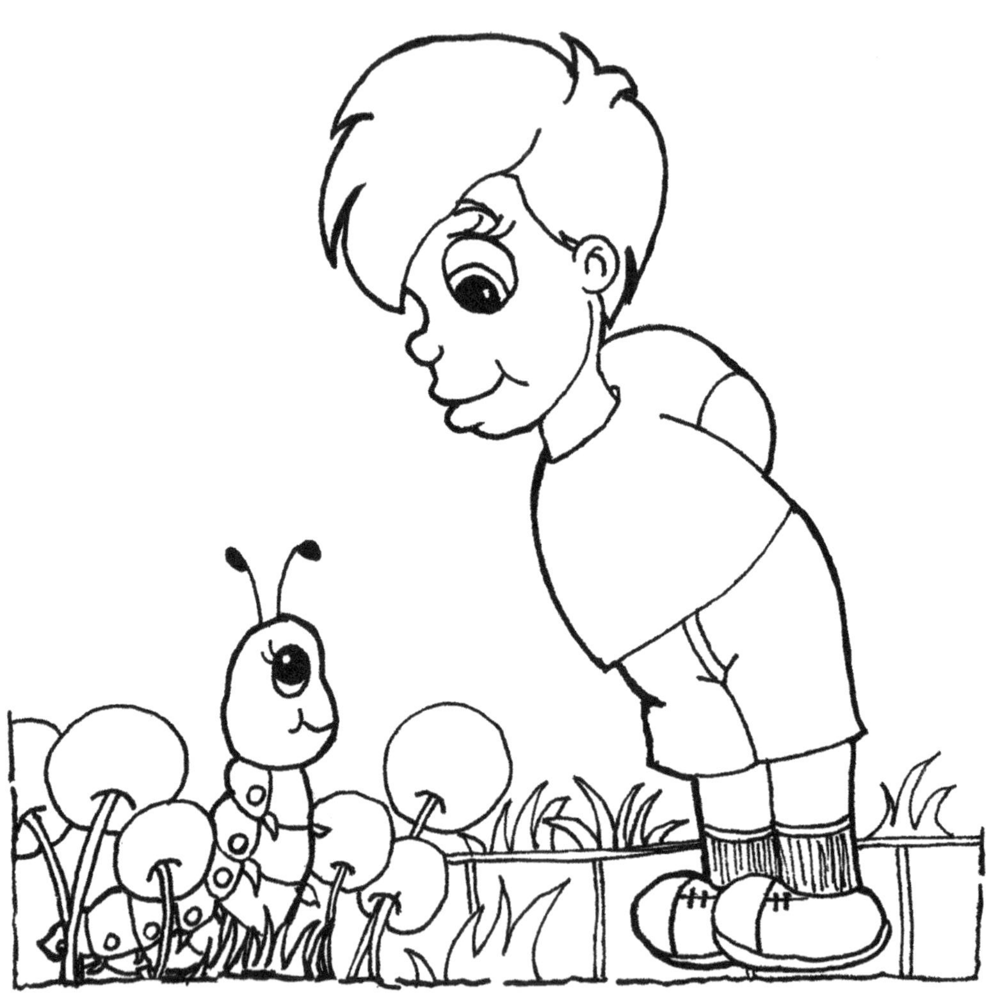

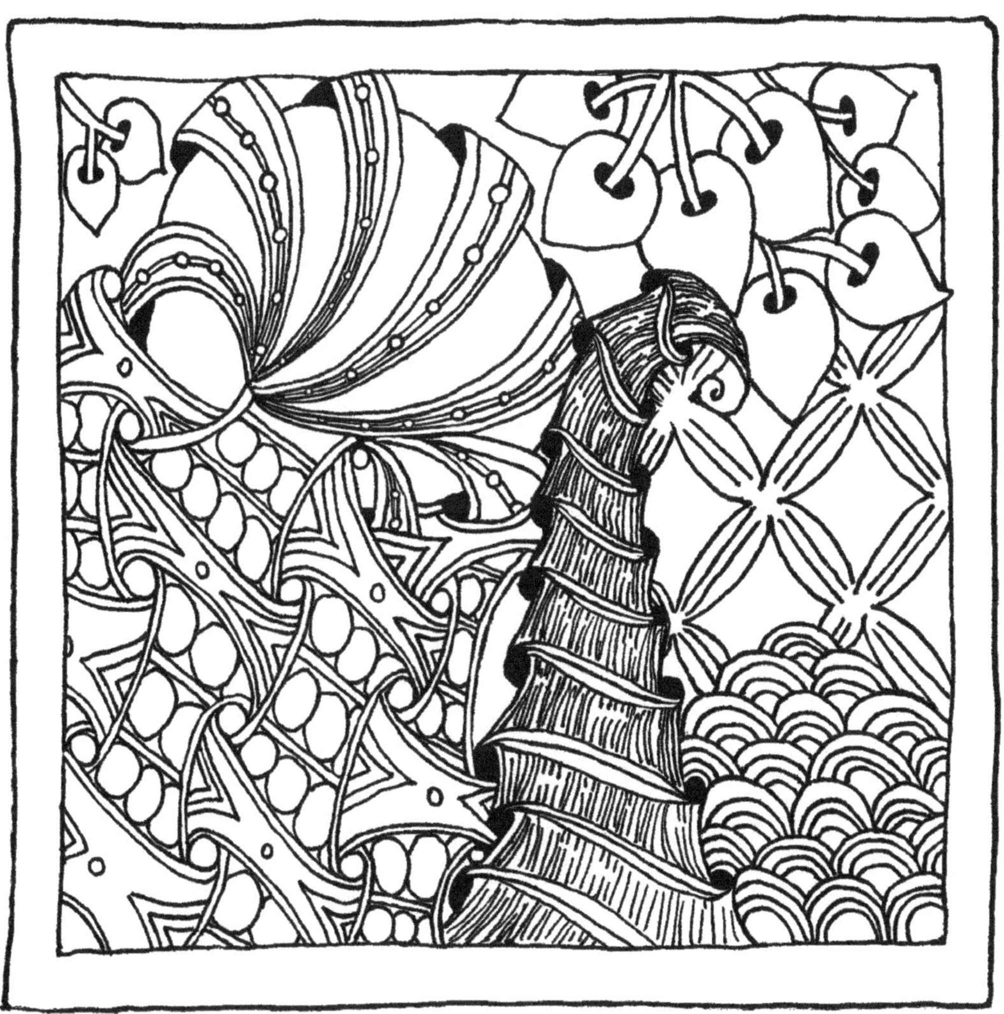

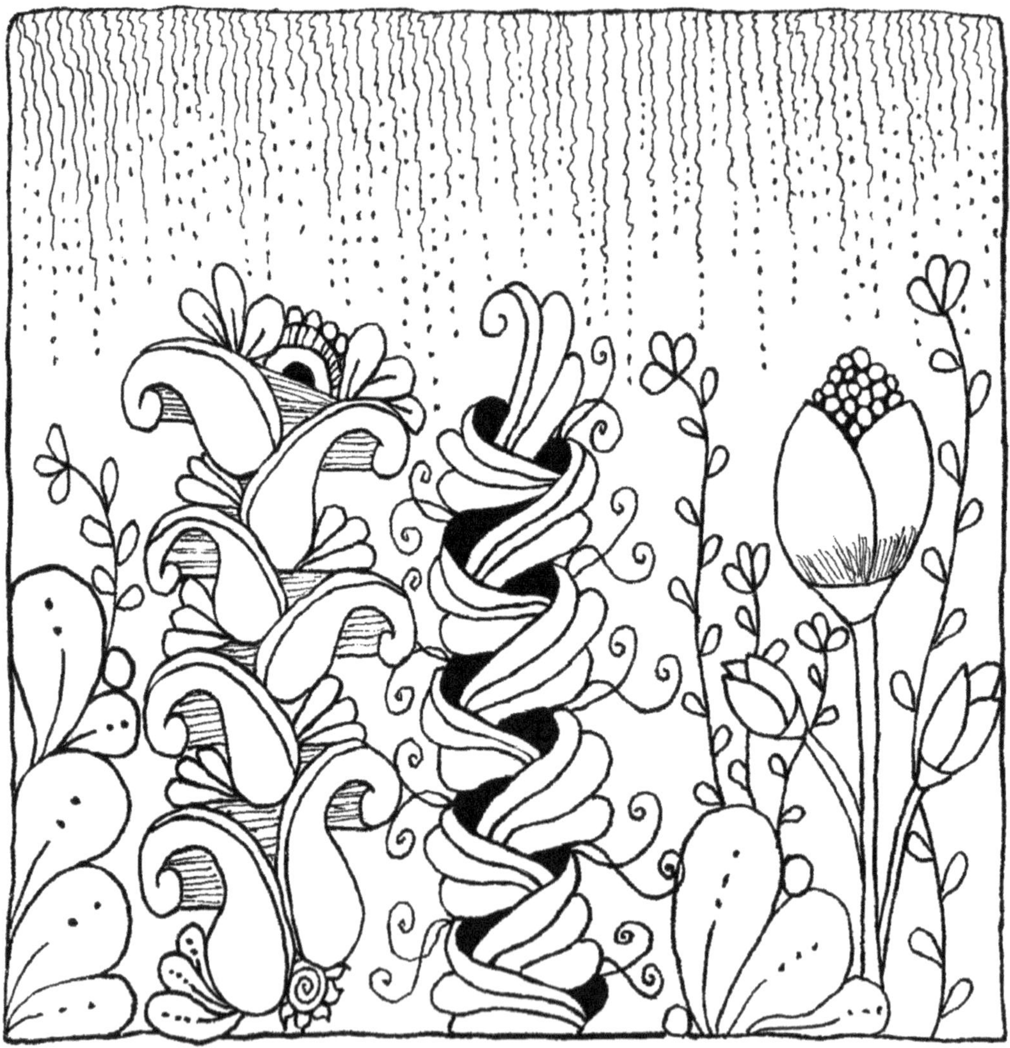

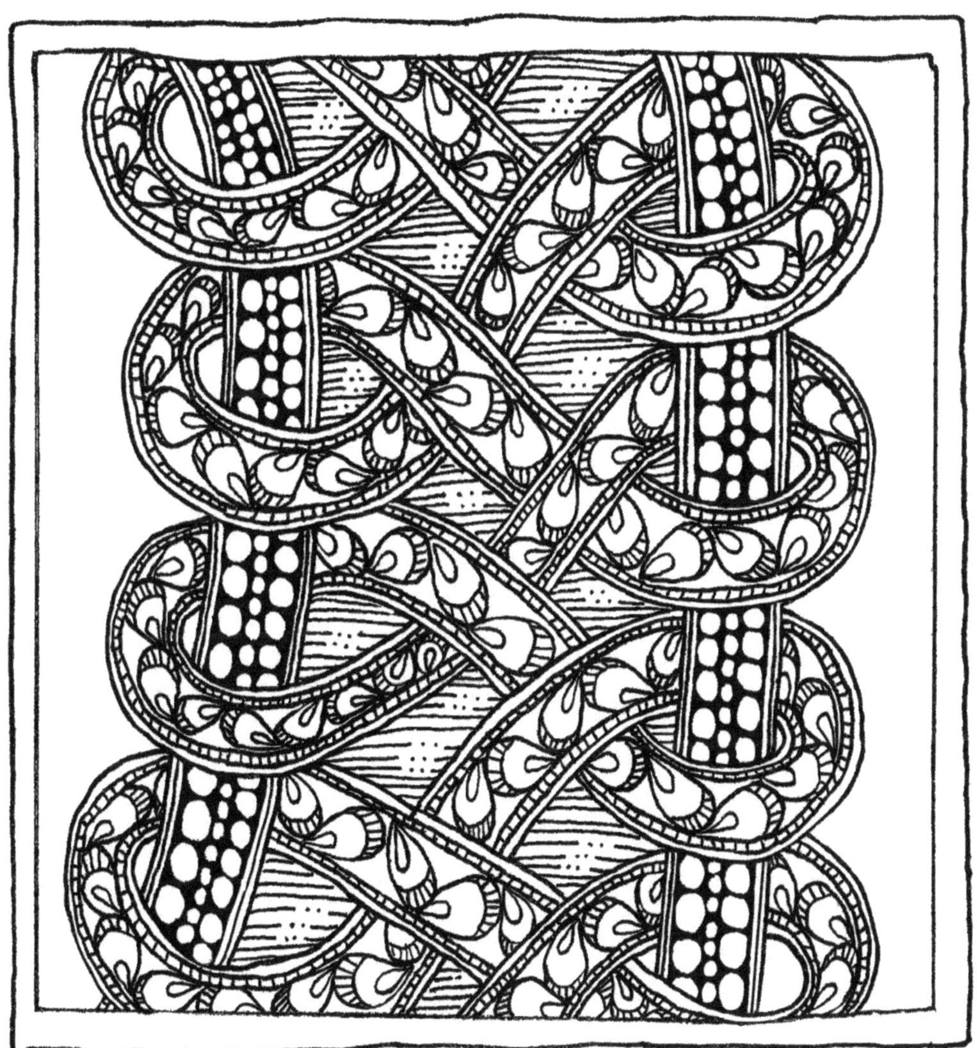

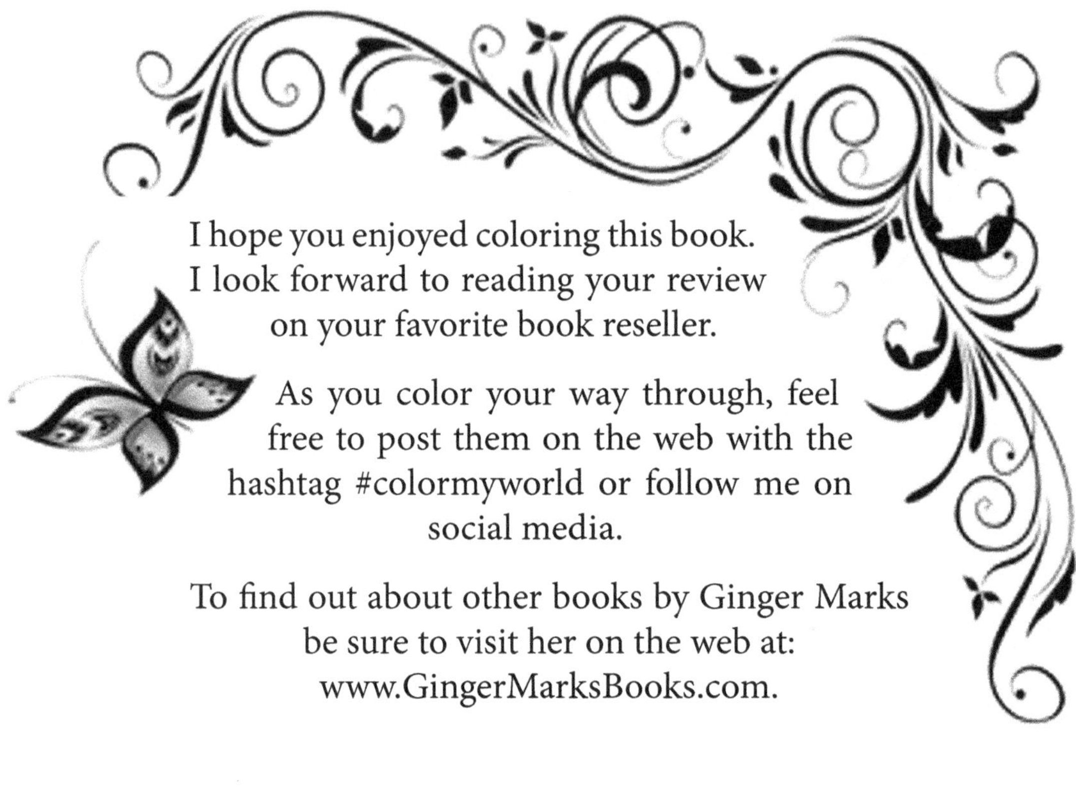

I hope you enjoyed coloring this book.
I look forward to reading your review
on your favorite book reseller.

As you color your way through, feel free to post them on the web with the hashtag #colormyworld or follow me on social media.

To find out about other books by Ginger Marks
be sure to visit her on the web at:
www.GingerMarksBooks.com.

www.ingramcontent.com/pod-product-compliance
Lightning Source LLC
LaVergne TN
LVHW060631110826
845147LV00014B/890

9781957832258